Sieges of the English Civil Wars

Sieges
of the English
Civil Wars

John Barratt

Pen & Sword
MILITARY

First published in Great Britain in 2009 by
Pen & Sword Military
an imprint of
Pen & Sword Books Ltd
47 Church Street
Barnsley
South Yorkshire
S70 2AS

ISBN 978 1 84415 832 4

A CIP catalogue record for this book is available from the British Library

Typeset in Ehrhardt by Phoenix Typesetting, Auldgirth Dumfriesshire

Printed by the MPG Books Group in the UK

Pen & Sword Books Ltd incorporates the Imprints of Pen & Sword Aviation,
Pen & Sword Maritime, Pen & Sword Military, Wharncliffe Local History,
Pen & Sword Select, Pen & Sword Military Classics and Leo Cooper.

For a complete list of Pen & Sword titles please contact
PEN & SWORD BOOKS LIMITED
47 Church Street, Barnsley, South Yorkshire, S70 2AS, England
E-mail: enquiries@pen-and-sword.co.uk
Website: www.pen-and-sword.co.uk

Contents

List of Plates and Maps

Plates

Fortifications
A cannon royal
A demi-cannon
A battery in action
Guns in position
Plundering
A sconce
Bristol in 1610
Storming
Beeston Castle
Sir Thomas Fairfax
Plymouth
Worcester
Prince Maurice
Thomas Mytton
Pendennis Castle
Denbigh
Basing House
Sir Arthur Aston
Colonel John Hewson

Maps

Introduction

The Civil Wars that ravaged the British Isles between 1641–1651 constitute the last great age of siege warfare in Britain. Hundreds of garrisons sprang up across the three kingdoms of England, Scotland and Ireland, and in many cases became a focus of prolonged siege operations. This book details the stories of a dozen such sieges, and of the men and women, soldiers and civilians, who – willingly or otherwise – were caught up in the bloody events that ensued.

I faced some difficult decisions on exactly which sieges to include – and even more on which to omit – out of the hundreds of possible choices. In the end I decided, reluctantly, to leave out some of those – such as the sieges of Chester and York – which have already been well documented by modern historians in favour of some lesser-known but equally interesting examples.

As usual, I must thank the staff of a number of libraries, notably those of the British Library and the Sydney Cohen Library, University of Liverpool, for their efficiency and patience. Charlotte Jones has skilfully deciphered my frequently illegible sketches to produce her excellent maps, and the team at Pen and Sword were, as ever, supportive and encouraging.

John Barratt
Henllan, 2008

Chapter One

The Military Background

The great battles of the English Civil Wars – such as Edgehill, Marston Moor and Naseby – have received a great deal of study, particularly over the last fifty years. Much less well known – with the exception of notorious episodes such as the siege of Drogheda (1649) and the 'Bolton Massacre' (1644) – are the siege operations, which had a vital influence on the course of the war, and which included some of its most colourful and bloody episodes.

It has been estimated that some 300 sieges took place across the British Isles in the two decades spanning 1640–1660. Involving cities, towns, castles, and often hastily fortified manor houses, the resulting military operations are thought to have incurred around 21,000 casualties, totalling 31 per cent of those sustained by the Parliamentarians and 21 per cent of those suffered by the Royalists.[1] The importance of siege warfare is highlighted by the fact that the First Civil War commenced in July 1642 with the unsuccessful Royalist siege of Hull, whilst the Second Civil War concluded with the fall of Pontefract Castle in March 1649. Indeed, over the whole Civil War period, siege operations occupied armies and senior commanders for much of the time. For example, during its first year of campaigning in 1645–1646 Parliament's New Model Army fought three major battles but a dozen sieges and stormings of defended garrisons; and Prince Rupert, best known in the popular imagination as a dashing cavalry commander, took part in six major field actions but around a dozen sieges and storms. Cromwell's Irish campaign of 1649–1650 consisted almost entirely of siege operations.

Sieges also had a major influence on campaigns and the strategy of major field armies. The summer campaign of 1643, involving the main field armies of the King and Parliament, was initiated by the Royalist siege of Parliamentarian-held Gloucester. In the following year the threat presented to York by the Allied Parliamentarian and Scottish armies resulted in a relief march by Prince Rupert, culminating on 2 July 1644 in the greatest battle of the war at Marston Moor. On 14 June 1645 the decisive encounter at Naseby was a direct consequence of the King's capture of Leicester two weeks earlier. The result of the Second Civil War in 1648 had partly revolved around the outcomes of the sieges of Pembroke and Colchester.

1

By the middle of the seventeenth century, after more than 100 years of almost continuous warfare, most of Europe was studded with fortifications, including major fortresses, castles, and settlements with defences of varying elaboration. But this was not the case with much of the British Isles. England had seen virtually no internal conflict since the battle of Stoke Field in 1487, which concluded the Wars of the Roses in favour of the Tudor dynasty. Scotland and Ireland had witnessed more strife, including foreign invasion, but had escaped relatively lightly in comparison with their European contemporaries. In England the most recently built fortifications – a series of coastal forts inspired by the threat of French invasion – had been erected by Henry VIII in the 1540s. The port of Hull had been refortified at the same time, although its design had been rendered obsolete by Continental advances even before completion. The only other permanent garrisons in England with fortifications worthy of modest European respect were those of Berwick upon Tweed (a constant bone of contention between a hostile England and Scotland) and the harbour of Portsmouth – a likely French target in case of war. In 1545 the antiquarian writer John Leland listed between 500 and 600 castles in England and Wales. It has been estimated that around ninety-one of these were in sufficiently good condition to be in normal use, usually as civilian occupation. Of the others, 30 were partially derelict and 137 ruinous, whilst the state of the remainder is unclear.[2]

Many towns in England and Wales had been fortified in the Middle Ages, and in some cases these defences originated in Roman times. Such fortifications might consist of a castle, with town walls and gates. Their condition varied. Some – especially inland towns in the peaceful Midlands and South of England, for example Leicester and Newark – were in a state of disrepair. Others – mainly coastal towns like Plymouth and Portsmouth, likely to be in the forefront of any European conflict involving England – were in somewhat better condition. The outbreak of the Irish rebellion of 1641 witnessed hasty efforts to refurbish the medieval fortifications of some Irish Sea-facing towns like Chester, together with several Welsh coastal castles. In Ireland, on the other hand, the threat of foreign invasion – most recently by Spain in 1601 – together with the ever-lurking possibility of rebellion, had resulted in both castle and town defences being kept in a somewhat better state of repair; whilst the turbulent state of Scottish affairs during the greater part of the sixteenth century resulted in fortifications there being maintained.

The non-involvement of the British kingdoms in the great Continental religious and dynastic conflict known as the Thirty Years War did not, however, preclude a number of their subjects from playing a part. Thousands of Scots and a significant number of English and Welsh saw military service in Europe. The armies of virtually every combatant (especially the Swedes of

King Gustavus Adolphus, the forces of the Palatinate, championed by King Charles I's sister Elizabeth of Bohemia, and of the Dutch Republic) included in their ranks a large numbers of volunteers and professional soldiers from the British Isles. The opposing Catholic and Imperialist armies had a smaller, though still significant, number of participants from the same source. As well as gaining experience on the battlefield, many of these foreign participants absorbed considerable knowledge of the art of fortification and siege warfare. Among them were the Welsh professional soldiers Charles Lloyd, Thomas Morgan, the Roman Catholic Royalist Sir Arthur Aston, and Parliament's Sir William Waller, who were all destined to play major roles during the Civil Wars.

Meanwhile, several veterans wrote military treatises or manuals that became standard texts during the course of the Civil Wars, although many of their recommendations were too elaborate and costly for provincial garrisons. Between 1600 and 1642 almost 100 military manuals were published in the British Isles. They included Henry Hexham's *Principles of the Art Militarie Practised in the Warres of the United Netherlands* (1637), and Robert Ward's *Animadversions of Warre* (1639). Most British fortification 'experts' – such as Sir Charles Lloyd and William Ellice (designer of the initial defence works at Chester) – had at least some knowledge of contemporary European theory and practice. Among them were David Papillon, whose book, *A Practical Abstract of the Arts of Fortification and Assaulting*, was published in 1645 (partly based on experiences of the English Civil War), and Robert Nye, Master Gunner of Worcester during the siege of 1646, who published *The Art of Gunnery* in 1647.

From the sixteenth century onwards, European fortifications were designed to withstand the devastating effects of modern artillery. This involved replacing or supplementing medieval stone fortifications of towns and fortresses with much lower stone walls, pierced with gunports for defending artillery. They had four-sided angled bastions at their corners, allowing flanking fire to command all possible angles of approach for an attacker. By 1642 Dutch military engineers were regarded as the most experienced in Europe, and the most widely copied. Lacking plentiful supplies of stone, they had developed fortifications constructed of earth, which were cheap and easy to build, though requiring more maintenance than stone defences. Earthen defences were better at withstanding artillery fire, absorbing many of the shots aimed at them, as well as being equally capable of withstanding assault.

Developments in fortification also led to changes in methods of siege warfare. One of the main functions of a besieged garrison was to tie down a besieging army, preventing it from being used elsewhere, and also to weaken it by means of a high rate of attrition in terms of casualties in action, sickness and desertion, together with a crippling expenditure in munitions and other supplies. In consequence, besiegers naturally sought to force a decision as rapidly and economically as possible. In order to achieve these aims, a besieger relied on bombardment, starvation, assault, and occasionally on treachery or mutiny from within.

There were essentially ten types of guns employed in siege warfare. The smallest fired shot of up to 4 pounds in weight, and were anti-personnel weapons. Guns used against fortifications included the saker of 4–7 pounds, the demi-culverin, ranging between 7 and 12 pounds, and the culverin with shot of 12–20 pounds. A saker weighed around 1,800 pounds, and was up to 10 feet long. A culverin, 13 feet long, weighed around 5,000 pounds.

Moving even small guns any distance was a major undertaking, particularly on the primitive roads of the seventeenth century. A demi-culverin required a team of a dozen horses and a crew of around thirty-five gunners and their 'matrosses' (assistants). Yet even culverins would take a long time to seriously damage a stone fortification in good repair. In order to breach such defences reasonably quickly, a demi-cannon, firing a shot of 20–40 pounds, or a full cannon, with shot of 60 pounds, was required. These weighed 4,500 to 6,000 pounds or more, and needed 100 men and 30 to 40 draught animals to move them. The largest gun of all, the cannon royal, fired shot weighing 80 pounds, but was rarely employed because of the enormous difficulties involved in transporting it, the huge amounts of gunpowder it consumed, and its very slow rate of fire, which sometimes made it possible for defenders to repair between shots some of the damage caused.

Mortars were widely employed on the Continent and also in the Civil War. These squat, short-barrelled pieces were used as much for their mortal effects as for the material damage they inflicted. They were used to lob solid shot and incendiary shells over defences, and were especially effective against the crowded thatched houses of towns, proving effective in undermining the resolution of civilians in besieged garrisons.

Nevertheless, the decision to besiege an enemy garrison was not one that ought to be taken lightly. As General George Monck observed:

> Every Commander knoweth that man's flesh is the best fortification that belongs to a Town; and where a Town is well-manned, the best way of taking it is by Starving, and when a Town is weakly manned, the best way of taking it is by Battery, Assault, or by Approaches, Mining Bribery and Assaults.[3]

Among the factors a general had to consider before beginning a siege was the cost involved, making only high-value targets worth the bother. Indeed, the expense to the besiegers of a prolonged operation was one reason for offering lenient terms, and there were sometimes grounds for hope that civilians and professional soldiers within a besieged garrison would press for them to be accepted rather than be forced to take worse conditions later.

Above all, it was accepted that prolonged sieges, particularly in bad weather or unhealthy conditions, could ruin an army. It was therefore incumbent on a general to resolve a siege as quickly as possible. Parliament's New Model Army, and the Royalists under Prince Rupert, followed the Swedish practice of bringing about a speedy conclusion by means of heavy bombardment and assault.

Sieges generally followed accepted procedures. The role of a besieged garrison was to hold out as long as possible, either in the hope of being relieved, or to delay and weaken an opponent as much as possible. If a besieging army could be held up long enough, particularly in bad weather or when disease was rampant, it might be crippled for an entire campaigning season. Operations would normally commence with the commander of a besieging force sending the governor of the garrison a summons to surrender. A governor who accepted this first demand was likely to face a court martial from his own side afterwards.

With his first summons rejected, as it usually was, the besieging commander began constructing siege lines. These would include emplacements for gun batteries, which ideally consisted of an assortment of guns of various calibres: heavy pieces to breach the enemy defences and smaller guns to act in an anti-personnel role to hinder the enemy in efforts to repair the damage. There would also be a series of trenches or 'approaches', along which the attackers might move closer to the enemy defences and eventually be in a position to assault them, or begin mining operations designed to create a breach. The siege works were generally termed 'lines of circumvallation', and might eventually be very extensive and elaborate, although those constructed during the Civil War were rarely as complex as Continental examples. Occasionally, if a major relief attempt was anticipated, a series of outward-facing defences, termed a 'line of contravallation', might be constructed outside the siegeworks, which could be manned by the besiegers against a relieving army. During this often lengthy process, a besieged garrison might receive several increasingly threatening further summons to surrender. However, unless faced by serious problems, such as mutiny, sickness or starvation, few governors would yield at this stage, being expected to bid defiance at any rate until their defences were breached.

The attackers' aim was to create one or more such breaches of sufficient extent as to be assailable. Both bombardment and mining were employed to this end. Mining was first used in England by Prince Rupert in 1643 at

Lichfield.[4] It required the use of a skilled labour force, often miners by trade, who were not always available. Even if they were, as at Gloucester in 1643, wet or otherwise unsuitable ground might severely hamper their efforts and an alert defender might countermine, with a view to blowing up the attackers' tunnel. A successful mine would also require a good deal of gunpowder, unless the tunnel itself might cause the collapse of the defences above it.

A breach was more commonly the result of bombardment and might be created over a period of hours or days, depending on the calibre of the siege guns and the condition of the defences. The thick walls of Denbigh Castle, for example, proved largely impervious to siege guns, which could not be employed at close range, whereas the soft sandstone medieval city walls of Chester crumbled after a few hours of steady bombardment.

The creation of an assailable breach by an attacker represented the 'moment of truth' for a besieged commander. He would now normally receive a final summons, which, if rejected, would – by the generally accepted 'laws' of war – render those soldiers and civilians within the garrison liable to no quarter, giving the attacking troops the right to sack the captured settlement. The terms 'on offer' generally became harsher the longer a garrison held out, often commencing with the defenders being allowed to march out with drums beating and colours flying, retaining all their arms and possessions, to make their way to a friendly garrison, through to a final offer that they surrender 'on mercy only'. This left their fate at the discretion of the besieging commander, and although it was usual for the majority of the defenders' lives to be spared, this was by no means automatic. In some cases, such as Cromwell's notorious action at Drogheda in 1649, a commander might decide to make an example of a stubborn garrison to deter others from a similar stance. Such was the attitude of Colonel Anthony Ashley Cooper at the capture of Royalist-held Abbotsbury in October 1644:

> The business was extreme hot for above six hours, we were forced to burn down an outgate to a court before we could get to the house, and then our men rushed in through the fire and got into the hall porch where with furze faggots they set fire to it, and plied the windows so hard with small shot, that the enemy durst not appear in the low rooms. In the meantime, one of our guns played on the other side of the house, and the guns with fireballs and the grenadiers with scaling ladders endeavoured to fire the second storey, but that not taking effect our soldiers were forced to breach open the window with iron balls, and forcing in faggots of fursefire set the whole house in a flaming fire, so thick it was not possible to be quenched. And then they cried for quarter, but having beat divers men before

it, and considering how many garrisons of the same make we had to deal with I gave command that there should be none given.[5]

There was, of course, no guarantee that terms agreed would actually be honoured. It was common for the men of a surrendered garrison to be forcibly relieved of their possessions by enemy soldiers, and, particularly in the later stages of the war, captured soldiers might be killed, particularly if they were claimed to be 'native' Irish or deserters from the victorious side.

Storming was a costly process in lives for both attackers and defenders. Attacking soldiers were often given 'Dutch' courage in the form of 'aqua vita' or other strong drink. An assault had to be planned with care, as evidenced by Royalist orders for the (unsuccessful) storming of Nantwich in 1644:

> Major Hawar with the regiment under his command, and the fire-locks, with the scaling ladders, they and all the dragoons armed with firelocks or snaphaunces, they to fall on first. Then to be seconded with a hundred musketeers; then a strong body of pikes, then a reserve of musketeers, and let the soldiers carry as many faggots as they can: this to be at five o'clock in the morning. Word: 'God and a Good Cause'.[6]

Commanders usually attempted to limit the bloodshed following a successful storming by urging that quarter should only be refused to those 'found in arms'. But such a fine distinction was often ignored or only partially observed, and it was common for non-combatants to find themselves caught up in the chaos and mayhem after a garrison fell. Fortunately – except in cases where there were strongly held religious or personal differences between the opposing troops – the average soldier's thoughts turned fairly rapidly from killing to looting. The result was that, in instances such as the Royalist storm of Leicester in May 1645, although scarcely a house was left unplundered, the loss of unarmed civilian life was minimal.

Chapter Two

The English Civil Wars
and Siege Warfare

When civil war broke out in the summer of 1642, there was a widespread hope that the conflict would be decided by a single pitched battle. As a result, although a number of towns began refurbishing existing defences or constructing new ones, the aim was to provide protection against generalised disorder rather than defences against a full-scale siege. At Chester, for example, although some repairs to medieval defences had begun in the previous year, as a result of alarm over the rebellion in Ireland, work on an extensive system of earthen outworks did not commence until early in 1643, when it was clear the war was likely to be prolonged. Many town councils clung to the hope that the conflict would pass them by, or were unwilling (or unable) to pay for the construction of effective defence works until it was too late. Birmingham was one such town, which, as a result, suffered the ravages of Prince Rupert's troops in the spring of 1643.

During the summer – a sign of things to come – the defences of the port of Hull saw off with ease a summons from King Charles in person, who found that royal authority did not compensate for lack of troops and siege artillery. At Portsmouth, held by the Royalists, strong seaward facing defences and an inadequate garrison could not withstand a Parliamentarian siege by sea and land.

In other places strenuous efforts to build fortifications began at once. In the summer of 1642 London was entirely without defences other than the Tower and the remains of its medieval walls, which the city had far outgrown. However, London had virtually inexhaustible supplies of money and labour. As with other towns and cities, its initial defences consisted of little more than posts and chains strung across the main routes into the city. But the defences were expanded rapidly. Even by the late autumn, when the Royalist advance on the capital was stalemated at Turnham Green, guns had been emplaced in earthen mounts and batteries. During the winter of 1642 some 20,000 women were labouring daily on the fortifications, and the massive workforce available was probably organised, and served in rota, by parish. The defences may well have been designed by Phillip Skippon, commander of the London Trained Bands, a soldier with many years' experience of European warfare. Eventually, the London defences would be 11 miles in circumference, with between 23 and 28 mounts and sconces, housing 200 guns, connected by an earthen rampart with turnpikes, gates and drawbridges on the main routes into the capital. By English, though not by Continental, standards, London's defences were regarded as formidable and certainly played a part in deterring any Royalist attack on the capital. However, it is debateable whether even the city's considerable numbers of trained men would have sufficed to man the full extent of its defences in the case of serious attack.

At the close of the 1642 campaign, King Charles established his headquarters and temporary capital at Oxford. Here too, from the winter of 1642 onwards, work began on fortifying the city. The inner defences were based on the surviving medieval walls, which were expanded with the customary earthworks and redoubts, also taking advantage of the natural defences provided by the Rivers Thames, Isis and Cherwell. Designed along approved European lines by Richard Rallingson of Queen's College, and built by the compulsory labour of the townspeople and soldiers, Oxford's defences were the most complex to be constructed during the war. Although they came under enemy attack on several occasions, no sustained siege was undertaken until the closing stages of the war in 1646. On that occasion, with the war effectively won, Parliament's New Model Army merely blockaded Oxford until realisation of their hopeless situation led to the garrison's surrender.[7]

During the winter and spring of 1642/3, with prolonged conflict inevitable, both sides established growing numbers of garrisons in virtually all parts of the country. These varied widely in type. Some strategically important towns and cities were clearly potential targets, and here work began quickly. In some cases, particularly in the North of England, where the threat of Scottish invasion had been real until less than fifty years earlier, town defences at such places as Carlisle, Berwick, Newcastle and York had been maintained in a better condition than elsewhere, and could be refurbished quickly and strengthened with earthen fortifications. In other towns, such as Chester, Hereford and Shrewsbury on the Welsh Borders – and still more so in the long peaceful areas of southern and eastern England – medieval town fortifications had been allowed to lapse into disrepair and much more work was needed, not only in clearing out silt-filled moats and ditches and repairing gates and drawbridges, but also in filling gaps in the original defences themselves.

Virtually all major towns had expanded considerably beyond their medieval walls, and the fate of the new suburbs raised many problems. The instinct of the soldiers was, in many cases, to demolish them or at any rate clear a belt of them outside the planned defence lines, in order to deny cover to a besieger. But such actions generally aroused a storm of protest both from the civilian authorities and those whose homes or livelihoods would be destroyed. The result was that, in many cases, such as Chester and Bristol, the new earthen defence lines were too extensive because of demands that much of the suburbs, and even some adjacent large country houses, should be included within them. At Bristol it was also necessary to control the high ground overlooking the city. In virtually every case, the defenders found they lacked the necessary manpower to hold these lines.

Particularly unfortunate were towns such as Reading and Newark, which found themselves on the contested military 'frontier' between the main territorial blocs of King and Parliament. In the case of Reading there were virtually no pre-war fortifications, but lying between the 'capitals' of the opposing sides, the town found itself thrust into the front line of the war. In December 1642, the Royalist garrison under Sir Arthur Aston, also employing forced civilian labour, began the construction of an earthen line and ditch, linking bastions. In the spring of 1643 Reading fell to the Parliamentarians after a siege of barely two weeks – a speedy surrender blamed by the Royalists on the weakness of Reading's defences. Reoccupied by the King's forces in the following autumn, Reading's defences were repaired, only to be demolished in the spring of 1644 when the Royalists evacuated the town. It then became a Parliamentarian garrison again, with the defences rebuilt once more.[8] Provided sufficient labour was available, earthen fortifications could be constructed surprisingly quickly. It was reckoned that a small town could be basically fortified in about a week. This, for example in the case of Manchester in July 1642, was often sufficient to repel assaults by untrained opponents.

More fortunate, at least in the eyes of their inhabitants, were towns such as Stamford in Lincolnshire. Although it lay in the hinterland between Parliament's Eastern Association and the Royalist territory centred on Newark, military experts were convinced that Stamford's topographical situation was such as rendered it indefensible. As a result the town came through the war relatively undisturbed and undamaged.[9] Cambridge was also fortunate – although strongly fortified in the course of the war – to be situated so deep within the Parliamentarian heartland that it was never seriously threatened with attack. Few if any Royalist-held towns were as lucky.

In the case of the King's 'Oxford' Army, it was necessary to billet troops in villages and country houses over a fairly wide area around the Royalist capital. Because of the danger of enemy raiding parties 'beating up' their quarters in surprise attacks, they tended to be at least partially fortified. Following

Continental practice, major strategic garrisons were frequently surrounded by a ring of smaller garrisons, often extending up to 20 miles in radius, both to provide additional protection to the main garrison itself and also to control a large area of the surrounding countryside, from which supplies could be drawn. These garrisons would be a mixture of fortified towns, villages, castles and country houses. Oxford's 'ring' included the towns of Abingdon, Faringdon, Banbury and Wallingford, with, in the latter three cases, a large manor house or castle forming the core of the defences. As well as these major outposts, Oxford was also surrounded by a number of smaller garrisons based on country houses such as Woodstock Manor, Greenland and Bletchingdon House and Godstow Manor. Their fortifications made use of any remaining medieval defences, but were principally earthen lines and ditches, strengthened with palisades of sharpened stakes and redoubts. If, as was often the case, a village church was situated close to the house, it was frequently included within the circle of the defences or fortified as an outpost.

London was fortunate in being relatively free from the danger of attack on its eastern approaches, but to the west, in the contested country between the capital and Oxford, similar 'satellite' garrisons were established at locations such as High Wycombe and Farnham Castle. Fortified 'complexes' of this kind were characteristic of a number of major garrisons. Newark on Trent was eventually supported by a ring of fortified villages; Chester had outposts at the villages of Chrisleton and Tarvin, and its approaches were at least partially commanded by the castles of Hawarden, Holt and Beeston. Similar clusters grew up around Parliamentarian-held Gloucester.

Growing demands for men and resources, as well as the need to control strategic roads and rivers and coastal ports, led to the spread of garrisons across the country. In many areas they would take the form of fortified country houses, each held by a small garrison of perhaps as few as fifty men. In some parts of the country medieval castles provided such outposts. By 1642 the majority of the surviving castles of England and Wales were in a semi-derelict or even ruinous condition; or had, in the previous couple of centuries, been adapted with residential rather than military needs in mind. In Scotland and Ireland, with their more recent stormy history, many castles had been maintained in defensible condition.

Only a small number of castles were immediately defensible but many others could be quickly refurbished, at least to acceptable standards, and even semi-ruinous castles – by virtue of their thick walls and strategic sites – could provide artillery-resistant defences that might prove costly to take by storm. Scarborough, Pontefract and a dozen other northern castles would enable the King to retain a potentially useful presence in the North of England for over a year after the effective destruction of his Northern Army at the battle of

Marston Moor in July 1644; and even in the closing stages of the war, following the Royalist defeat at Naseby (14 June 1645), the numerous garrisons, many of them based in castles, which dotted Royalist territory, enabled the King's men to prolong their resistance for over a year.

Although there were some British professional soldiers and veterans of European warfare with knowledge of current developments in the art of fortification, they did not produce many classic examples in the course of the English Civil War. In many cases the defences of individual garrisons, particularly those of country houses and castles, were the work of their owners, who might lack both the means, knowledge and willingness to carry out necessary demolitions to produce effective fortifications. Sir Thomas Fairfax's Chaplain, Joshua Sprigge, who wrote the 'official' history of the New Model Army, felt that fortified manor houses were rarely able to resist a determined siege, and that garrisoning them was therefore a waste of resources.[10] In some cases owners of houses with military significance were reluctant to attract attention from the enemy by fortifying them. Increasingly, more ruthless military commanders such as Prince Rupert would take matters into their own hands by garrisoning or demolishing such places – with or without the cooperation of their owners.

Many towns began the war with hastily improvised defences. At Manchester and Nantwich, for example, they at first consisted of posts and chains or other moveable barricades at the ends of streets, with other barricades on bridges and key defensive points. Where stone defences such as medieval walls already existed, it was recommended they be surrounded by additional fortifications of the modern European type. At Worcester some stone bastions were added to the existing walls and, commonly, earth outworks were constructed beyond them.

Many Parliamentarian-held towns, among them London and Liverpool, were defended by forts connected by a ditch and bank. At Liverpool the ditch was 36 feet wide and 9 feet deep. The Royalists at Chester had a similar system of 'outworks' and the King's garrisons also occasionally employed what was termed a 'continuous bastioned enceinte', which was seen as being superior to the Parliamentarian pattern. It could be seen in its most elaborate form in the defences of Oxford, and was also employed or planned in simpler forms at Reading, Newark and Liverpool. These defences would have angular bastions at intervals, often with cannon mounted on them, their gunners protected from enemy fire by 'gabions' (baskets filled with earth or stones) or by woolpacks. Separate forts or mounts outside the main defence lines, such as the Queen's Sconce at Newark and the 'Forts Royal' at Chester and Worcester, were common. These were often star-shaped or irregular in form, made of earth and protected with wooden palisades or sharp-ended 'storm–poles' jutting at an angle from the outer face of the fort. Other detached outworks were termed 'half-moons' and 'horn-works', according to shape or purpose.

Additional obstacles to an attacker might be provided by star-shaped pointed metal objects known as 'caltrops', aimed specifically at cavalry horses, and pits, similar to animal traps, filled with sharpened stakes and known as 'pitfalls' – 'two rows of holes the height of a man in depth, and so near it might hinder their sudden assaulting of the works . . .' Few if any fortifications actually employed the full range of these defences. However, with the passage of time, basic defences hastily constructed on the onset of war might be significantly elaborated, particularly if a town or other garrison was situated in an area of active military operations. An initial defensive system might have the height of its bank and the depth of its ditch increased, and, if close to a source of water such as a river, the ditch might be flooded to form a moat. Palisades and 'storm-poles', sometimes with iron tips, could be added. Medieval stone walls were often given an inner lining of earth, designed to cushion the effects of artillery bombardment. Whilst a heavy gun could pierce an 8-foot stone wall, it was claimed that, if increased to a thickness of 20 feet by an earth backing, it could absorb any artillery fire.

All of these refinements might be thought desirable but they were rarely all achieved, due to disruption, expense, or lack of materials or enthusiasm. It generally took the threat of storming to unite all within a garrison – men and women, young and old, civilian and soldier – in an effort to strengthen or repair their defences. In normal circumstances a military governor had either to pay civilians to work on defences or take the unpopular step of introducing conscription. Both methods had a serious effect on a local economy and were strongly disliked. Even if compulsion was used, many civilians found means to evade the work. At Oxford in December 1642, only 12 men of an expected labour force of 122 turned up. In 1643, with the city likely to come under Parliamentarian attack, all able-bodied men between sixteen and sixty years of age were ordered to spend one day a week working on the defences, using their own tools. But even then considerable difficulty was encountered in enforcing this. In the following winter a fine of 1 shilling was decreed for every day missed without good reason. Soldiers tended to regard themselves as being 'too good' to labour on defences and frequently had to be compelled, or paid extra, to do such work.

Siege works were not dissimilar to defensive works in design. They also generally consisted of ditches, whose 'spoil' was used as the basis for earthen walls or embankments, together with sconces or mounts, staked or pallisaded against sorties by the besieged garrison, with the pioneers and others involved in the siege sheltering behind gabions or the earthen walls. At the siege of Donnington in 1644 the Parliamentarians

> made a mount upon the said level some 200 paces of the Castle, trench[ed] and pallisaded it, the walls being high, cannon proof, and the top made of great thickness and strong, as covered with bricks and earth propped up with great beams and laid over with packs of wool to prevent the execution of mortar grenades.[11]

Both sides used foreign experts. Perhaps the best known of them was a Walloon, Bernard de Gomme, who accompanied Prince Rupert to England in 1642. Eventually becoming the Prince's Engineer-General, de Gomme spent much time redesigning Royalist fortifications built by others. Bristol, Liverpool, Chester and Lathom House were among those for which de Gomme produced amended designs, some of which were put into practice. A Swede, Martin Beckman, was highly valued by the King, and advised on the Oxford defences.

The Parliamentarians also employed European professional military engineers. The German Johann Roswurm designed the defences of Manchester, which in 1644 were deemed by Prince Rupert as too strong to attack, and was also involved in the construction of the first fortifications at Liverpool. A Dutchman, John Dalbier, was Engineer-General to the Earl of Essex, and later with the New Model Army, and probably advised on the construction of fortifications at Newport Pagnell.

If the design of fortifications during the earlier part of the Civil War was imperfect, the same could be said of the practice of siegecraft. Both sides initially lacked the powerful siege trains essential for the speedy reduction of enemy fortifications. The Parliamentarians had the advantage of retaining control of the major arsenals and magazines of Hull and the Tower of London, as well as the gun-founding facilities of the Kentish Weald. The Thirty Years War in Europe saw the use of massive siege trains of 80–100 guns, but neither side in the Civil War had the funds or other resources for this. In 1641 the siege train of King Charles's army consisted of twenty-seven guns of various calibres, including two demi-cannon, two culverins and two-demi-culverins. A year later he had added another demi-cannon and culverin. In the 1644 campaign he fielded four demi-culverins and four sakers, and in 1645 two demi-cannon and three culverins. Parliament's New Model Army began its campaign in 1645 with two demi-cannon and three culverins, to which it added the Royalist artillery train taken at Naseby, giving it the most formidable array of siege artillery seen during the war, enabling it to strike very effectively at Royalist garrisons. In his 1649 campaign in Ireland Cromwell mustered the largest siege train of the war, with eleven siege pieces.

Siege guns were a rare enough commodity to acquire individual nicknames. Queen Henrietta Maria gave two demi-culverin, which arrived at Bridlington in 1643 as part of her large shipment of munitions from the Continent, to the Earl of Newcastle's Northern Royalist army. They were known as 'the Queen's pocket-pistols' or 'Gog and Magog', and employed at the siege of Hull, where one was taken by the Parliamentarians, who captured the other at the fall of York in July 1644. Both were later used to reduce Royalist garrisons in Yorkshire. At the start of the war a demi-cannon in Parliamentarian-held Hull was known as 'Sweet Lips', allegedly in honour of a well-known prostitute of the town. The gun was used by Sir John Meldrum at the siege of Newark in 1644 and captured by Prince Rupert, after which it formed part of Newark's defences until the end of the war.

In the later stages of the war Parliament stationed heavy guns at Portsmouth, Northampton, Hull, Manchester and Stafford, from where they were loaned out, often reluctantly, to local commanders according to their needs. Mortars were also in short supply. During his siege of Chester Sir William Brereton, with some difficulty, borrowed one from Stafford but then had problems obtaining sufficient ammunition for it; whilst the Royalists' siege of Gloucester in 1643 was hindered when their mortar blew up, a replacement eventually being provided from the Queen's jealously guarded magazine at Oxford.

Siege guns were notoriously difficult to transport along England's primitive road system. On occasion it was possible to move them by river or by sea, with Parliament's naval supremacy assisting in the latter. On land large teams of thirty or forty horses or oxen would be needed for each gun.

As well as guns, siege trains sometimes included several hundred wagons, carrying a vast assortment of items. Among them were barrels of gunpowder, cannon shot and mortar shells, grenades and other incendiary devices, nails, tools, shovels and spades. The draught animals required – horses and oxen – would often be conscripted, along with their owners, who acted as drivers. Particularly in the later stages of the war – and especially in the often contested and exhausted Royalist-held territory – it was difficult to obtain sufficient numbers. In the spring of 1645 the start of the King's operations was delayed for several vital days after a raid by Cromwell carried off many of the draught animals in the Oxford area.

As siege operations became increasingly important, Parliament, with its greater resources, enjoyed a distinct advantage: in fact, the Royalists seldom, if ever, had sufficient of the heaviest guns to have a realistic chance of breaching the defences of the strongest enemy garrisons. On numerous occasions, for example at Hull, Gloucester, Lyme and Plymouth, their siege operations failed largely because of this. And so the Royalists had to employ other methods in their efforts to reduce enemy garrisons. At Lichfield in April 1643 Prince Rupert exploded what was said to have been the first mine employed in England in order to blast a breach in the defences of Lichfield Cathedral Close, and mining was attempted, with little success because of the wet ground, at Gloucester.

On many occasions the Royalists' best hope of capturing enemy strongholds lay in storming them. To this end they made large-scale use of incendiary and explosive devices. When he arrived in England in 1642, Prince Rupert brought with him a French explosives expert or 'fireworker', named Bartholomew la Roche. La Roche, almost as fiery in nature as some of his devices, became the King's Master Fireworker, and was eventually knighted for his efforts. Although he sometimes – as at Bristol in July 1643 and Gloucester in the following month – accompanied the Royalist forces in the field with his wagon loaded with 'infernal' devices, much of la Roche's time was spent in Oxford supervising the manufacture of these weapons.

Among the devices employed were firepikes, which basically consisted of a pike with cord or other material soaked in gunpowder attached to its head, which could be ignited and then thrust or waved at the enemy, especially useful in scaring cavalry mounts. Grenades, or 'granadoes', were used in large numbers, some 800 being in store at Oxford in May 1643. These consisted of small containers, usually of clay or pottery, which were filled with a mixture of gunpowder and nails, small pieces of metal or stone or inflammable tar or pitch, with a length of cord soaked in gunpowder as a fuse. This would be lit, and the grenade hurled to explode among the enemy. They were used with considerable effect at the storming of Bristol in 1643 and at Leicester two years later. Also used were fire arrows tipped with tar or other inflammable materials, which were ignited and then fired by bow or short-barrelled musket at the thatched roofs of buildings within the besieged garrison. Particularly hazardous to those employed in it was 'petarding'. A petard – a cone-shaped container on a pole – was filled with explosives and fitted with a fuse, then fixed against the gate of the besieged garrison and exploded to blow a hole in it. These devices occasionally succeeded, as in the Parliamentarian capture of Oswestry in 1644, but more commonly they failed to explode or those carrying them were shot down before they could fix them in place.

With their knowledge of classical and medieval siege warfare, Civil War commanders – especially the educated amateurs rather than professional soldiers – were often attracted by the notion of employing siege engines of various types. Among them were 'sows', which were wheeled vehicles covered with boards or hides – effectively small-scale versions of medieval siege engines, which in theory could be pushed up to the enemy defences or to a breach carrying storming parties. In March 1644 the Cheshire Parliamentarian commander, Sir William Brereton, had three 'moveable breastworks fittest to storm any place or enter any breach and will shelter from the enemy's shot 18 musketeers . . . these also will be of use to barricade suddenly any bridge, lane or narrow pass.'[12] One of them was possibly deployed at the siege of Beeston Castle in 1644, though to no effect.

Among the most remarkable of these 'engines' were those built by the Royalist academic Dr William Chillingworth, based on classical design, for use at the siege of Gloucester in 1643. Apparently fitted with movable bridges and carrying troops, they were intended to be pushed close to the enemy defences, which they would overtop, and the bridges would then be lowered to allow the troops on board to storm the fortifications. Unsurprisingly, they were never used: possibly because they were unable to cross ditches and moats, and were found abandoned in a bog when the siege was raised.

Chapter Three

Garrisons

In most seventeenth-century conflicts garrisons multiplied to an alarming extent. They were regarded as one of the plagues of the Thirty Years War in Germany, and similar mushrooming growth was a feature of the English Civil War. They were viewed as a necessary evil by most soldiers, and as an almost unmitigated menace by many civilians.

Once it became obvious (by the winter of 1642) that the war would not, after all, be decided by the outcome of its first major battle, the need to secure as much territory as possible was clear to both sides. The only way this could be done, especially in hostile and contested areas, was by establishing garrisons. The Parliamentarians were fortunate in having large areas, particularly in the Eastern Association and South East England, where, for much of the war, their control was largely undisputed. Here garrisons could be kept to a minimum and disruption to civilian life greatly reduced. The Royalists, with few areas, except initially parts of Wales and Northern England, free from danger, were less fortunate. Particularly in disputed areas such as the Midlands, the numbers of garrisons established by both sides increased steadily. In the spring of 1645 a Royalist writer estimated there were thirty-nine of the King's and thirty-six Parliamentarian garrisons in Wales and the Midlands, but this was a considerable underestimate, for more detailed research has identified thirty garrisons in Shropshire alone.[13]

Garrisons absorbed much military manpower, especially for the Royalists. In the spring of 1645, at a time when his field armies needed every available soldier to meet the threat of the New Model Army, around 48 per cent of the King's troops were tied up in garrison duties, and between June 1645 and the surrender of Harlech (the last Royalist mainland fortress) in March 1647, at least eighty-one Royalist garrisons were captured, their garrisons ranging from several thousand men to a mere handful.[14]

Garrison duty was usually popular with soldiers. For much of the time life was uneventful – boredom a greater threat than an often distant enemy. Accommodation would generally be superior to that available for troops serving in the field armies, and in inactive garrisons life might take on civilian overtones, with wives and children of the soldiers allowed to join them. Both the ordinary soldiers and their commanders often did well for themselves at the expense of the civilian population, and some commentators feared that the growth of garrisons would prolong the war, as the troops serving in them would have no desire to see their comfortable lifestyles threatened by the return of peace.

Garrison commanders, particularly those distant from their high commands, could often be their own masters. It was inevitable that some became little better than 'robber barons', with a nominal allegiance to their proclaimed cause. Particularly in the later stages of the war, as the Royalist administrative system broke down, some of the King's garrison commanders operated increasingly to agendas of their own. Sir William Vaughan, for example (a veteran of the Irish war, known as 'the Devil of Shrawardine' after the name of his principal garrison) ran a virtually independent 'fiefdom' in North Shropshire, his troopers enforcing contributions on the local civilian population and frequently robbing them as well, whilst fiercely contesting any enemy incursions into their domain.

So notorious had Vaughan's men become by the end of the war that the Governor of Ludlow, Sir Michael Woodhouse – himself no paragon of virtue – refused them admission into the town. Another West Midlands Royalist, Sir Thomas Leveson, Governor of Dudley Castle, on his surrender in 1646 had to be provided with an escort out of the area by the Parliamentarians, so hated was he by the local civilian population. Of the Royalist garrison of Lichfield it was said: 'There is a great rabble of all sorts of people convened there, being neither disciplined nor armed.'[15]

A community would greet the establishment of a garrison in its midst with mixed feelings. It might provide protection from plundering, but it would make demands of its own, and the presence of troops in its midst would have a variety of effects on the community. In the case of a large town or key strategic location a garrison might be several thousand strong, but in its outposts, or in the smaller strongholds which dotted the countryside, a more typical garrison might number between 100 and 200 men.

In an area uncontested by the enemy, a garrison aimed to control the surrounding area within a 20-mile radius – one day's ride for a troop of horse. All the villages and farms within this area would be expected to support the upkeep of the garrison by means of financial and material contributions. In theory these would be decided and regulated by the civil and military authorities by means of 'assessments', with rates and quotas laid down for each community and individual householder, and ideally administered and collected by the constable, and either delivered by him to the garrison or collected by troops. In practice the system rarely operated smoothly. Civilians frequently professed themselves unable to meet the demands imposed on them, or at least proved slow in doing so. The consequences for them were usually unpleasant. A Royalist Governor of Worcester informed one such dilatory community:

> Know you that unless you bring to me the monthly contributions for six months you are to expect an unsanctified troop of horse among you, from whom if you hide yourselves, they shall fire your houses, without mercy, hang up your bodies wherever they find them, and scare your ghosts.[16]

Unsurprisingly, even when the required contributions were ready on the arrival of the party sent to collect them, a wise village constable would ensure that in addition suitable refreshments were available for the troops.

The penalty for non-cooperation was usually the threat of burning of property. This threat was most commonly made against villages, for the economic effects on larger communities would probably be too great. Because it was not in the interests of a garrison to destroy the economic infrastructure that supported it, the taking of hostages to ensure compliance was an alternative.

Whilst it might be hard enough for a community to support the demands of a single garrison, many found themselves in a disputed area, subject to the demands of opposing garrisons. Here they would have to contribute twice over, with the added probability of suffering reprisals at the hands of whichever garrison regarded the community concerned as being part of its 'home' territory. In 1644 Lincolnshire was described as:

> a ruinated county . . . no man hath anything to call his own or assure himself a quiet night's sleep they are so surrounded with garrisons both of the king's and the parliament's what one leaves the other takes.[17]

The impact of a garrison on its locality varied. In the case of a castle or country house, a new governor would have several concerns. A castle might be in a poor state of repair, and as well as mending breaches in its walls and beginning construction of earthen outworks, accommodation for the soldiers, their horses and supplies, would also be needed. Very often the original buildings, which had been constructed in the bailey or courtyard for this purpose, had decayed and needed to be replaced, or some of the rooms in towers and gatehouses repaired. A particularly powerful or uncooperative owner might seriously hinder or frustrate military plans. The eccentric Lord Herbert, owner of Montgomery Castle, refused to allow it to be garrisoned by the Royalists, only then to turn the castle over to the Parliamentarians, on condition that they did not set foot in the library! The owner of Bletchingdon

House in Oxfordshire proved similarly obstructive regarding the fortification of his house, with fatal results for its governor, Frank Windebanke, who was executed for his quick surrender to Oliver Cromwell.[18]

In these cases, the effect on the local civilian population might be limited to demands for their labour on the garrison defences and meeting the assessments set for its upkeep.

Much more far-reaching was the impact of garrison troops in towns. Inhabitants preferred a garrison to be made up of local troops, who were likely to be more considerate towards the community within which they were stationed. On the surrender of York to the Parliamentarians in July 1644 it was agreed that the new garrison should consist of Yorkshire troops. It was also common for part of a town's garrison to consist of units of citizens, often based on the pre-war Trained Band. Chester and Worcester, for example, had 'Town Regiments', usually officered by local merchants and other leading citizens, and consisting largely of their employees. Military governors had limited enthusiasm for such units, feeling, with some justification, that their members placed the interests of their own community and families above harsher military needs.

Such local units were largely billeted in their own homes and, as part-time soldiers except in emergency, could supply their own needs. This was not the case for the 'strangers' who frequently formed the bulk of town garrisons. The citizens were expected to provide the funds required for their up-keep, usually in the form of weekly 'assessments'. These could be crippling, especially in the case of a town under siege, whose economic life and income came to a standstill. In December 1645, for example, despite having been under close blockade for three months, a weekly assessment of £200 (around £10,000 in modern values) was demanded of the citizens of Chester.

Even more unpopular was the system of 'free quarter'. Under this a house-holder had a set number of troops billeted on him or her, and was required to provide them with board and lodging at an agreed rate. If fortunate, the householder might be recompensed for this in money, usually raised by deductions from the soldiers' pay. More commonly, however, the unwilling 'host' would receive in lieu a receipt known as a 'ticket' or 'billet' theoretically redeemable from the authorities at a later date. In practice such payments were made in a very laggardly fashion and frequently not at all. And on many occasions, dissatisfied with the rations allocated to them, soldiers forced the householder to supplement their diet at his own expense. It was not uncommon for an unfortunate civilian to have a considerable number of troops billeted on him. In the crowded condition of Chester in the final weeks of the siege, some residents had half a dozen or more soldiers billeted on them.[19]

The life of a civilian community was affected in numerous other ways by the presence of an alien garrison in its midst. Whilst some of the financial cost might be recovered as a result of what the soldiers spent in the town, other effects were certainly less desirable. It was generally felt that the presence of troops – with their tendency to seize goods, money and livestock with little regard for legal nicety – discouraged traders from attending fairs and markets in the town. Still more resented was the behaviour of the soldiers. In 1644 Chester became unwilling host to several thousand English troops brought over from Ireland to fight for the King. These soldiers had arrived dressed virtually in rags, and collections of shoes and clothing for them were made in Chester and across North Wales. Yet within a few days of the soldiers' arrival the city council was offering their commanders gifts of the civic plate on condition that the 'Irish' (as they were often inaccurately described) left the town.[20] But in January, following defeat at the battle of Nantwich, the 'Irish' were back, now largely confined to Chester and its immediate vicinity, and the citizens soon presented their commander, John Lord Byron, with a catalogue of complaints. In order to obtain beer money, the soldiers were selling the clothing they had been given. Men wounded in the fighting at Nantwich were reported to be idling around the town with no attempt to return them to duty, and armed soldiers were brawling in the streets and threatening civilians. The soldiers' women and children were accused of various misdemeanours. There were allegations of robbery, whilst the citizens' religious sensibilities were injured by the alleged failure of many of the troops to attend church on Sundays.[21]

Byron attempted to meet these complaints by the well-tried expedient of hanging a couple of offenders. Unless he had overwhelming military strength available, the governor of a town had to maintain a delicately judged balance between military needs and the requirement to retain the support – or at least the acquiescence – of the community. Most governors cordially detested the civilian leadership with whom they had to deal, and who would understandably tend vociferously to oppose such measures as the demolition of suburbs and the financial demands made upon them. In general, a governor would find it easier to impose his wishes if his charge was under actual, or imminent threat of, attack, when the well-being of the citizens themselves might be at risk. But even then, non-military factors had to play a part in his actions. The demolition of buildings, for example, was limited by the need to keep sufficient housing both for the troops and for civilians who lost their homes in the process, and to minimise both economic disruption and the amount of civilian hostility created. For civilian unrest, particularly as a result of the privations of a prolonged siege, was always a major factor. In Chester, for example, in the early weeks of 1646, sustained demonstrations by the women of the town did much to force Lord Byron to surrender.[22]

For much of the time boredom was a greater threat than enemy action to the soldiers of the average garrison. Certainly more of them died from the effects of disease than at the hands of their opponents. For those troops unfortunate enough to be stationed in contested areas, however, life was considerably more eventful. In November 1643 a Parliamentarian soldier in the garrison of Farnham Castle, lying close to Royalist forces at Odiham, reported: 'We never want constant alarms, so that we have a hellish life.' [23] More typical of garrison actions were the innumerable minor skirmishes, raid and counter-raid, which occurred over wide areas of the British Isles. A typical action was witnessed by the Shropshire antiquarian Richard Gough, as a schoolboy in the village of Myddle:

> There was one Cornet Collins, an Irishman, who was a Garrison soldier for the King, at Shrawardine Castle. This Collins made his excursions very often into this parish, and took away Cattle, provision, and bedding, and what he pleased. On the day before this conflict, he had been at Myddle taking away bedding, and when Margaret, the wife of Allen Challinor, the Smith, had brought out and showed him her best bed, he thinking it too coarse, cast it into the lake, before the door, and trod it under his horse's feet. This Cornet, on the day this contest happened, came to Myddle and seven soldiers with him, and his horse having cast a shoe, he alighted at Allen Challinor's Shop to have a new one put on. There was one Richard Manning, a Garrison soldier at Moreton Corbet, for the Parliament. This Manning was brought up as a servant under Thomas Jukes, of Newton, with whom he lived many years, and finding that Nat. Owen did trouble this neighbourhood, he had a grudge against him, and came with seven more soldiers with him, hoping to find Owen at Myddle with his wife. This Manning and his companions came to Webscott, and so over Myddle Park, and came into Myddle at the gate by Mr Gittin's house at what time the Cornet's horse was a-shoeing. The Cornet hearing the gate clap, looked by the end of the shop and saw the soldiers coming, and thereupon he, and his men mounted their horses; and as the Cornet came at the end of the shop, a brisk young fellow shot him through the body with a carbine shot, and he fell down in the lake at Allen Challinor's door. His men fled, two were taken, and as Manning was pursuing them in Myddle Wood Field, which was then unenclosed, Manning having the best horse overtook them, while his partners were far behind, but one of the Cornet's men shot Manning's horse which fell down dead under him, and Manning had been taken

prisoner had not some of his men come to rescue him. He took the saddle under his arm, and the bridle in his hand, and went the next way to Wem, which was then a garrison for the Parliament . . . The Cornet was carried into Allen Challinor's house, and laid on the floor; he desired to have a bed laid under him, but Margaret told him, she had none but that which he saw yesterday; he prayed her to forgive him, and lay that under him, which she did. Mr Roderick [a schoolmaster] was sent for to pray with him. I went with him, and saw the Cornet lying on the bed, and much blood running along the floor. In the night following, a Troop of horse came from Shrawardine, and pressed a team in Myddle, and so took the Cornet to Shrawardine, where he died the next day.[24]

Chapter Four

Taken by Storm:
The Fall of Bristol 1643 and 1645

Most costly in terms of lives, and most terrifying and horrific for those caught up in it, was the taking of a fortress or town by storm. The sack of Magdeburg in the Thirty Years War, when 30,000 allegedly died, was the comparison most often made by Civil War propagandists when describing similar events in the English Civil Wars. And although no British examples actually approached such notorious Continental cases in terms of destruction or loss of life, there were instances, such as the Royalist stormings of Liverpool, Bolton and Leicester, where the toll was sufficiently high to invite such comparisons.

Storming an enemy garrison was usually a last resort. It inevitably took a high toll in lives among the attackers, and destruction and looting of property by the victors – often followed by large-scale desertion as soldiers made off with their booty – was almost inevitable. Consequently, generals would only storm an enemy garrison if time was at a premium (requiring a speedy resolution of the siege) or they lacked an adequate siege train, or if the garrison was thought to be inadequate to put up an effective defence.

The stormings of Bristol in 1643 and 1645 involved all these factors. In 1642 Bristol was described by the Parliamentarians as 'a place of greatest consequence of any in England, next to London.'[25] It was an important administrative and economic centre and a leading mercantile port, which also had considerable naval significance, especially for control of the southern Irish Sea. Its population of 15,000 made Bristol England's second largest city. As was often the case, the predominant feeling among the citizens of Bristol as civil war approached was one of neutralism. Work began on refurbishing the defences but the hope was for a short war, which would be concluded without an irreconcilable breach between the supporters of King and Parliament, both substantially represented among the population of Bristol.

In the event, control was initially established by Parliament, with the arrival in November of troops under Colonel Thomas Essex. Plans for resistance by the local Royalists collapsed and the Parliamentarian occupation took

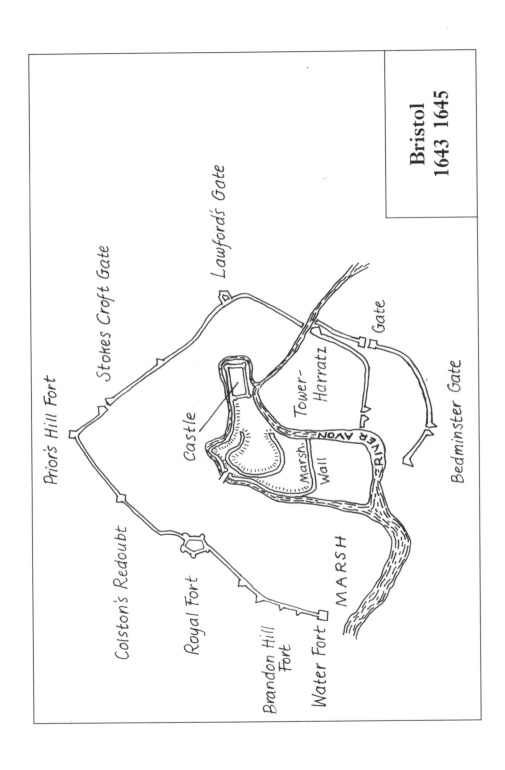

Bristol
1643 1645

Prior's Hill Fort

Stokes Croft Gate

Lawford's Gate

Colston's Redoubt

Royal Fort

Brandon Hill Fort

Water Fort

Castle

MARSH

Marsh Wall

Tower-Harratz

RIVER AVON

Gate

Bedminster Gate

place without opposition. Essex was a tough professional soldier whose rule proved unwelcome to the citizens. Partly because of this he was suspected of disloyalty and on 2 February was arrested by the newly arrived Colonel Nathaniel Fiennes, a politician and lawyer who lacked military experience or proven ability, but a member of an influential Parliamentarian family. Fiennes took over as governor but his attempts to strengthen the defences of Bristol were partially undermined by the demands placed on the garrison by the field army of Sir William Waller. Fiennes was aware of his own limitations and took advice from those with greater experience when surveying Bristol's defences, and was energetic in his efforts to improve them. Bristol's existing defences were based on its castle and medieval walls, and were over-looked by high ground to the north and west. To add to these difficulties, the suburbs had spread considerably beyond Bristol's medieval defences, and the two rivers around which the town was built made the rapid movement of troops between different locations difficult.

During the summer of 1642 the then Royalist-controlled town council had ordered the medieval gates to be repaired and guns mounted to defend the walls. In November, following the arrival of Essex, a new floor, strong enough to bear the weight of artillery, was ordered for the castle, and earthworks were to be constructed at various points. None of this work was actually commenced until February, when an earthen fort was constructed on Brandon Hill on the southern side of the town, though the medieval walls remained the principal defence. These were 7 feet thick with towers at intervals and a ditch, 24 feet wide and 9 feet deep, in front. The church of St Mary Redcliff was converted into a fortified outwork, armed with three guns, to support the twenty-five artillery pieces already positioned on the town walls. The military headquarters and core of Bristol's defences was intended to be the castle, described as 'a very large stronghold, fortified with a very broad deep ditch, or graf, in part wet and dry, having a very good well in it.'[26] It stood upon a steep mount, with keep and curtain walls, its towers mounting twenty guns. A line of earthworks was constructed to the north and east of the city, though they were far from perfect. They stretched for some 3 miles from Limekiln Dock in the west along the high ground to the north of the city, and meeting the River Avon at Tower Haritz. According to the Royalist military engineer Bernard de Gomme:

> Its height commonly about a yard and a half or six feet where highest. The thickness on the top, above a yard, usually. The graf, or ditch, commonly two yards broad, but somewhere a foot or two more. The depth scarcely considerable; as being hardly five foot, usually; and in many rocky places not so deep.[27]

The line was bolstered by a series of forts or mounts, the principal Prior's Hill Fort, square in shape mounting three medium and one light gun. Brandon Hill, at the highest point of the line, was again square, with its defences 18 feet high, though according to de Gomme 'its graf or moat but shallow and narrow, by reason of the rockiness of the ground.' [28] It mounted four guns.

The construction of these fortifications made huge demands in money (about £1,000 per week – perhaps £50,000 in modern values – borne by the city) and in labour, and were not completed in time for the Royalist attack. The forts were mostly finished, although they lacked outworks.

Such extensive defences required a large garrison to man them, but the troops available fluctuated in both numbers and quality. A considerable number were called away in the summer of 1643 to reinforce the army of Sir William Waller, and some were probably lost in his defeat on Roundway Down (14 July). Fiennes would claim later to have had at the time of the Royalist attack in July only about 1,500 foot and 300 horse, notwithstanding desperate efforts to recruit. In fact he seems to have underestimated his strength, for counting the 700 men of the original garrison, he had about 1,100 newly raised recruits, as well as some city volunteers and various other odds and ends of units, giving him probably 2,500 foot in all, mostly well armed. He also had at least ninety-eight guns, not counting a considerable number available on ships in the harbour. There was no shortage of other firearms, for as well as those purchased by the city, a considerable number had been manufactured locally. Fiennes had added at least 1,000 muskets, obtained either by purchase or confiscation from the local Trained Band.[29] He had also bought or had manufactured considerable quantities of gunpowder. Later, placed on trial for his role in the loss of Bristol, Fiennes would be very evasive on this issue: he admitted to surrendering fifty barrels of powder, although in fact he probably had at least ninety.[30]

In March Royalist supporters in Bristol hatched a plot to admit Rupert's forces but were discovered and a number executed. The Royalist armies were too short of arms and ammunition to consider an attack on Bristol before the summer: indeed, the Oxford Army was largely on the defensive until July, when arms convoys from the North of England partially improved the situation. Although the Royalists still lacked an adequate siege train, the decision was taken, apparently mainly on the urging of Prince Rupert, to move against Bristol.

The Oxford Army probably provided around 4,500 foot and up to 6,000 horse. There was an artillery train of eight guns, limited partly because of a shortage of draught horses. The train included four heavy siege guns; two of them 27-pounder demi-cannon and two 15-pounder culverins. There were also two demi-culverins and two lighter field pieces. The effectiveness of this inadequate siege train was further limited by the persisting ammunition shortage. Only forty-two shot were available for each demi-cannon, a totally inadequate provision for prolonged bombardment.[31] Also present were two of Prince Rupert's foreign experts, his engineer Bernard de Gomme and the Frenchman Bartholomew la Roche, 'Captain General of all Masters of Artificial Fires', more prosaically in charge of pyrotechnical devices such as firepikes, petards and 'granadoes'. La Roche brought with him four carts laden with such materials. Another fireworker, Captain Samuel Fawcett, was in charge of a mortar piece.

Also present was the Royalist Western Army under Prince Maurice, with probably about 3,000 foot and 1,500 horse, making a total Royalist force of around 7,000 foot and 7,000 horse. The Oxford Army was to attack on the northern side of Bristol, with its foot organised into three brigades or 'Tertias' under Lord Grandison, Henry Wentworth and John Bellasis. Its horse formed two 'wings', commanded by Sir Arthur Aston and Colonel Charles Gerrard. The organisation of the Western Army is more obscure, but its foot may have been organised in three small Tertias.

The Royalists began to close in on Bristol on 23 July. Rupert established his headquarters at Westbury and during the day dragoons under Colonel Henry Washington occupied the dominating high ground around Clifton Church, opposite Brandon Hill Fort, giving them an important geographical advantage, for, as de Gomme noted: 'the city of Bristol stands in a hole'.[32] Skirmishing continued into the evening and next morning the ring around Bristol closed tighter as the Western Army crossed the River Avon at Keynsham and drove back Parliamentarian outposts on the southern side of the city. Maurice established gun batteries opposite Temple Gate, whilst Royalist sympathisers gained control of ships anchored at Kingswood, effectively severing Bristol's links by sea.

Rupert, meanwhile, paraded his troops on the high ground in a bid to intimidate his opponents, and then summoned Fiennes to surrender. The latter made a rather less than determined reply, stating that 'being instructed to keep the town for King and Parliament he could not yet relinquish that trust 'till he were brought to more extremity'.[33] Meanwhile, work continued on establishing the Royalist artillery positions, which would fire on Windmill Hill and Prior's Hill Forts. At the same time skirmishing continued and there was a brisk little action near Brandon Hill Fort, against which a battery mounting two culverins was being prepared, when Royalist Lieutenant Colonel Anthony Thelwall of Sir Edward Fitton's Regiment of Foot was sent with 200 men:

to lodge himself in the bottom of Brandon Hill: where he was well sheltered by the ferns and bushes, and bolstered by the two hills before and behind. The enemies made some sallies now and then, by twenties and thirties in a party, but were still repulsed by Lieutenant Colonel Thelwall . . . he often sent up some of his, to skirmish with the works, within a pistol shot. Our ordnance also sent them a bullet now and then, though with little effect upon their forts, the interest being only to alarm and keep them in, that they did ours the less mischief, only, as we heard, one of their cannoniers, vapouring in his shirt on the top of the fort, was killed there for his foolhardiness. Thus you have all our Tertias lodged at their designed posts, where they were to fall on afterwards, where from that time forward they were incessantly plied with great shot, case-shot, prick shot, iron drugs, slugs, or anything, from all the works and along the curtain, with all of which we received but little harm, our men as cheerfully them again with leaden courtesies.[34]

There was a lull in fighting at nightfall, but later hostilities resumed:

It was a beautiful piece of danger, to see so many fires incessantly in the dark from the pieces on both sides, for a whole hour together . . . And in these military masquerades was this Monday night passed.[35]

Rupert and Maurice met next day (25 July) to make their final plans. Fiennes's lukewarm response to their summons played a part in their decision not to mount a formal siege but to storm the defences. Other considerations included shortage of artillery ammunition and increasing sickness among their troops. Whilst skirmishing continued, orders were drawn up for a general attack by both armies to be launched at dawn next day.

In the days before reliable communications, synchronising attacks was always difficult. The intention was that the assault should be signalled by the firing of the two demi-cannon, but with skirmishing continuing throughout the night, there was potential for confusion, and the Western Army went into action prematurely, at around 3am. Rupert hastily ordered the signal to be given for the Oxford Army to begin its own attacks. Lord Grandison's Tertia was to advance on Prior's Hill Fort, and if successful, to reinforce Bellasis to his left. Grandison's force was spearheaded by two parties each of about fifty musketeers, which aimed to penetrate the line on either side of Prior's Hill Fort and isolate it. However, a larger attack by 300 men under Lieutenant Colonel Lunsford, directed at a point near the Fort, was repulsed. At Stokes Croft:

Major Sanders, Major Perkins, Major Burgess, the two Captains Aston and Captain Nowell and some two hundred and fifty men, fell directly upon the spur itself, came up to pistol and push of pike with the defendants through the bars [of the stockade] and threw nine hand-grenades in the works after which, Captain Fawcett, who behaved himself skilfully and stoutly in all this service, fastened a petard upon the port, which, though it blew well enough, yet it only broke two or three bars, but made no way for entrance. Plainly both works and line were so well defended, that ours, being able to do no more than give testimony of their valour, and having lost Captain Nowell and nineteen men, after an hour and a half fight, perceived there was no more good to be done upon them.[36]

Grandison now directed his efforts against Prior's Hill Fort itself, seeing that its approaches were not pallisaded. His soldiers got into the ditch below the fort, but as this stage of the assault had begun earlier than planned, scaling ladders had not yet been brought up:

and the enemy made too hot with shot and stones out of the fort, with muskets and case shot from the line and other batteries, our men were forced to quit it, some of them ran along by the line, others directly down the hill, and others standing to their arms, and shooting gallantly. Colonel Sir Ralph Dutton that day leading on the pikes, very gallantly with one in his hand into the ditch, charged upon the foot with it. In the meantime, his pikes being fallen back from the fort, he went out to bring them on again, when, finding my Lord Grandison, who behaved himself most gallantly all that day, persuading with them to return, he brought them up after him. Colonel Lunsford finding a ladder of the enemy's in the field, got up the fort with it as high as the palisades; which not being able to get over, he was fain to come down again. Lieutenant Ellis had once gotten upon the line, but receiving two shots, fell off again. Our men retreating, my Lord Grandison again took horse, to fetch them up the third time, which they obeyed very willingly, following even to the very ditch. Into this, since our retreat, some of the defendants were descended, and by one of them was my Lord Grandison shot in the right leg, who, thus hurt, desired Colonel [John] Owen to lead on the men, which he doing, was presently shot in the face; whereupon, the soldiers perceiving two of their chief commanders hurt, pressed on no further, but retreated.[37]

Elsewhere, the Royalists were also running into trouble. The Western Army's assault was already failing even before Rupert's men went into action. The Western foot advanced in three columns, the centre one under one of the best of the Cornish regimental commanders, Sir Nicholas Slanning, with Colonel Brutus Buck on his right and Sir Thomas Bassett to his left. The plan was to bridge the dry ditch with wagons but it was discovered to be too deep and the troops were forced to fill up the ditch, whilst under fire, with bundles of sticks before they could bring up their scaling ladders:

> These three divisions fell on together with that courage and resolution, as nothing but death can control; and though the middle division got into the graf and so near filled it that some mounted the wall, yet by the prodigious disadvantage of the ground and the full defence the besieged made within, they were driven back with a great slaughter; the common soldiers, after their chief officers were killed, or desperately wounded, finding it a bootless attempt.[38]

After half an hour of savage fighting the attack by the Western troops began to collapse, although Prince Maurice at least succeeded in tying down the Parliamentarian defenders on the southern side of Bristol.

Meanwhile, Rupert's assault seemed to be faring no better. John Bellasis's brigade had attacked around Windmill Hill Fort and soon encountered 'hot service'. Bellasis had spearheaded his attack with a 'forlorn hope' consisting of thirty musketeers, six firepikes and six granadoemen from John Stradling's South Wales regiment, seconded by Bellasis's, Lunsford's and the remainder of Stradling's Regiments:

> All these advancing as fast as they could well run, to the very trench or ditch of the spur-work, and finding there an impossibility of entering, for that they wanted faggots to fill up the ditch, and ladders to scale the work, were to fall down upon the line, to the right hand of the Windmill Fort, to a stone wall.[39]

At this critical moment Major Will Legge brought news that Henry Wentworth's Tertia had broken through the defences:

> upon which Lieutenant Colonel Moyle crying, 'They run! They run!' encouraged our men again. Rupert himself rallied some waverers, having a horse shot under him in the process, and Belasyse's men followed Wentworth's through the line.

Wentworth's Brigade had made the vital breakthrough:

> And this was the manner of it: About twelve the night before, by a council of the officers of the Tertia, the line between the two forts

of Brandon Hill and the Windmill fort was resolved to be first fallen upon . . . The second Tertia, with Colonel Washington's and Sir Robert Howard's dragoons, was to have been divided into van, battle and rear, Sir Jacob Astley's and Sir Edward Fitton's regiments being ordered to lead, Colonel Bolles and Colonel Herbert to follow, and Colonel Washington to bring up the rear. But the furze and unevenness of the ground not suffering them to observe the agreed order, every man, according to his courage served him, fell on as he could come at it. In the advance up, being full under the command of both forts, they were saluted with iron-slugs, pike-shot, and what they pleased, from their cannon. Here were Lieutenant Stapleton and Ancient [Ensign] Middleton shot, and four or five soldiers killed. This made our men run close up to the works, as fast as they could: Colonel Wentworth, Sir Edward Fitton, Colonel Washington, Lieutenant-Colonel Thelwall, and other brave commanders, leading the way gallantly. Having recovered up to the line, they were almost in cover under St Michael's hill, and so under the hill, that the Windmill fort could not see them . . . the spur and barn on their right sheltered the forwardest of them from Brandon fort also. Being gotten to the line, Lieutenant Wright, Lieutenant Baxter, with others, throwing hand grenades over among the enemies, made them stagger and recoil a little: so that ours more courageously coming on to storm over the line, the enemies quitted it, and ran towards the town. Ours, thereupon, helping over one another, fell presently to fling down the work with their hands, halberds, and partisans, as they could, to let in their fellows. In the meantime, Lieutenant-Colonel Littleton, riding along the inside of the line with a fire-pike, quite cleared the place of the defendants: some of them crying out wildfire.[40]

The Royalists had broken in at a weak point in the defences, which was not covered by the Parliamentarian guns. But their position was extremely critical. Fiennes had placed in reserve here his own troop of horse under Major Hercules Langrish. The latter had a reputation for cowardice, and, for whatever reason, failed to counter-attack. The Royalists were given enough breathing space to bring up two or three hundred men, but they were still in disorder when some of Fiennes's horse at length charged:

Our pikes staggered at the charge; but some fifty or sixty musketeers from a hedge giving them a round salvo, they retreated with some loss. By that we had ranked the men already gotten over the line, the enemy's horse rallied again; so that wheeling on the side of the Windmill-hill, they gave us another charge. Our pikes, which should have staved them off, could not yet be made stand: but some six of our dragoons firing on them, and other musketeers first discharging and then laying at them with their musket-stocks, they again retreated. But the truth is, Captain Clerk, Ancient Hodgkinson, and some others, running upon them with fire-pikes, neither men nor horses were able to endure it. These fire-pikes did the feat . . . [41]

Wentworth's men cleared 'Essex's work' at the end of a lane and were supported by several parties of horse. The Royalists pressed on into the suburbs, engaging in vicious house-to-house fighting, musketeers exchanging fire from neighbouring houses 'like scolding at one another out of windows.'[42] A musket ball hit the bar of Lieutenant Colonel Thelwall's headpiece, and ricocheting off, wounded a captain in the arm.

Some of the Parliamentarians attempted to contain the break-in, but Fiennes ordered the troops on the northern line and in the forts to retire into the city. His officers tried to dissuade him and urged that a counter-attack be launched, but Fiennes angrily refused, accusing them of mutiny and threatening them with execution. He would claim later that he had feared that the defenders would be isolated in small groups and cut down, and that the reserves in the city would not support them. There may have been some truth in this, but the effect of Fiennes's orders was that panic set in among his men:

> A heap of them [Royalists] now newly gotten over the line and being there charged by the enemy's horse, before they could range themselves into order: made up all together with such good speed into a lane towards the town, the enemy retreating still before them and here (all unknown to ours) the enemy had a strong work: and they in it suspecting our men's running haste, to be the courage of such as pursued the victory, and were resolved to carry all before them with as much haste ran out of it.[43]

This was the work at the end of the modern Park Street, and its fall opened the way for thrusts towards College Green and the Quay. Wentworth's men, still under fire from Brandon Hill and Water Forts, and from guns across the river, occupied College Green, but enemy foot, with some light field pieces, still held the houses surrounding the Green. As street fighting continued, some Royalist officers asked leave from Rupert to set fire to ships in the harbour as a diversion but the Prince refused, fearing that the blaze would get out of control. Bellasis's men, supported by Sir Arthur Aston's cavalry, pushed on towards the Frome Gate, taking significant losses:

Here, in two hours' space, were two or three brisk bouts, for Sir Arthur Aston's, Major Marrow's and other horse . . . had several charges with them. Here, upon steps (since called Lunsford's Steps) was the gallant Colonel Lunsford shot through the heart, who had that day before been shot through the arm; Colonel Bellasyse, also, was slightly hurt in the forehead. A party of Colonel Washington's and Colonel Stradling's men going on, Lieutenant Blunt and Lieutenant Ward were both shot through the thighs. The fight grew hard, and our men much tired, when, by the coming in of Lieutenant Colonel Herbert Lunsford, with part of the Lord General's Tertia of foot, and others, with fresh horses, the enemies were beaten down the stairs again, through the Frome gate into the town. Here was Lieutenant Colonel Moyle shot in the bladder, of which he died afterwards.[44]

A Parliamentarian wrote:

When the news came into the said city on the Wednesday morning, that some of the enemies were entered within the line, this deponent and divers other women, and maids, with the help of some men, did with wool sacks and earth, stopt up Frome gate to keep out the enemy from entering the said city, being the only passage by which the enemy must enter.[45]

The barrier was about 16 feet thick, and by around 9am Wentworth and Bellasis were bogged down. In the south, the attack by the Western Army had been completely repulsed, whilst in the north the attackers had yet to penetrate the inner defences, their only remaining reserves being some cavalry. At Fiennes's trial his accusers would claim that the Royalists had already lost around 700–1,000 dead and 700 wounded. This was almost certainly an exaggeration, but there had been significant casualties among officers and the known toll of between 100–300 Cornish losses might suggest perhaps 1,100–1,400 among the Oxford Army troops: something like 23–31 per cent of their total strength.[46]

The defenders still held the forts on the high ground, and the inner defences presented a potentially very formidable obstacle. The Parliamentarians, with comparatively light casualties, had considerable reserves uncommitted. However, Fiennes failed to inspire his men, and morale began to falter:

the said Langrish, afterwards coming back to Froom Gate; his troop came along with him whom he had brought from the lime-kilns or thereabouts, and upon the sound of the trumpet he was let in at

Froom Gate. All men then crying shame that the soldiers were called off the line, and complaining that they were betrayed: I further say, that one of the soldiers drawn off the line then reported, they were commanded to retreat into the city upon pain of death, for that city was like to be lost.[47]

Many of the reserves who had been mustered in the centre of the town now quietly disbanded themselves and went home, and only about 200 men out of an expected 1,000–1,200 actually rallied to Fiennes's call. The discouraged Governor sent out a request to Rupert for a parley but this was rejected by the Royalists, who suspected trickery. How near to defeat the King's men actually were was now demonstrated when the garrison made a sally, lasting for about an hour and a half, in which only one of their number was killed and during which a number of Royalists attempted to surrender. However, Fiennes once again requested a parley:

Which the Prince willingly embracing and getting their hostages into his hands sent Colonel Gerrard and another officer to the governor to treat, The treaty began at 2 o'clock in the afternoon and before 10 at night the articles were agreed upon and signed.[48]

Fiennes met great difficulty in enforcing acceptance of the surrender among his men, especially as the conditions granted were harsh, the defenders being disarmed and denied the honours of war. Fiennes accepted the terms without consulting a Council of War, and suffered further humiliation, when, according to the Royalists as a result of marching out of the wrong gate at the wrong time, the Parliamentarians were robbed of their possessions by Rupert's men.

After the storm it was the turn of the civilian population to feel the wrath of the victors. Although they claimed to have plundered only Parliamentarian supporters, in reality the sack of Bristol was fairly indiscriminate. Nor did the end of hostilities do much to ease the plight of Bristol's inhabitants, who found the influx of Royalist soldiery a highly unpleasant experience:

They quartered soldiers upon all sorts as well malignants [Royalists] as others and all upon free quarter, placing 20 and 30 soldiers in a house upon men of but reasonable estates, which puts them to an unreasonable charge, and the more because divers of the Cavaliers will have a variety of victuals at each meal, and will not be content to feed upon good beef, but must have mutton and veal and chickens with wine and tobacco etc, and much ado to please them all; causing also men, women and children to lay upon boards, or as they make shift, while the Cavaliers possess their beds, which they fill with lice.[49]

Furthermore:

> they fill their houses with swearing and cursing insomuch that they corrupt men's servants and children, that those who were once civil have learnt to curse and swear almost as bad as they: and on the Sabbath these guests, or rather these beasts, spend their time in dicing, drinking, carding and other such abominations.[50]

Fiennes was rather more fortunate than those he had abandoned. Although he was brought to trial in London, charged with cowardice and treason, his family influence was sufficient to secure his acquittal, although he was never re-employed by Parliament.

The capture of Bristol was a pyrrhic victory for the Royalists. Of the 4,000–5,000 foot of the Oxford Army who had taken part in the attack, only about 1,400 could be mustered afterwards, and Bellasis's Tertia had lost so heavily that it was broken up, its regiments initially forming the new garrison of Bristol, their ranks filled out with prisoners-of-war.

The heavy casualties suffered at Bristol had a major influence on Royalist strategy for the remainder of the campaign. The loss of life horrified King Charles, who, a few weeks later, rejected his generals' suggestion that he storm Parliamentarian-held Gloucester. As a result the town held out until relieved by the Parliamentarian army under the Earl of Essex, which itself avoided defeat at the First Battle of Newbury, arguably the turning point of the First Civil War.

During the next two years Bristol became steadily more important to the Royalist war effort. In particular, it was a major centre for the mustering of recruits, arms manufacturing and supply. Both the garrison and defences of Bristol were reorganised. Lord Francis Hawley's Regiment of Foot, recruited locally, became a permanent part of the garrison, together with Trained Band and other auxiliary units. In theory, the Trained Bands totalled 1,000 men, though in practice probably never reached that figure. The auxiliary units were formed in March 1644 and a year later were six in number, each of 600–800 men, and remained under the control of the city authorities. By then there were two Trained Band regiments, under Colonels Thomas Colston and John Taylor, although in the summer of 1645 Prince Rupert complained they could only muster 800 men between them.

The Second Siege

There is uncertainty concerning the size of Bristol's garrison when the second siege began in the summer of 1645. The Parliamentarians claimed it was 4,000 strong, whilst Rupert, though initially saying that 'We never were in better condition than now', [51] later claimed only 500–600 effective foot out of a total of 3,600 regulars and 800 Trained Band and auxiliaries. He also admitted to only 150 horse, which may only have included the cavalry of the regular garrison, as during the summer the Prince had also had his own and Prince Maurice's veteran units, of around 700–800 men, together with at least two newly raised Welsh infantry regiments. A reasonably accurate total for the Royalist garrison might be around 1,000 cavalry, together with 2,500 regular infantry and 800–1,000 Trained Band and auxiliaries.

There was similar dispute regarding the state of Bristol's defences. Immediately after they captured the town, the Royalists had begun repairing and extending the fortifications. The forts along the outer lines were certainly improved, although much of the lines themselves were left unaltered. Brandon Hill Fort was converted into a huge bastion carrying six guns. Windmill Hill Fort was also extended and fitted out with twenty-two guns. Prior's Hill Fort was rebuilt and armed with thirteen cannon. A number of the smaller forts were also strengthened under the supervision of Bernard de Gomme, utilising a labour force conscripted in the city and the surrounding area. As usual there were difficulties of finance and manpower, and work was still incomplete in August 1645, although by then the defences mounted a total of 151 guns.

The major Royalist defeats at Naseby and Langport, in the summer of 1645, faced Bristol with attack by the victorious New Model Army. Prince Rupert – now General of a field army that no longer existed and knowing that the war was lost – took personal charge of the defence of Bristol. Orders were issued for the civilian population to stockpile six months' supply of food in preparation for a siege, though it was later discovered that 60 per cent had been unable or unwilling to comply. The Prince also complained of a shortage of ammunition, despite having 130 barrels of gunpowder. He gave orders for the suburbs to be demolished, although the customary reluctance of the civilian population and the speed of the enemy advance left this incomplete. Parliament's victories in Somerset meant that Bristol was isolated from the remaining Royalist forces in South West England and elsewhere.

Sir Thomas Fairfax, General of the New Model Army, saw his first task as being to take Bristol's outlying garrisons, such as Bath. The reduction of Bristol was a priority and he was unwilling to advance any deeper into the South West so long as Rupert and his garrison remained defiant. As Fairfax knew, Rupert was endeavouring to raise more levies from among the war-weary inhabitants of South Wales and hoped for reinforcements from Gerrard's troops there. For a time it seemed the King himself, with his remaining 3,000 or so cavalry, might join him. However, the defeat at

Langport and opposition to the plan by his Secretary of State, Lord George Digby, persuaded the King to abandon this idea.

The change of plan was not known to Fairfax, when, on 21 August, the first troops of the New Model Army approached Bristol. Fairfax established his headquarters at Keynsham. Rupert, meanwhile, was trying to burn the remaining suburbs of Bristol, together with outlying villages such as Bedminster and Clifton, but was driven back by Parliamentarian cavalry. Fairfax sent Commissary General Henry Ireton, with five regiments of horse, one regiment of dragoons and five hundred foot to protect the villages lying to the north of Bristol. On the south side of the River Avon Fairfax's outposts were again attacked by Royalist cavalry on 22 August. They were once again repulsed, Sir Richard Crane, commanding Rupert's Lifeguard, being mortally wounded.

During the next two days more Parliamentarian troops moved up from Somerset and, crossing the Avon at Keynsham, deployed on the eastern side of the city. Edward Mountagu's Brigade was stationed between the Rivers Frome and Avon, within musket shot of the Royalist defences, whilst to their right, Thomas Rainsborough's Brigade took up position on Durdon Down, its flanks protected by Ireton's horse.

On 23 August Fairfax shifted his headquarters to Stone House in Stapleton. Cromwell admitted that the Parliamentarian besieging forces were thinly spread. Whilst the troops on the southern side of Bristol were setting up siegeworks, the Parliamentarians tried without success to incite an uprising within the city. Rupert, meanwhile, continued to hit back. On 23 August the Royalists attacked Rainsborough's outposts, though with little effect. Next day, a stronger force issued out of Prior's Hill Fort and surprised some of Colonel John Okey's dragoons, before being driven back by reinforcements. On the 26th an attack was made at 4am against Weldon's Brigade, stationed on the Somerset side of the town. Because of Parliamentarian negligence, the Royalists achieved a surprise, killing ten of the enemy and taking ten others prisoner. However, in the afternoon a senior Royalist officer, Sir Bernard Astley, was mortally wounded and captured in another skirmish.

On 27 August the Parliamentarians were forewarned of an intended Royalist sally from Lawford's Gate, and the attack was repulsed, as was a similar sortie next day. On 1 September, in the biggest raid so far, 1,000 horse and 600 foot, led personally by Rupert, sallied from the vicinity of the Royal Fort, concealed by mist and rain. They achieved initial surprise, capturing Colonel Okey, but were forced to withdraw when the Parliamentarian outposts were reinforced.

The Royalists argued that their series of sallies had succeeded. They claimed that on 24 August Rupert, with 300 horse and 500 foot, had 'killed 37, in an instant, and disordered the whole body'.[52] On the 26th the Prince had sortied from the Radcliffe Gate with 120 horse and 300 foot, and

> fell on the rebels guard at Bedminster, killed six score, cut off their whole guard, pursued them quite through the streets, and brought off seven score arms . . . Thursday noon (the rebels being at dinner) His Highness sallied forth near Lawford's Gate with 500 foot and 50 horse, slew eight score rebels, cut off the whole guard, brought off all provisions, clothes and arms, Colonel John Russell commanded here. Saturday last His Highness early sallied at Watergate Fort with 400 horse and 120 foot, fell on the body of the rebels' quarters, slew their foot, killed three officers (a major and two captains) brought in Colonel Okey himself and most of his regiment. Colonel Cary commanded the horse.[53]

Cromwell, however, said that the Parliamentarians lost a total of no more than thirty men in all of the Royalist sallies. Not only did they fail to disrupt the operations of the New Model Army, but the latter also obtained the services of several thousand local volunteers who were sent to support Rainsborough's Brigade. By 3 September, according to a contemporary report:

> Great store of ladders are brought into the leaguer by the country, and the first and second of September instant at night every soldier in the guards was commanded to take a faggot, many cannon baskets are made.[54]

On 2 September the Parliamentarian Council of War initially decided against an assault on Bristol, 'through the unseasonableness of the weather, and other great difficulties'. However, no sooner was this decision reached 'when the difficulties were removed'. A sub-committee was set up to plan an assault. This change of mind was probably influenced by increasing sickness among the besiegers, fear of a Royalist relief attempt, and the political consideration that Parliament wanted a quick victory.

The sub-committee felt that an attack on the strongly defended northern side of Bristol would be too costly, and instead recommended assaults on the south and east. Weldon's Brigade, supported by three regiments of horse, would attack from the south. Edward Mountagu's men, backed by two regiments of horse, would attack around Lawford's Gate and the line between the Rivers Frome and Avon. Between the Avon and Prior's Hill Fort, Rainsborough's Brigade, with two regiments of horse, were to make the Fort their main objective, detaching one regiment of horse and another of foot to prevent the defenders being reinforced from the Royal Fort. Another 200 men, supported by sailors landed from the fleet, were to attack the Water

Fort. A brigade of horse would be stationed on Durdham Down to guard against any Royalist breakout attempt and was also to tie down the Royalists in the Brandon Hill area.

On 4 September Fairfax summoned Rupert to surrender. According to the Royalists, the Prince's reaction was 'God damn me! It's a summons!' However, Fairfax's plea that Rupert should surrender in order to avoid needless bloodshed and pointless destruction may have struck a chord with the Prince's own view that the war was effectively lost. He did not reject Sir Thomas's demands outright but asked to be allowed to send a messenger to ascertain the wishes of the King. Fairfax rejected this proposal as a ploy to gain time.

On 5 September the Royalists held a Council of War, at which they agreed to send Fairfax their own proposals, gaining a breathing space during which they

> might strengthen our works within, hear from the king, and had [Fairfax] assented to our demands, we should have required a confirmation of them by the Parliament, which protraction of time would have been to our advantage.[55]

The Royalist demands included an amnesty for all citizens of Bristol and no garrisoning by the Parliamentarians. The latter was an impossible request but desultory negotiations continued until 9 September when, after issuing a final ultimatum, Fairfax ordered the assault to take place next day.

Both sides had continued warlike preparations throughout the period of talks. At around midnight, Fairfax moved up to his siege lines in order to supervise the final deployment of his 8,000 assault troops. At 2am on 10 September a huge bonfire, lit at Fairfax's command post on Ashby Hill, and the discharge of four heavy guns against Prior's Hill Fort, signalled the attack. Rainsborough claimed that his men were 'shouting with joy', although 'the service was very hot'.[56] The Royalists had been warned of the impending attack by a Parliamentarian deserter and were in full readiness. On the south side of the defences the attackers' scaling ladders proved too short and they were thrown back with the loss of over 100 men. The attacks on the eastern side of Bristol were made by foot regiments operating in pairs, which breached the lines at several points, forcing back the disorganised defenders. Mountagu and Pickering's Regiments attacked near Lawford's Gate:

> a great double work well-filled with men and cannon, presently ordered, and with great resolution beat the enemy from their works, and possessed their cannon; their expedition was such, that they forced the enemy from their advantages without any considerable loss to themselves, they laid down bridges for the horse to enter.[57]

The Parliamentarians claimed to have taken here twenty-six guns and many prisoners. This attack was supported by foot soldiers who had broken through the defences to the north, whilst Major John Desborough of Fairfax's Regiment of Horse pushed the defenders back behind the medieval walls and secured a gate near Castle Street. Rupert explained the Royalist collapse by claiming that the Parliamentarian assault had fallen on a part of the line held by townsmen and raw Welsh levies, whilst de Gomme said that the defences were weak at this point.

Meanwhile, the foot regiments of Sir Hardress Waller and Fairfax attacked further along the line towards the River Frome, where de Gomme, without explaining the reason why, said that the defences were 'decayed' and the ditch only 5 feet wide and deep.[58] In any event, the Parliamentarians again achieved a quick breakthrough and advanced into the rear of the defenders of Lawford's Gate, isolating them.

Phillip Skippon's and John Birch's Regiments attacked just to the north of the River Frome, seizing control of the Royalist guns and turning their fire against their former owners. Here the attackers opened a way for the supporting cavalry led by Major Hugh Bethell, who was just in time to counter-charge 500 horse moving up to 'scour the line'. A melee ensued, in which Bethell 'did behave himself very gallantly, and was shot in the thigh, had one or two shot more, and had his horse shot under him'.[59] However, reinforced by the cavalry regiments of Edward Whalley, Robert Rich and part of Samuel Greaves's, the Parliamentarians forced their opponents to retreat to the shelter of the Royal Fort and nearby Coulston's Fort.

To the south, the planned attack on the Water Fort was frustrated by a high tide, and some of the sailors were instead landed to support Rainsborough, who had detached half of Colonel Thomas Pride's foot to skirmish against the Royal Fort, in the course of which they took 'a little fort of Welshmen'.

The bitterest fighting of the day took place around Prior's Hill Fort. This was attacked by Rainsborough, with Edward Hammond's and part of Pride's Regiments. Its capture was vital for the success of the whole operation:

> this strong fort, without which all the rest of the line to Frome river would have done us little good; and indeed, neither horse or foot would have stood in all that way, in any manner of security, had not the fort been taken.[60]

Hammond thrust forward below and behind the fort, in order to cut off the retreat of its defenders, and allowed in cavalry, which moved forward to prevent Royalist reinforcements from coming up. Among the latter were city troops led by the Mayor of Bristol, who was killed in the fighting. Rainsborough's

Regiment attacked the Fort itself. Fierce hand-to-hand fighting followed. The attackers' ladders once again proved too short, as the fort was 'exceeding high'. However, Hammond's Regiment attacked the weaker inner face of the Fort and climbed in through the firing positions, the soldiers, in a state of fury and probably terror, laughing dementedly as they did so:

> In the end we forced the enemy within to run below into the inner rooms of the work, hoping to receive quarter, but our soldiers were so little prepared for to show mercy, by the opposition they had met withal the storm, and the refusal of quarter when it was offered, that they put to the sword the commander (one Major Price, a Welshman) and almost all the officers, soldiers and others in the fort, except a very few, which at the great entreaty of some of our officers, had their lives spared.[61]

By dawn much of the outer defences of Bristol were in Parliamentarian hands, though the Castle remained defiant, and a shot fired from its guns narrowly missed Fairfax and Cromwell as they were conferring on the ramparts of Prior's Hill Fort. The Royalists

> found them in full possession of the line and fort which caused our horse to retire to the Great Fort, who were presently ordered into the city to make that good, leaving other works insufficiently manned, Coulster's Work, Brandon Hill, and the new redoubt without the line, finding ourselves in this condition and considering the engagement of those within the city and castle and that Lord Hawley, Sir Matthew Appleyard, Colonel [Walter] Slingsby and their men were being in danger of being cut off, the enemy betwixt us and them, his highness moved the officers to entertain a treaty this time, before they were lost.[62]

Parts of the city were on fire and Fairfax set many of his men to work fighting the flames, 'fearing to see a great city burnt to ashes before our faces'. At 9am he agreed to Rupert's request for negotiations, provided the Royalists assisted in extinguishing the blaze. Talks were at times difficult, partly perhaps because not all of Rupert's officers shared his view that further resistance was hopeless. The castle, for example, was still intact and well provisioned. However, the outcome was inevitable and the Royalists accepted terms by which they were granted the honours of war and allowed to make their way to Oxford. On 11 September a Parliamentarian writer reported:

> Yesterday, according to the articles, Prince Rupert marched out in this manner, having drawn all his foot into the Royal Fort and the

Castle, his horse, standing in the green under the fort, within the line, those wagons appointed for him being laden with his baggage, in all not above eight. He drew out part of his horse and foot before his wagons and part following, himself next with his lifeguard of firelocks came forth, all in red coats before him and his lifeguard of horse following . . . Colonel Hammond's regiment of foot standing at the port to receive the keys of the fort and marched in. Lieut-General Cromwell, Col Montague, Col Rainsborough and some other officers waited at the port of the fort for his coming out, and waited upon him to the general, who stood with the convoy of horse without the line, and accompanied him over Durdum Down, being almost 2 miles. The Prince was clad in scarlet, very richly laid with silver lace, mounted upon a very gallant black Barbury horse; the General and the Prince rid together, the General giving the Prince the right hand all the way; the number of the Princes foot was about 2000, the horse with the designated number of 250 and the lifeguard altogether, made 400; I think there might be noblemen and gentlemen to the number of several hundred more.[63]

The Royalists had lost Bristol for similar reasons to those which had cost Nathaniel Fiennes the town. The garrison were too few to man the extensive defences and some were poorly motivated. But Rupert had put up a less fierce resistance than the defenders in 1643, and the attackers' losses were much lighter. The Prince was certainly accurate in his assessment that further resistance was futile, for, although the Castle might have held out for a while longer, the defenders of the isolated forts were doomed and there was no possibility of relief. This realism bore little weight with King Charles, influenced by opponents of Rupert such as Lord George Digby. Accused of treachery, the Prince was dismissed from all his commands and never again fought for the King on English soil.

Chapter Five

'Castle of the Rock':
The Leaguer of Beeston Castle 1643–1645

It was quickly apparent that medieval fortifications could still prove an effective defence. This was still more the case if the garrison concerned was sited in a naturally strong defensive location. A prime example of this type of stronghold was Beeston Castle in Cheshire.

Towering 160 metres above sea level on its sandstone crag, with precipitous drops on two sides, Beeston Castle dominates the surrounding countryside. It had been a place of strategic importance since prehistoric times, but following the Roman Conquest passed into obscurity until the arrival of the Normans. The long struggle between the Norman Earls of Chester and the Welsh Princedoms to the west meant that Beeston Crag was once again of military significance, controlling the route through the Peckforton Gap from Chester to the English Midlands, and with a panoramic view which made it a superb observation post. In 1236 Ranulf de Blundeville, sixth Earl of Chester, began the construction of Beeston Castle, referred to in contemporary documents as Castellum de Rupe, the 'Castle of the Rock'.[64]

Beeston's history had been comparatively uneventful. It was used as a military store and secure hold for prisoners, and was notable as a rumoured hiding place for the fabled treasure of King Richard II. However, in 1642, as Civil War burst upon England, Beeston's significance once more became apparent.

Parliamentarian Beeston

The defences of Beeston Castle consisted of a large Outer Ward on the lower eastern slopes of the crag, with a fortified gatehouse, and a curtain wall with an uncertain number of towers at intervals around it, and, occupying the summit of the crag and separated from the Outer Ward by a deep dry ditch cut into the rock, an Inner Ward with gatehouse, walls and towers, protected on its three outer sides by precipitous cliffs dropping to the plain below. Described in the previous century, by the Tudor historian John Camden, as 'A place well guarded by walls of a very great compass, by a great number of

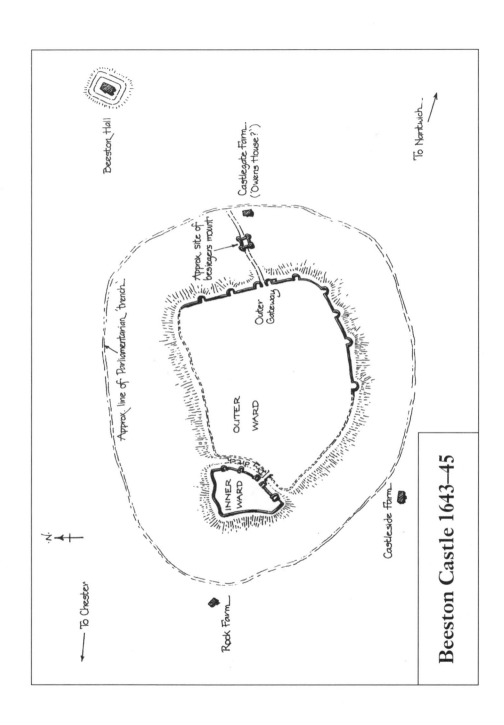

To Chester

N

Beeston Hall

To Nantwich

Approx. line of Parliamentarian 'trench'

Approx. site of besiegers mount

Castlegate Farm
(Owens House?)

Outer
Gateway

OUTER
WARD

INNER
WARD

Castleside Farm

Rock Farm

Beeston Castle 1643–45

towers and by a mountain of very steep ascent',[65] by 1642 Beeston Castle had fallen into disrepair and was dismissed scornfully by Nathaniel Lancaster as 'no more than the Skeleton or bare Anatomy of a Castle.'[66] Nonetheless, it was clear that if conflict between King and Parliament were to be prolonged, and hostilities spread to Cheshire, securing Beeston would be of great importance to both sides.

In January 1643 Sir William Brereton arrived in Cheshire to take command of Parliament's forces there, and, as he 'prized it by its situation',[67] lost no time in occupying Beeston Castle. On 20 February he placed a force of 200–300 men in the Castle.

The Parliamentarians set to work to repair Beeston's defences and to make their new quarters reasonably habitable. Brereton gave orders that 'the breaches [in the walls of the Outer Ward] be made up with mud walls, the well of the outer ward to be cleansed, and a few rooms erected'.[68] Archaeological evidence suggests that the latter consisted of some timber buildings in the Outer Ward, replacing earlier ones that had fallen into ruin. These would have been used as barracks for the soldiers, stables for their horses, and as store-houses for their equipment and supplies. The Parliamentarian governors of Beeston seem to have made their personal quarters in the towers of the Outer Gatehouse, which was further strengthened at this time by some fairly rudimentary earthworks beyond it, together with a new wooden gateway.

Not much else seems to have been done at this stage to strengthen or modernise Beeston's defences, and during the spring and summer of 1643, as Brereton gained the upper hand in the war in Cheshire, so Beeston came to be seen as a quiet backwater, precautions relaxed and the size of the garrison reduced. Its Governor, Captain Thomas Steele, was a cheese-dealer from Nantwich, who received a universally bad press from Parliamentarian writers. In part this seems to have been because his private life did not meet with the approval of his more godly comrades. His military performance also left much to be desired:

> A captain or two being wearied out of the charge of such a prison, it was committed to Captain [Thomas] Steele (a rough-hewn man; no soldier) whose care was more to see it repaired, victualled and live quietly there, than the safe custody of it.[69]

Steele, in fact, was typical of the kind of officer put in charge of garrisons that were not expected to see any action. By the autumn of 1643 Beeston was being used as a supply depot, possibly as a store for arms and equipment, and as a safe deposit for the valuables of a number of the leading Parliamentarian gentry of the Nantwich area. The garrison had been reduced to about sixty men of the local Trained Band, all second-line troops.

Beeston Surprised

This peaceful interlude came to an abrupt end in November 1643, when
several thousand veteran English soldiers from Ireland landed in North Wales
in support of King Charles. They formed the basis of a powerful new Royalist
army, which, under the command of John, Lord Byron, was tasked with
restoring the King's control of Cheshire and North West England and
capturing the Parliamentarian headquarters at Nantwich. As a first step, it
was obviously important to secure control of Beeston Castle, a formidable task
indeed, especially when speed was essential. On the night of 12/13
December, a Royalist force, evidently consisting of some companies of
Colonel Francis Gamull's Chester Regiment of Foot, and Captain Thomas
Sandford's company of firelocks, appeared before Beeston.

Sandford was a colourful character, a fire-eating soldier who, with his 'firelocks' (elite commando–type troops) originally raised on the Welsh Border,
had gained a ferocious reputation during the fighting in Ireland, and whose
blood-curdling threats had terrified the King's enemies since his return to
England. But what happened next is uncertain. It appears that Gamull and
the bulk of the Royalist force staged a demonstration before the Outer Gate
of the Castle. Steele seems to have drawn virtually all of his men down into
the Outer Ward to meet this threat, leaving the way clear for Sandford and
eight of his firelocks to gain entry to the Castle and occupy its dominating
Inner Ward. It is usually stated that they achieved this by scaling the virtually
sheer western face of the crag, which was generally regarded as impregnable,
with the result that the curtain wall here was very low. However, no surviving
contemporary account confirms that this was how Sandford gained entry. It
is true that, until recent times, local boys continued to emulate Sandford's
supposed feat and the less agile can trace a theoretically feasible route. But
could a party of troops encumbered with firelocks and other equipment have
undertaken such a climb in silence in pitch darkness, 'betwixt moonset and
dawn'? A Chester Royalist, Randle Holme, wrote:

> Colonel Gamull with the assistance of Captain Sandford and his
> firelocks, in the midst of a dark night, surprised the innermost ward
> of Beeston Castle and garrisoned it for the King.[70]

A Parliamentarian version simply stated that Sandford and his men gained
entry by 'a byeway, through treachery, as is supposed'. [71]

The fullest Royalist account, in their news journal *Mercurius Aulicus*, also
makes no suggestion of such a climb, reporting that on the night of 12 December:

> Lord Byron sent out the firelocks and about 200 commanded
> musketeers to Beeston Castle . . . and having two men to be their

guide that had formerly been very conversant in the Castle, assaulted the Outer Ward, and presently forced the entrance, after that they fell upon the river [*sic*] ward (where the greater part of their provision and all their ammunition was stored up) and very courageously soon made themselves masters of it, we caused the Rebels to betake themselves to the several Towers of the castle, where having little provision and no ammunition, they desired a treaty, which was presently granted, wherein it was concluded that they should march away with such baggage as did properly belong to the soldiers, leaving all the ordnance and ammunition behind them with all plate and other goods laid up in that Castle, which was the place wherein the Rebels of that County chiefly confided.[72]

A possible explanation is that Sandford and men stealthily approached the Outer Ward on its northern side, where the slope of the hill, though still steep enough for the perimeter wall to be less formidable than elsewhere, was relatively easy to climb. The Royalists were perhaps led by their guides to a sally port known to have existed here, slipped inside, and made their way undetected to the entrance to the Inner Ward. They may have stormed its gatehouse, although examination of the dry ditch shows several points at which its inner side could have been scaled. In fact the Inner Ward may have been undefended, for Lancaster says that 'there was nothing there but stones and a good prospect'.[73]

Threatened with attack by Gamull's men at the Outer Gateway and with the terrifying Sandford loose in his rear, Steele lost his nerve and surrendered. He might (just) have been forgiven for this, but Steele now made the fatal error of entertaining Sandford to dinner in his quarters, and sent a supply of beer up to the firelocks guarding the Inner Ward. For the Cheshire Parliamentarian leadership, alarmed by the ignominious fall of such a supposedly impregnable stronghold, and doubtless infuriated by the loss of their valuables, Steele's fraternisation with the enemy was the final insult. On reaching Nantwich at the head of his surrendered men, Steele was court-martialled and shot.

Royalist Beeston

Thomas Sandford was apparently appointed as first Royalist Governor.[74] But his tenure was brief, as the fire-eating Captain was killed in Byron's unsuccessful assault on Nantwich on 17 January 1644. The only other Royalist Governor of Beeston who can definitely be identified was Captain William Vallett, who was in command by April 1645, although the exact date of his appointment is unknown. Vallett seems to have been a professional soldier, who served in Lord Byron's Regiment of Horse. As for the garrison, its composition remains unclear, although it probably fluctuated according to circumstances. There is some slight evidence that in the spring of 1645 the defenders of Beeston included soldiers claimed by the Parliamentarians to be 'native' Irish. This may indicate that some of the defenders of Beeston came from Lord Byron's Regiment of Foot, which was partly raised in Ireland.

We know from archaeological evidence that the Royalists made strenuous efforts to strengthen the defences of Beeston. The Royalist Governor, doubt-less taking heed of the fate of the hapless Captain Steele, established his private quarters in the South West Tower of the Inner Ward, whose defences were further improved. It was probably after the Royalist takeover that arrow slits in the flanking towers of the Inner Gatehouse were partially blocked in order to convert them into musket loopholes. To the south of the East Tower is a blocked opening, which was probably a gunport, and a second has been identified between the South East Tower and the eastern Gatehouse Tower, although there is no evidence that any cannon were actually mounted. Surviving artefacts suggest that the South East Tower may have been used as an equipment store, and fragments of lead shot moulds have been found in the South West Tower.

Undoubtedly, the Outer Ward will have continued to be the main centre of activity, with its timber barracks, storehouses and stables providing accom-modation for livestock, including sheep and cattle, which in quieter times would have been driven out each day to graze. In at least two of the towers arrow slits were widened to permit the use of muskets, and many fragments of military equipment found in and around the Outer Gatehouse suggest intensive use.

Beeston remained in largely undisturbed Royalist possession until the late autumn of 1644, when Byron's defeat at Montgomery, followed soon after-wards by the fall of Liverpool, enabled Sir William Brereton to resume operations against the main Royalist regional stronghold of Chester. The capture – or at least the neutralisation – of Beeston, a Royalist observation post and base for raiding cavalry, was a major Parliamentarian objective.

The Leaguer Begins

Late in October, Brereton began setting up a series of fortified outposts around Chester, aiming eventually to cut off the communications of the Royalist garrison there. The Parliamentarians, whose forward headquarters at Tarvin was only about 6 miles from Beeston, would be seriously incon-venienced if this Royalist garrison remained operational so close in their rear.

As a first step towards containing Beeston, detachments of troops were sent from Nantwich and Tarvin with orders to seize the garrison cattle grazing at the foot of the crag. A Parliamentarian writer, Thomas Malbon, describes the incident, saying that a report reached headquarters at Nantwich that:

> the King's party at Beeston had an intent to have robbed and spoiled Nantwich market folks on their return home. But the forces from Tarvin did prevent them, and sent 12 of the Soldiers near the Castle who brought away the Enemy's cattle, which they in the Castle perceived, issued forth to have rescued them. But the body of the horse from Nantwich being on Tilstone heath, and Lieutenant Colonel Massey having laid some his company in Ambushment drew from the Castle towards Tilstone heath, and Tarvin forces being gotten betwixt the Enemy and the Castle, upon the retreat of the Enemy towards the Castle, having espied the Body of Nantwich horse on Tilstone heath did set upon them, and took about 20 of them prisoners, and 12 of their horse, and the rest fled into the Castle, without loss of any in the Parliament force.[75]

On 26 October, Captain Gimbart and a party of his Parliamentarian fire-locks, who may have included some of the same men who had taken part in the Royalist capture of Beeston, but who had changed sides after being taken prisoner at the battle of Nantwich, made a nocturnal raid, capturing thirty-seven cattle and oxen; and a few nights later, Major Croxton's men from Nantwich took another sixty, losing two men wounded. On 28 October Brereton reported to the Parliamentarian Committee of Both Kingdoms:

> On Saturday a party of our men from Tarvin took away divers cattle belonging to the Governor of Beeston Castle, and enticed the enemy into an ambuscade, killing several and taking seventeen prisoners, whereof one was an ensign, besides thirty stand of arms, without loss of one man.[76]

On 16 November Brereton, 'receiving intelligence that they in Beeston Castle were in want of match, fuel and other necessities', increased the pressure by bringing up a strong force of troops to cover the establishment of a series of outposts surrounding Beeston. One of these was at Beeston Hall, about half a mile to the north-east of the Castle, and others were in several farms around the foot of the crag itself. On the same night the garrison struck back, making a sally in which they 'fired one Owen's Barn standing at the foot of the hill, and burned down the same Barn and the Wheat therein'.[77]

Brereton's immediate aim was not to reduce Beeston but prevent further raids by its garrison. He was not successful initially, for as well as attacks by the Royalists from Chester, the most successful counterstroke was mounted from Beeston itself, when on 7 December a party of forty or fifty troops slipped out of a sally port and surprised the Parliamentarian outpost in 'Owen's House' (very possibly on the site now occupied by Castlegate Farm), firing the building whilst the troops inside were at dinner, killing twenty-four of the thirty-six men present. The survivors were carried off to the Castle as prisoners. Nevertheless, the blockade was maintained and on 17 January 1645 Brereton was writing hopefully to the Committee of Both Kingdoms that 'we still maintain the siege of Beeston Castle, which we hope cannot hold out long.' [78]

Unfortunately for Sir William, the plight of Chester and its satellite garrisons had by now attracted the attention of the Royalist high command in Oxford, and their preservation would be a major consideration in Royalist strategy for much of the remainder of the war. As a first step, troops under Prince Maurice were despatched to relieve Chester. On 19 February this was accomplished but they were unable to assist Beeston, as a relief attempt mounted from Holt Castle was repulsed. However, Maurice was reinforced by his redoubtable brother, Prince Rupert, and following the latter's arrival Royalist efforts proved more successful. On 18 March Brereton was forced to abandon the leaguer of Beeston. A Royalist diarist recorded:

> the enemy, having intelligence of our intention to relieve Beeston, quitted the siege; left their works undemolished and a sow behind them. No distress; 8000 weight of biscuit; plenty of beef, only some want of fire and beer.[79]

The 'sow' was a siege tower of some kind, which may have been intended for use in an assault on Beeston's Outer Gateway.

Before departing, Rupert's men burnt Beeston Hall, probably demolished the enemy siegeworks, and ordered the long-suffering neighbourhood to pay the garrison all of the contributions outstanding since the start of the siege – a heavy burden, as the local population will also have been supporting the besiegers.

The Leaguer Resumed

With the departure of Rupert's forces, Brereton ordered troops from Tarporley to resume the blockade of Beeston, but quickly encountered difficulties. It was reported on 10 April that most of Captain Gregg's Company of Brereton's Regiment of Foot, which had been manning an outpost at Tilston, had deserted, complaining that in their absence their homes were being plundered by Parliamentarian troops from elsewhere. The Parliamentarian

Deputy Lieutenants at Nantwich warned Brereton: 'If not prevented or supplied by others, that part of the county which lieth within the power of Beeston Castle will be absolutely ruinated and those few left at Tilstone subjected to being lost.' [80] Captain Holford's Company and Gimbart's fire-locks were ordered to the scene.

An interesting sidelight on the Beeston garrison, and of the bitterness with which the war was now being waged, is contained in a letter of 12 April to Brereton from Major Thomas Croxton, Governor of Nantwich:

> I received a command from you for the executing of some of Beeston's soldiers. I could have wished that no quarter had been given to them when they were first taken, but having quarter given them I know of no order or ordnance that authoriseth the taking away of their lives. But if you please to send a warrant to the Marshal I shall see it put into Execution. Those that were taken last were pressed for pioneers and had overrun [deserted] the castle since the raising of the siege. Therefore I conceive the giving of quarter to them was fit. The castle soldiers have taken divers of our men prisoners since theirs were taken, who must expect no more mercy than we intend to them. I refer this to your further order.[81]

The ordnance referred to by Major Croxton had been passed by Parliament, ordering its commanders to execute any 'native' Irish found in arms for the King. In practice there was a good deal of variation in its observance, and during the spring of 1645 both sides carried out a number of executions, either under the terms of the ordnance, or in the case of the Royalists, as reprisals for the execution of their men. It may be that some of Beeston's garrison were 'native' Irish, possibly from Lord Byron's own Foot Regiment, or were men of uncertain origin who had come over with the forces from Ireland, or had simply been chosen as scapegoats. Brereton, in common with other Parliamentarian commanders, displayed considerable flexibility in enforcing the ordnance, and it may be that Major Croxton's obvious doubts about the wisdom of any executions also swayed him, as there is no evidence that these at least were carried out.

By this stage, Brereton's men had recognised that it would be very difficult – and costly in lives – to attempt a direct assault on Beeston, and they were concentrating their main efforts on the capture of Hawarden Castle, another of Chester's satellite garrisons, whilst confining operations at Beeston to sealing the garrison off from the outside world. In furtherance of this, work began on extending the siegeworks. At some stage, possibly rather later in the siege, an entrenchment was dug around the entire base of the crag. The besiegers also began the construction of a small mount, or earth fort, about a musket shot (150 yards or a little less) beyond the Outer Gateway. Malbon recorded that the besiegers 'had begun to have raised a brave mount with a strong ditch about the same, and had placed good buildings therein, which were scarce finished'[82] by early May. Croxton's letter suggests that the Royalists attempted to disrupt the work.

The Parliamentarians were still encountering difficulties in maintaining their forces, as indicated by a letter of 8 April from Colonel Robert Duckenfield to Sir George Booth of the County Committee in Nantwich:

> My regiment hath lain so long at the siege of Beeston without pay that many of them are grown sick and discontented so that I cannot persuade them to march presently unless your gentlemen of the county would be pleased to order some pay for them.[83]

On 8 May Brereton reported to the Committee of Both Kingdoms:

> We have almost finished a mount before Beeston Castle gate, which is encompassed with a strong deep trench. This will command and keep them in the castle, so that they dare not issue out in strong parties to annoy the country or bring in provisions.[84]

And Parliamentarian activities triggered a colourful exchange of letters between the opposing commanders. On 9 May Captain William Vallett wrote to Captain Godfrey Gimbart, evidently currently in command of siege operations:

> I understand by the bearer that you intend to burn the house [evidently 'Owen's House', situated at the foot of the crag, below the Outer Gateway]. Indeed it should not have been left for you to have done it, but that I did commiserate a poor widow and two poor orphans in so much that I was content rather to show that extremity to suffer it to be a den of thieves and traitors. But if you take this course you prevent that which I might, upon good reasons, do myself and I shall make it such a precedent as the surveyors of your works – Aldersley, Spurstowe, Metcalf *cum multis altis* [i.e. 'with many others' – ed.] of your traitorous faction shall repent. And whereas you flatter yourself with hopes of taking this place, I scorn your threats and attempts and the forces of your best general, for all his great ram's head.[85]

Possibly stung by Vallett's words, though also, one suspects, rather enjoying himself, Captain Gimbart retorted:

> From my royal fort which stands for the confusion of a den of traitors in Beeston Castle. Governor, I have received your civil

expressions in a scandalous paper. You said you delighted in civility; it appears in your beastlike expressions. You told me you would not be tied by conditions. And do you think to tie me, that am at liberty, and that by you whom I keep close prisoner amongst your anti-Christian Babylonian crew and will wait to expend my dearest blood upon the destruction of such traitors to King and state as that den of blasphemers are whereof you are the chief. You cause me to burn the house by your expressions. For your scandals to my general, you put it upon him, whose shoes you are not worthy to clean. But I suppose you take the counsel to write this letter with the asses whom you took prisoners.[86]

But within a few days the Parliamentarians were again forced to abandon operations against Beeston on the approach of the King's main army in the early stages of the campaign which was to end on 14 June with its crushing defeat at the battle of Naseby.

The Final Round

Following the raising of the leaguer, the Beeston garrison made at least one major sortie, on 4 June, aimed at a small Parliamentarian outpost at Ridley Hall, about 2 miles to the south-east of the castle, which was held by a garrison of sixteen men. Parliamentarian operations against Beeston were evidently resumed in late July. The first task of the besiegers, commanded by Lieutenant General Michael Jones and Major General James Lothian, in the temporary absence of Sir William Brereton, was to complete the siegeworks which had been begun in the spring, and which had not apparently since been completely demolished by the Royalists. Much of the labour was carried out by the Trained Bands of Nantwich, Northwich and Bucklow Hundreds. Nathaniel Lancaster gives some details of their activities:

To make work sure (which formerly proved abortive), they erected a strong Fort within musket shot of the Castle, before the Castle Gate, furnished it in seven days, built a convenient House in it [apparently a barn brought over from Beeston Hall] which they stored with provision and ammunition, afterwards made a Counterscarp, whereby all hope of relief to the Castle was utterly cut off, and enabled to call off the greatest part of their Force, when called thereto.

Lancaster claimed that the support of divine providence had been demon-strated by the fact that

> in all the dangerous work of the Fort, we lost not a man, not a drop of Blood, though perpetually a fair mark to a violent enemy.[87]

One reason for this, Lancaster claimed, was that a pro-Parliamentarian gunsmith had been infiltrated into Beeston in the days after the blockade had been raised, and employed by the garrison to overhaul their weapons, and 'so rested their arms in the firing of them that none could take such aim as to come near the mark'.[88] This interesting claim is not directly supported by any other evidence, although the remains of several damaged weapons have been uncovered in the Outer Gateway. More likely is that when the blockade had been firmly re-established neither side would have been anxious to incur unnecessary casualties in what had effectively become a stand-off. Excavators have found the remains of three young males, dated to the Civil War period, buried in the Inner Ward. They may all have died from natural causes, and although there may be other bodies so far undiscovered, the evidence does not point to a high fatality rate on either side.

By the middle of September Beeston had been so closely blocked up that it was 'gasping for everything necessary but air and water'. So secure were the besiegers that on the night of 19 September they were able to detach a con-siderable force under cover of darkness to surprise the suburbs of Chester.

After the major Royalist defeat at Rowton Heath (24 September) the chances of Beeston again being relieved grew increasingly remote, and the besiegers were content to allow starvation to do their work for them. Jones was determined to take no unnecessary risks at this late stage, writing on 28 October to Brereton (who had resumed command):

> I think it best not to draw off any Beeston forces. I have given Mr Dod directions to have a trench cast above each guard there and have promised each guard £3. I have sent 12 lean cattle to help them [the besiegers] at Beeston.'[89]

Brereton was still encountering continual problems in finding money with which to pay his men and sufficient supplies with which to feed them, and on 29 October Major General Lothian warned him:

> My lieutenant will inform you of the condition of our men at Beeston. If you have not an eye to them to prevent it I much fear the consequence, the care of which I refer to your wisdom.'[90]

The garrison was maintaining some communication with the other Royalist forces remaining in the area, possibly by means of signal fires. The defenders of Beeston were able to inform Royalist-held Holt Castle of their desperate plight, and a new relief attempt was organised. It is uncertain whether Vallett knew of this when, on 15 November, he at last asked for terms. Negotiations began next day, Vallett being represented by Captain Robert Barrow and a Mr William Smith. Brereton himself may have represented the Parliamentarians. No agreement was reached that day, and when talks were resumed on 15 November the Parliamentarians were represented by Colonel Thomas Croxton and Lieutenant Colonel Chidley Coote. By now Vallett was probably aware of the proposed relief attempt – certainly the besiegers were – and the prospect caused them considerable alarm. The forces immediately blockading Beeston were commanded by a Captain Thomas Walley, to whom Lothian wrote from Chester suburbs on 15 November, warning him that an attempt might be made 'this night or very suddenly'. Colonel Robert Duckenfield added a postscript to the letter, addressed to Captain Smith, commanding one of his own companies of foot at Beeston:

> I do verily believe the enemy in Beeston expect this night to be relieved and that they will make a desperate sally out upon you. Engage not your horse without your foot and do not pursue too hastily. I hope the enemy are more desperate than strong. You may easily deal with them if you are careful, but use all means and haste to get Colonel Greaves's horse and what foot you can from Nantwich to make all haste to you this night.[91]

Unfortunately, the besiegers were far from confident that they could 'easily deal' with the combined efforts of the Beeston garrison and a determined relief force, as Brereton later admitted:

> Our guards about the castle were not in so good a condition as were to be desired, very many of our men being straggled abroad, secure upon the confidence of the castle being to be delivered up the next day . . . Upon which grounds the gents. that there treated were induced to consent to better conditions than otherwise.[92]

As it happened, the relief force of about eighty horse and forty foot, escorting packhorses laden with cheese and meat, which had been prepared at Holt, had hardly begun their march when a dispute among some of the troops about pay caused the expedition to be called off. But by then Vallett had obtained slightly better terms than those originally on offer.

The Surrender

It was agreed that the garrison should surrender Beeston on 16 November

1645, before 10am, giving up all arms, ammunition and other supplies, the officers and men being allowed to carry their own weapons, and be given escort to the North Wales Royalist garrisons and 'march away from the said castle with complete arms, drums beating and colours flying . . .' [93] In fact, it was not until midnight that the Royalists quit Beeston, and as they marched out the Parliamentarians realised how skilfully Vallett had played his weak hand. Malbon said that there were fifty-six soldiers with Vallett on his surrender, of whom twenty took the opportunity to go home. Brereton estimated that there were ninety, of whom fifty marched away with their commander, and the remainder went home. According to Nathaniel Lancaster, the defenders of Beeston Castle 'had eaten their cats and had not proven [provisions] for that night'. Reporting to the Committee of Both Kingdoms that 'The Lord hath been pleased this day to restore unto us the strong castle of Beeston . . .' Brereton went on to say of the defenders, 'We found their horses in a weak and languishing condition, the governor's own horse being scarcely able to go out of the castle.' [94]

On the Parliamentarians entering Beeston, the true plight of the defenders became apparent. According to Malbon: 'there was neither meat, ale, nor beer found in the castle, save only a piece of turkey pie, two biscuits, a live peacock and a peahen.'[95] Vallett had carried through a well-executed bluff and obtained better terms than he would have been granted had the enemy known the true weakness of his situation. It was an outcome that raised a number of Parliamentarian eyebrows, and one which Brereton, unsurprisingly, was defensive about.

Vallett and his men made their way to Denbigh, where Vallett himself remained until the surrender of that fortress in 1646. Some of his men, with others from recently surrendered Lathom House, went on to Conwy, where they were 'much commended for their carriage', and formed part of its garrison for the remainder of the war.

Beeston Castle's active role in the war was over. On the day after its occupation Brereton gave orders for the local countryfolk to be employed in dismantling the mount and other siegeworks. A garrison was maintained in the castle until the following spring, when orders were given for it to be slighted. Parliament was determined that Beeston should never again be such a thorn in its flesh.

All too often nothing is known of the thousands of ordinary men who fought for King or Parliament, but in the case of Beeston there is a poignant reminder of the wider human cost resulting from the deaths of two of the Parliamentarian soldiers slaughtered in the Royalist sortie from Beeston on 7 December 1644. In 1650 a petition for assistance was presented to the Cheshire Committee of Justices of the Peace:

The Humble Petition of Thomas Collier of the Parish of Mottram in Longendale Most humbly showeth unto your Worships that your Petitioner Thomas Collier a poor inhabitant near Mottram in Longendale has been a great pains taker and lived in good repute, by the trade of a woollen Webster, and now through age and infirmity is not able any longer to maintain himself and wife being either of them four score years of age or thereabouts and as it hath pleased the Lord to add more sorrow unto his old age, had two sons quartered or listed under the Command of Colonel Robert Duckenfield from the beginning and in the last siege of Beeston Castle, were in their sentry house run through and utterly burnt and consumed to ashes, which were the only stay and relief for him and their present maintenance the one son, being married, having a wife and two small children, the wife's heart was burst and as it apparently appeared died for grief, and has left the two small children upon the charge of the two old people who have not any maintainance for themselves but lie languishing under most miserable conditions for the present. May it therefore please the worshipful Committee or the Several Justices of the Peace, whom this may concern, taking into serious consideration the most miserable sad and weak condition of this poor suppliant that some speedy order might be taken for the relief of himself, wife and two small father-less and mother-less children that lie upon his hands through the barbarous cruelty of those wicked murderers . . . [96]

Chapter Six

Ports Under Siege:
The Defence of Plymouth 1642–1646

Possession of seaports was of vital concern to both King and Parliament. As it became evident that the conflict was likely to be prolonged, the combatants were eager to gain control of maritime trade – and the revenues associated with it – and also to ship in supplies, munitions and perhaps foreign troops.

Parliament held most of the advantages. London, England's greatest port, was firmly in its hands from the start of the war, whilst the only major ports in Royalist hands were Newcastle upon Tyne and Portsmouth, and the latter quickly fell to the Parliamentarians. And thanks to the prompt action of Robert Rich, Earl of Warwick, its commander, most of the fleet, including all of its larger vessels, was secured for Parliament on the outbreak of war. Thus, despite energetic efforts to improvise a navy of their own, the Royalists were never able to match their opponents at sea.

Parliament's control of the seas – ultimately a decisive card – presented a major obstacle to Royalist efforts to capture more ports. Apart from rare instances, such as Exeter and Dartmouth, where they were able to control entry to the port by means of artillery mounted at its approaches, they were unable to mount a seaward blockade. As a result Parliament could bring supplies, money and reinforcements into threatened ports, often without serious opposition.

Lack of heavy artillery meant that the Royalists were usually forced to attempt the capture of enemy ports by means of storming. This was always costly and by no means certain of success. Prince Rupert stormed Bristol in July 1643, gaining for King Charles England's second most important port, but the losses his troops incurred effectively crippled his army for several weeks at a critical stage of the war, and made Charles reluctant to countenance similar tactics for the rest of the war. In September 1644 he baulked at the prospect of storming the defences of Plymouth, at a time when its defenders were highly vulnerable. On other occasions, such as the siege of Lyme in 1644 and in several instances at Plymouth, lack of resources – particularly of siege artillery – led to assaults being repulsed with heavy losses.

Parliament's ability to supply coastal garrisons by sea enabled it to maintain outposts deep in enemy territory. The Parliamentarians retained control of the key east coast port and arsenal of Hull throughout the war, notwithstanding two sieges and treachery from within. In the autumn of 1643, at a critical stage of the war, the Northern Royalist army led by the Earl of Newcastle was unable to fulfil the King's wishes to invade the Eastern Association, partly because Newcastle's Yorkshire Royalists were unwilling to march further south as long as the enemy based on Hull could mount raids into their unprotected home territory. In consequence, Newcastle had no option but to sit down before Hull's powerful defences in a siege he knew from the outset to be doomed to failure.

Other Parliamentarian-held ports exerted similar influence. Throughout the first half of 1644, the Royalist Western Army under Prince Maurice, whose presence was urgently needed elsewhere, was tied down in the siege of Lyme, on the Dorset coast. Of itself, the small port was of limited value, but so long as it remained in enemy hands it provided a base from which raids could be mounted deep into Royalist-held territory, and despite the surrounding terrain favouring the Royalists – and the town's defences being not particularly formidable – Maurice proved unable to break its defenders' resistance.

But although Parliament's coastal garrisons were often able to withstand enemy attack, thanks to support from the sea, this alone was not generally sufficient to raise a siege. In the case of Hull, threats and reverses elsewhere – as well as the aggressive defence mounted by the garrison – caused Newcastle to abandon his siege in October 1643. In other cases, however – particularly in 1644 in the West Country – the threat to Parliamentarian-held ports had a major effect on strategy. The decision by the Earl of Essex to lead his army deep into the South West, allegedly with the aim of relieving Lyme and Plymouth, would lead to the surrender of a large part of his army in September at Lostwithiel, in the greatest Royalist victory of the war.

The Siege of Plymouth

For those who endured it, the long siege and blockade of Plymouth, lasting almost continuously for three and a half years, was one of the most destructive experiences of the war. Plymouth was of major significance, not only because of its role as a port and naval base, but because – so long as it remained in Parliamentarian hands – it presented a constant threat that made the Cornish Royalists unwilling to commit a large part of their forces far from home.

Plymouth had grown in importance in Tudor times, when it had become increasingly significant as a naval base in England's wars with France and

Spain. In consequence, Plymouth's seaward defences had been steadily strengthened. A major fort had been constructed on Lembay Point, over-looking the harbour, the Cattewater and Plymouth Sound, and in addition several fortified blockhouses were built, protecting the approaches to Plymouth along the River Tamar and several inland creeks. The approaches to the harbour were covered by fortified St Nicholas Island.

Plymouth, by the early decades of the seventeenth century, had become a centre of Puritanism. In the early years of Charles I's reign Plymouth had been a principal base for the disastrous expeditions against Cadiz and La Rochelle. Discontent with the Stuart regime had been heightened in Plymouth as a result of disorder among the troops quartered in the area, and disease spread in the town by the soldiers. There were about 2,000 fatalities from the total population of 7,000–8,000.[97] Thus it was not surprising that, on the outbreak of civil war, Plymouth declared for Parliament, and several regiments were also mustered by the Devon Parliamentarians. Parliament's control of Plymouth was consolidated towards the end of 1642, when Colonel William Ruthven and 200 Scottish professional soldiers were driven into the port by a storm and joined the town's defence. In the meantime, Cornwall had been secured for the King by the local Royalists and Sir Ralph Hopton, and they were hard at work recruiting a Cornish Royalist army. Whilst Plymouth was relatively well protected on its seaward side, the land approaches to the town were virtually defenceless, and the construction of new fortifications was therefore a priority. Mainstay of the defence at this time was the newly elected Mayor, Philip Francis, a wool merchant.

Francis and Sir Alexander Carew now took charge of Plymouth's prepara-tions for war. Arms from the town's magazine were distributed to the local Trained Band and several volunteer companies. The town also had to bear most of the initial expense of constructing landward defences. Plymouth lay at the tip of a peninsula, with, at its base, several prominent ridges running from east to west across it – ideal sites for defences. Initially work was con-centrated on a bank and ditch stretching from the Hoe Gate to the East Gate of the town. Seamen were landed from ships in the harbour to assist in the work.

These initial defences were far from satisfactory: the town was dominated by the high ground to its north. Fortunately however, the Cornish Royalists, constructing an army from scratch, were initially in no position to take advan-tage of Plymouth's weaknesses. Hopton's first move was to occupy the house and blockhouse at Mount Edgecumbe, on the western bank of the River Tamar, so putting Plymouth under a partial blockade. The defenders of the town responded with nocturnal raiding by small parties of troops brought across the Tamar by boat.

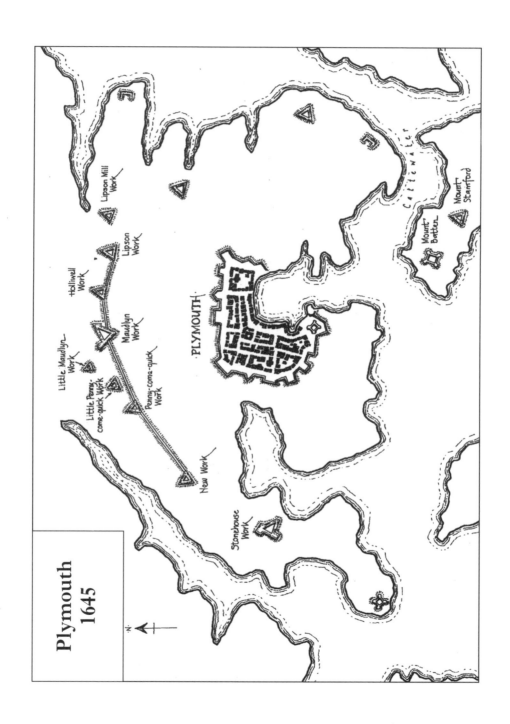

Plymouth
1645

Lipson Mill
Work

Lipson
Work

Halliwell
Work

Little Maudlyn
Work

Maudlyn
Work

Little Penny-
come-quick Work

Penny-come-quick
Work

New Work

Stonehouse
Work

PLYMOUTH

Causeway

Mount
Batten

Mount
Stamford

On 11 November the Cornish Parliamentarian County Committee, in exile in Plymouth, wrote to the Parliamentarian leader, John Pym, protesting at lack of support provided by Westminster. They asked especially for arms and ammunition. Their concern was justified, for Hopton was about to take the offensive. Encouraged by promises of support from the Devonshire Royalists, Sir Ralph decided to move directly against Plymouth.

By now William Ruthven was in military command in the town and sent out daily patrols to watch for enemy activity. On 30 November a detachment of his troops abandoned the village of Plympton, 5 miles east of Plymouth, which now became Hopton's headquarters. Sir Ralph realised, however, that he needed considerably more infantry than he currently had if he were to stand any chance of taking Plymouth by assault, and urged the Devon Royalists to raise additional troops.

Hopton was not prepared to make his own assault on Plymouth's slowly burgeoning defences and remained on the defensive around Plympton whilst the Parliamentarians began marking out the plan of Plymouth's outer line of defences, at the same time strengthening their existing fortifications with guns landed from ships in the harbour.

As his own forces increased, Hopton established additional outposts in outlying villages and country houses, and on 5 December the Royalists cut Plymouth's main water supply, carried from Dartmoor in a 20-mile-long leat. This proved, however, to have little effect, as there were ample additional sources of water within the town and further supplies were brought in by ship. Meanwhile, Hopton hoped to benefit from treachery within Plymouth, where pro-Royalist plotters were attempting to disrupt work on the town's defences. But their activities were temporarily dampened when one of them, a local gentleman called Robert Trelawney, was arrested and sent by sea to be imprisoned in London. Finally, the Devon Royalists begun to muster support at the town of Modbury, but the gathering soon took on the aspect of a jolly country fair, and on 7 December the raw recruits were dispersed in a surprise raid by Ruthven and 300 Plymouth horse. Discouraged, Hopton broke off his blockade of Plymouth in favour of a wildly optimistic scheme to capture Exeter, leaving small blockading forces at Edgecumbe, Millbrook and Saltash. At the end of December, his project at Exeter having predictably failed, Sir Ralph fell back into Cornwall.

Plymouth, meanwhile, had been reinforced and Parliamentarian ships began a desultory bombardment of Saltash, whose garrison Hopton re-inforced with the regiment of Colonel John Trevanion and some foot soldiers under Captain William Arundell. They were able to frustrate attempts by the Parliamentarians to assault the town using boats in the Tamar.

Parliament had, meanwhile, appointed a new commander for the South

West, Henry Grey, Earl of Stamford. Knowing he was about to be superceded, Ruthven decided to make a bid for military glory by launching an invasion of Cornwall. His expedition began well, with the occupation of Saltash (abandoned by the Royalists), but came to grief on 21 January 1643 at Braddock Down, where Ruthven was routed by Hopton and driven back in disorder towards Plymouth.[98]

The Parliamentarian garrison was saved by the arrival on 22 January of Stamford with 800 foot and 13 troops of horse. The 500 demoralised troops left by Ruthven with orders to hold Saltash were less fortunate. On the day following his victory at Braddock Down Hopton advanced on the town at the head of William Godolphin and Lord Mohun's Regiments of Foot. At 4pm Hopton began his assault. The defenders of Saltash resisted for about three hours, but by 7pm had run out of ammunition and decided to withdraw to Plymouth by boat, under cover of darkness. Such operations are always difficult, and discipline broke down, followed by panic. About 100 of the fleeing Parliamentarians were drowned in the Tamar, another 140 captured, only 260 joining Ruthven in Plymouth.

With fears of an imminent Royalist assault, all able-bodied men were called to arms, whilst the outposts at Millbrook and Mount Edgecumbe were abandoned. Although the alarm proved groundless, Mayor Francis ordered the strengthening of Plymouth's existing defences and the construction of a new outpost overlooking the town, called Mount Stamford. Additional food supplies were brought in by sea, together with two handmills for grinding corn. In the event, it was late January before Hopton felt ready to move against Plymouth. Royalist outposts were established at St Budeaux and Plympton, and skirmishing followed as the Royalists established additional fortified positions. Stamford wrote to Parliament, asking urgently for money and munitions. The garrison of Plymouth now consisted of around 3,000 men, including Sir John Merrick's regiment of London greycoats under Lieutenant Colonel Vincent Calmedy. Stamford praised the role of Philip Francis in the defence: 'The mayor of Plymouth is as brave a man as ever breathed.' [99]

The opposing forces were approximately equal in numbers. The besiegers were divided in two by the River Plym, and neither side felt strong enough to take the offensive. Hopton had recently reoccupied Modbury, garrisoning the town with Sir Nicholas Slanning's and John Trevanion's Foot. The Modbury garrison blocked the road from Plymouth to the South Hams of Devon, and collected supplies for Hopton's forces. The remainder of the Royalist forces were quartered around Plympton, Stoke and Mannamead, each detachment too far apart to assist each other in case of attack.

The Parliamentarians took advantage of this weakness by mounting a two-pronged assault on Modbury, involving an advance from Kingsbury in the east by a force under the energetic James Chudleigh, claimed to be 7,000 strong – though many of them were ill-armed levies – supported by a smaller force moving out from Plymouth. The attack on Modbury, defended by around 1,500 Royalists, began at midday on 22 February and continued throughout the remaining hours of daylight. Most of the fighting consisted of not particularly effective exchanges of fire between opposing musketeers positioned in the thick hedgerows on the approaches to the town, and ended at nightfall as the Royalists, still in good order, fell back through Modbury and mostly made their escape, losing around 100 dead, 200 wounded and 150 prisoners.

The defeat at Modbury forced Hopton to raise his blockade of Plymouth yet again, and withdraw into Cornwall. Both sides had by now fought each other to a standstill and a truce was agreed, mainly to give the combatants a breathing space in which to build up their forces.

The Plymouth garrison now consisted of around 3,500 foot, including a number of sailors and the 400 men of the Plymouth Trained Band, together with 500 horse. A further 1,200 foot under Sir John Northcote were camped outside the town on Roborough Down. A succession of ships were bringing supplies into the port, although there were still shortages as a result of the large number of Parliamentarian sympathisers who had taken refuge in Plymouth. Philip Francis detained a number of grain ships on their way through the port on their way to Spain and compulsorily purchased their cargoes.

The truce expired at midnight on 22 April, and James Chudleigh immediately launched an advance across the Tamar against the town of Launceston. A day of fierce fighting ended in partial Royalist victory, though the arrival of reinforcements from Plymouth saved Chudleigh from disaster. His setback was partially compensated by a farcical Royalist reverse on Sourton Down, but Hopton decisively gained the upper hand in May with his crushing defeat of the Earl of Stamford at Stratton.[100]

The bulk of the Cornish Royalist forces now marched eastwards into Somerset to join up with reinforcements from the Oxford Army, leaving beyond a small force, supported by the Cornish Trained Bands, to occupy Millbrook and Saltash and maintain a partial blockade of Plymouth. And so, for the next three months, Plymouth's defenders were largely left in peace, which was fortunate as morale in the town slumped along with her maritime trade, badly hit by Royalist privateers. On 15 June Philip Francis warned Plymouth's MP, John Yonge: 'We are here in a deplorable condition, our whole country being harrowed by Sir Ralph Hopton.' [101]

The Plymouth Parliamentarian leadership was aware that it had gained only a temporary respite, and work on strengthening the town's defences continued. An outer line of defence was taking shape, with four main forts at key points on the high ground overlooking Plymouth, linked by trenches and a number of intermediate smaller 'mounts'. The most likely avenue of attack was via Maudlyn Ridge, whose defences were consequently the strongest. On the left of the line, Lipson Fort overlooked the creek of the same name, with Holywell Work to its left, commanding the higher part of Lipson Creek and part of Maudlyn Ridge. Maudlyn Fort (also known as the 'Great Work'), covering the main road into Plymouth from the north, was the keystone of the Parliamentarian defences. To its left was the Pennycomequick Work, covering the Saltash road and Stonehouse Creek. Guns from ships in the harbour, mostly manned by seamen, were emplaced in the forts and further defences were planned. Sir Alexander Carew was still in command of St Nicholas Island, which with Plymouth Fort and various blockhouses controlled all of the approaches to the harbour.

Thus Plymouth seemed adequately protected and throughout the summer Parliament continued to reinforce the port by sea whenever resources were available, which was fortunate, as the tide of war had turned firmly in favour of the Royalists, climaxing with their capture of Bristol on 25 July. During the late summer and autumn the Royalist Western Army, now under the command of Prince Maurice, overran most of the South West, its conquests including Exeter and Dartmouth.

A Royalist force of 3,600 men under Colonel Sir John Digby had taken the North Devon towns of Barnstaple and Bideford, and now moved against Plymouth. Digby, undoubtedly correctly, felt himself too weak to make a direct assault on the town's defences, although his cavalry was able to isolate Plymouth on its landward side, and he also isolated the fortification at Fort Stamford, bringing guns to bear on shipping entering Plymouth harbour.

By now the King's successes were emboldening a number of Royalist supporters in Plymouth, among them Sir Alexander Carew, who sought to place himself on the winning side by entering prolonged secret negotiations with the Royalists regarding handing over St Nicholas Island to them. However, in his anxiety to secure the guarantee of a royal pardon before he committed himself, Carew hesitated too long. His furtive nocturnal activities, including visits to Royalist-held Mount Edgecumbe, had aroused the suspicions of Philip Francis. Carew attempted to hole up in St Nicholas Island but was arrested by his own men and despatched to London, where he was eventually tried and executed for treason. It had been a lucky escape for Parliamentarian Plymouth, for if St Nicholas Island had fallen, Plymouth's seaward supply line would have been effectively blocked. Around the same time Plymouth's defenders had a further scare when the captain of the frigate *Providence* was detected as he was about to defect to the enemy.

Throughout the summer work continued on strengthening Plymouth's defences. The forts of the interior line were faced with stone and the ditch in front of them deepened, whilst the surviving medieval gates of the town were refurbished. Some additional small mounts were added to the outer line, although isolated Fort Stamford remained vulnerable.

In September Philip Francis was succeeded as Mayor by John Cawse, a much less tactful and efficient administrator, who soon found himself at odds with the military leadership in the town. Parliament had decided that an effective military commander was needed to oversee Plymouth's defence. A reinforcement of 600 men of Colonel William Gould's Regiment of Foot was despatched by sea from Portsmouth, along with arms and ammunition and 200 barrels of powder, as well as £4,000. In overall command, earmarked as Plymouth's Governor, was a Scottish professional soldier, Colonel James Wardlaw, who had led a dragoon regiment at the battle of Edgehill. Gould was a Devon man, and a strong Puritan, who as Wardlaw's second-in-command would inspire Plymouth's defence and would eventually become governor.

The reinforcements sailed into Plymouth Sound on 30 September, met by cheering crowds, and although Wardlaw and Cawse were soon at odds, the new arrivals did much to raise the morale of the townspeople, especially after Wardlaw made it clear that he would not surrender.

The Crisis

This boost came just in time, for Plymouth was about to face its sternest test, at the hands of Prince Maurice. The Prince captured Dartmouth on 6 October, leaving him free to turn his full force against Plymouth. The defenders had recently rejected a summons from John Digby, who had attempted to persuade soldiers of the garrison to defect, with offers of payment of 6 shillings a week to any who went over to the Royalists. He had met with no response.

Prince Maurice was a competent, if not very imaginative, soldier, without the charisma of his elder brother Rupert.[102] He was happier in the company of fellow soldiers than among civilians and his men had created a good deal of hostility in the West Country as a result of their looting and disorder. They were now at the end of a long campaign and both the Prince and many of his soldiers were suffering from the effects of illness, including typhus and a strain of influenza, which weakened their effectiveness. This advantage for the defenders was soon neutralised when the same illnesses began to flourish in the overcrowded conditions of beleaguered Plymouth. Nevertheless, the sickness among the Royalists gained Wardlaw a month free from serious attack, giving him opportunity to hit back in a series of raids. Early on 8 October he took three hundred men in small boats across the Cattewater to attack a Royalist outpost at Hooe, catching the enemy by surprise, taking fifty-four prisoners, along with two colours and three barrels of gunpowder. A week later, on 15 October, Wardlaw mounted a second raid, when 200 musketeers and a body of horse headed north towards the village of Knackershole, 2 miles beyond the Plymouth defences, where some Royalist horse were surprised in their quarters, losing 30 prisoners. However, the Parliamentarians chased the fleeing Cavaliers too far, running into reinforcements, from whom Wardlaw's men extricated themselves only with difficulty.

As October dragged by, Digby was steadily reinforced by Maurice's troops and was able to intensify his blockade of the northern side of Plymouth. On 22 October the Royalists prepared an attack on isolated Fort Stamford. The besiegers now consisted of 9 regiments of foot and 5 of horse, totalling around 10,000 men. Maurice and his main force were on the north side of the town, whilst Digby, with three foot regiments, five troops of horse and some guns, was at Radford. Wardlaw knew attack was imminent and expected it to be amphibious, directed against a fort on the banks of the Tamar at Prince Rock. He had left the 300-strong garrison of Fort Stamford dangerously isolated, not realising that Digby had decided to make it his first objective. The Royalist commander saw that if he could turn the left flank of the fort, it would be completely cut off. Fort Stamford's flank was protected by a small fortlet to its east, whilst Stamford itself was held by a party of naval gunners and men from Colonel William Herbert's Regiment, Calmady's London Greycoats and William Gould's Regiment.

During the night of 21 October a party of Royalist foot moved stealthily towards Fort Stamford, constructing a small earthen fortification within musket shot and isolating the small fortlet. At dawn the proximity of the enemy came as a rude shock to the Parliamentarians, but the garrison of Fort Stamford mounted a hasty counter-attack by men from Gould's Regiment under Captain Richard Corbett. They were thrown back by the fire of the Royalists within their entrenchment, but after three hours succeeded in overrunning the Royalist defence work, taking fifty-one prisoners. An ensign and thirty men were left to hold the captured work, only to lose it again in another stealthy Royalist attack on the night of 22 October.

On the 23rd the Parliamentarians renewed their counter-attacks, regaining the much-contested outpost but losing twenty dead, including Captain Corbett. The pleas of the defenders of Fort Stamford for reinforcements had gone unanswered and they worked desperately to strengthen their own defences, incorporating some of those recently thrown up by the Royalists. They were critically short of men and Wardlaw was unwilling to reinforce what he regarded as a doomed outpost. But the fall of Fort Stamford would not only give the Royalists complete control of the eastern bank of the River Plym, but also allow the Royalists to establish artillery batteries to fire into the lower part of Plymouth itself. By now Digby's gunners were closing the range against Fort Stamford. On 5 November they opened fire with guns ranging in weight from 6 to 24 pounds, and also fired on ships anchored in Sutton Pool. These vessels were forced to withdraw behind the shelter of Saint Nicholas Island.

Under concentrated fire, the earth and timber defences of Fort Stamford gradually disintegrated, whilst pleas to Wardlaw for assistance continued to go unanswered. On 6 October Digby prepared a final assault to be carried out by some of his own cavalry regiment and those of Sir Francis Hawley and Lieutenant Colonel Thomas Monk, and three regiments of foot. By now gunfire had made a large breach in the Parliamentarian defences, and the Royalists, wearing a bay leaf in their hats as a field sign and yelling their watchword, 'Victory', surged forward. The fortlet was stormed, with forty Parliamentarians killed or taken, and then, using movable breastworks and ladders, the attackers moved against Fort Stamford itself, advancing on three sides, covered by the fire of their own guns and filling the surrounding ditch with faggots. With their own ammunition exhausted the garrison of Fort Stamford surrendered and at 4pm marched out with colours flying, to be evacuated to Plymouth by boat. The Royalists could now fire on the enemy shipping in Sutton Pool and observe movements within the town, although Parliamentarian ships could still anchor in Mill Bay. Whilst the assault on Fort Stamford was going on, the Royalists launched a secondary assault on Lipson Work, which was repulsed.

With enemy pressure on Plymouth mounting, Wardlaw tightened military control in the town, arrested a number of suspected Royalist supporters, and declared that he would set Plymouth ablaze rather than surrender it. Everyone in the town was ordered to take an oath of loyalty, but supplies were running low and there were too few troops to man all the defences. There was also trouble between Wardlaw and Cawse regarding control of the Plymouth Trained Bands, whom Gould blamed for the loss of Fort Stamford, although Wardlaw felt that on balance its loss had actually been an advantage for the defence. However, he placed the castle, fort, St Nicholas Island and the magazine under military control, distrusting the reliability of the civilian population.

On 18 November Digby once again summoned Plymouth to surrender, offering a general pardon. This followed a demonstration of strength the previous day, when Prince Maurice had paraded his army in full view on the high ground on the northern side of the town, and also began emplacing artillery there. The Parliamentarians predictably rejected the latest enemy summons, whilst Wardlaw worked to strengthen Plymouth's defences, replanting high hedges connecting the outer line of forts as rudimentary defensive positions. Maudlyn Fort was strengthened and the fortlet in the gap between Lipson Fort and the River Plym was extended.

On 11 November the importance of seapower in the defence of Plymouth was emphasised when the fleet commander, the Earl of Warwick, wrote to Parliament saying that he planned to keep Plymouth supplied by sea.[103] On 4 December a half-completed regiment of foot under Edward Harley was ordered to be despatched to Plymouth by ship.

After a plot to blow up the fort of Maudlyn magazine failed, two deserters reached Royalist lines with full details of Plymouth's defences. Prince Maurice had concentrated the bulk of his cannon in five batteries along the high ground above Lipson Creek, and on 28 November they opened up, aiming most of their fire at Lipson Fort, though they did little damage, and an initial attempt to put troops across Lipson Creek failed. Maurice now decided on a diversionary attack against the small Liara Point fort, further to the east. Sunday, 3 December was a cold windy day and the Parliamentarian garrison of the fort was evidently off guard. The two deserters led four hundred Royalist musketeers at low tide across Lipson Creek and quickly overwhelmed the defenders of the fort, though one of them managed to fire off a warning shot alerting Plymouth itself. The garrison prepared a force of 450 men to regain the fort, whilst at the same time there was growing alarm onboard a flotilla of supply ships anchored in the Plym near Liara Point, which were now within cannon range of the enemy, and, possibly in order to spin out time whilst the situation clarified, agreed to discuss surrender terms with the Royalists.

Maurice had drawn up his main force near the village of Compton and sent around 2,000 foot down towards Lipson Creek, employing the cover of the hedgerows. They were in the process of crossing the Creek when the Parliamentarian counter-attack began. Eventually the outnumbered Parliamentarians were forced back and then broke, fleeing across three fields to take refuge in Lipson Fort. A party of Royalist horse advanced to within a short distance of Plymouth's inner defence line near Resolution Fort but were driven back by musket fire.

Meanwhile, the disordered Parliamentarians had rallied at Lipson Fort and Colonel Gould arrived to direct operations, drawing men from other forts despite the possibility of further Royalist attacks elsewhere, and eventually mustered between 1,000 and 1,500 men. The situation remained critical: if Maurice could take Lipson Fort he would be able to roll up the entire outer line of Plymouth's defences. But Maurice's troops – never the best disciplined of Royalist forces – hesitated, possibly concerned about the intentions of Gould's force. As the Parliamentarians continued to bring up men the Royalists mounted one or two half-hearted attacks, whilst Gould sent sixty musketeers, using the cover of rising ground, to attack the Royalist left flank, following up with a full-blooded counter-attack. Gould himself was twice unhorsed in the fierce fighting which followed, but as his flanking force appeared in the enemy rear and opened fire, the Royalists panicked and fell back in increasing disorder towards Lipson Creek, only to find that the tide was now in, and their retreat cut off.

As they retreated down the slope under heavy fire, some of Maurice's men were driven into the Creek and drowned, and others also came under fire from the Parliamentarian ships in the River Plym, whose crews had reconsidered their thoughts of surrender. The repulse cost the Royalists around 300 casualties, a large quantity of weapons and 13 barrels of powder, compared with Parliamentarian losses of about 150 men.

However, Maurice remained determined and on 13 December John Digby's regiment of horse and Colonel Bullen Reymes's foot attacked Lipson Mill Work but were repulsed. The Parliamentarians expected the next enemy attempt to be against Maudlyn Fort, which Wardlaw strengthened, adding a demi-culverin to its ordnance. On Monday 18 December the Royalists began to bombard Maudlyn and the Parliamentarian guns replied, claiming to have silenced one Royalist piece. The artillery exchange continued until Wednesday evening and that night a party of 200 Royalist musketeers, using the cover of hedgerows, made their way across Maudlyn Ridge and came up close to the Parliamentarian line between Maudlyn and Pennycomequick Forts without being detected. The Royalist musketeers spent the remainder of the night quietly constructing a small earthwork. At dawn sixty Parliamentarians from Maudlyn Fort counter-attacked but were repulsed. However, as the situation clarified with daylight, Gould collected a considerable force of horse and foot from elsewhere in the defences and at 9am began a major counter-attack. The earthwork changed hands several times until, in a fourth attack, the Royalists were eventually driven out in fierce hand-to-hand fighting and the earthwork demolished.

This was Maurice's final effort: his army was devastated by sickness and on Christmas Day he pulled back into Devon to rest and reorganise his forces for the coming year's campaign. Digby was once again left to maintain a loose blockade of Plymouth, unable to prevent further supplies and reinforcements arriving by sea. Within the town William Gould had replaced Wardlaw as Governor and tightened discipline among the defenders whilst continuing to strengthen his fortifications.

'Skellum' Grenville

Throughout the first half of 1644 indecisive skirmishing, raid and counter-raid, continued. Digby was joined by the notorious Parliamentarian defector, Sir Richard 'Skellum' Grenville, whilst William Gould died in March from the sickness contracted from Maurice's forces, which was ravaging Plymouth, carrying off up to 400 people in a month, including entire families. Gould was replaced as Governor by another Scottish professional soldier, Colonel James Kerr, who also had an uneasy relationship with the civilian authorities, whilst John Digby was seriously wounded in a skirmish, leaving Grenville in command of a small blockading force.

In July, Plymouth found itself in the forefront of events, as the main Parliamentarian field army under the Earl of Essex marched west, followed by the Royalist armies of the King and Prince Maurice. One of Essex's objectives was the relief of Plymouth, although Grenville's forces were too few to present any serious threat to the town.

Grenville retreated into Cornwall in the face of Essex's advance, and the Parliamentarian commander, encouraged by optimistic promises of support from local Parliamentarian leaders such as Lord Robartes, crossed the Tamar in pursuit. He took with him about 1,000 troops from Plymouth, seriously depleting the garrison. The Earl of Warwick, still supplying Plymouth by sea, was horrified, saying that only 1,000 soldiers and seamen remained to man 4 miles of defences, and that 200 of them were garrisoning Saltash.[104] He sent 160 of his crewmen to reinforce the latter garrison and added to the Plymouth artillery 16 guns from a captured Royalist vessel, the *Frederick and William*. For the moment Warwick took over as effective commander at Plymouth and summoned the Royalist outpost at Mount Edgecumbe to surrender, in an attempt to reduce the danger to ships entering Plymouth. His summons was rejected and Warwick could only mount an ineffective retaliatory bombardment of the Royalist defences.

On 18 August Warwick sent a gloomy report to the Committee of Both Kingdoms, explaining that Colonel Kerr and Mayor Cawse were still at loggerheads and warning that if Plymouth fell, the whole of the South West would effectively be lost.[105] His concern mounted when Essex was trapped by superior numbers around Lostwithiel and Fowey. He had hoped that Warwick would be able to supply and perhaps evacuate his army by sea, but contrary winds prevented the fleet from advancing further west than Plymouth.

Although Essex's cavalry were able to escape, followed by the Earl and Lord Robartes in a fishing boat, the Parliamentarian foot, and the Plymouth detachment, were forced to surrender on 1 September. Plymouth was the obvious next target for the victorious Royalists and Warwick detached Vice Admiral

William Batten, with a squadron of eight ships, to support the garrison. On 3 September the net tightened as Grenville stormed Saltash in a surprise attack, the surviving defenders fleeing by boat across the Tamar to Plymouth. Lord Robartes – left by Essex as Governor of Plymouth – now had to face (with an exhausted and depleted garrison) an estimated 15,000 Royalists.

On 9 September King Charles summoned Plymouth to surrender, and next day his troops took up position around the town, bringing up twenty-eight guns. Despite their strong defences, Plymouth's 3,000 defenders were in a desperate situation. Batten reinforced them with all the sailors he could spare, and the Committee of Both Kingdoms ordered that all available troops be shipped to Plymouth, although these were unlikely to arrive in time, and indeed only Colonel John Birch's foot from Weymouth actually appeared.

Despite his previously undistinguished performance, John, Lord Robartes, proved an inspirational commander. A strict Puritan, Robartes – a leading West Country wool merchant – had the twin advantages of being a local man and Warwick's son-in-law. Robartes expected an imminent assault but although small-scale skirmishing continued for several days, no large-scale attack materialised. By delaying a follow-up to his victory at Lostwithiel, the King had lost his chance of attacking Plymouth when its defenders were at their weakest. He made a futile attempt to bribe Robartes into surrendering, and then, on 12 September – unwilling to incur the losses and time involved in a major assault or prolonged siege – drew off his forces and continued his march eastwards.

This did not mean that Plymouth was yet safe. On 26 September Robartes warned the Committee of Both Kingdoms that many officers of the garrison were threatening to quit their posts due to lack of pay:

> The inhabitants are so exhausted that they are not able to support a third part of the garrison, which I conceive in the lowest proportion should be 2,500 foot besides the townsmen and 400 horse.[106]

The King had left Sir Richard Grenville, initially with only 800 foot, to resume the blockade of Plymouth. Grenville, in a sideswipe at its Parliamentarian owner, Sir Francis Drake, established his headquarters at Buckland Abbey and reoccupied his former outposts at Plympton and Saltash, whilst endeavouring, with a good deal of success, to recruit additional troops. Among them were 4 additional regiments of foot, known as Grenville's 'New Cornish Tertia', which included about 2,000 deserters from Prince Maurice's army. Grenville, though savage and unrelenting towards the enemy and the civilian population, was a firm disciplinarian who proved better able to maintain his forces than many other contemporary commanders.

Although his forces slowly increased, for most of the autumn Grenville remained too weak to mount a direct attack. In mid–September Sir Richard attempted to gain Plymouth by means of treachery. Joseph Grenville, a sixteen-year-old kinsman (possibly an illegitimate son) of Grenville, entered the town, posing as a deserter. He offered £3,000 to a Parliamentarian officer, Colonel Searle, if he would betray Plymouth's outworks to the Royalists. However, Searle informed Robartes and Joseph Grenville was arrested and executed, despite Sir Richard, with unwonted generosity, offering any ransom or exchange demanded for his life.[107]

Perhaps this personal loss, if such it was, darkened Grenville's mood further. He soon found opportunity to exact characteristically bloody revenge. On 4 October 700 troops from Plymouth, crossing by boat, seized Saltash in a surprise attack. This was a serious blow to Grenville, threatening his communications with Cornwall, and he quickly struck back. His first assault, on 5 October, was repulsed. Next day the Royalists managed to establish a foothold in the lower town but were thrown back by fire from a Parliamentarian ship in the river, and the fierce resistance of the defenders holding the upper town, who, when their ammunition ran short, threw rocks.

On the night of 8 October, Grenville launched a third assault. He claimed afterwards that three calls to the defenders to surrender had been rejected, so that he 'resolved to storm them, having 500 stout Cornish foot'. At about 1am the Royalists attacked Saltash on two sides and in a couple of hours of fierce fighting drove the Parliamentarians down the steep main street to the banks of the Tamar, where some managed to escape by boat, although Grenville claimed to have killed 400–500 of the enemy and to have taken 300 prisoners.

By rejecting a summons to surrender, if one had been made, the Parliamentarians had, by the laws of war, forfeited their right to mercy and Grenville was not in any mood to grant clemency. He declared that 'after he hath given god thanks for his victory, he intends to hang 300 of the prisoners'. King Charles apparently wrote to Grenville urging him to spare them but was apparently too late, for a Cornish Royalist reported that Grenville 'hanged many in cold blood'.[108]

Though Grenville's reported boast that he would take Plymouth by Christmas proved ill-founded, by early 1645 he had mustered 5,000 foot and 1,000 horse, and could go on to the offensive. On 10 January he launched a major assault on Plymouth's outworks. The largest attacks were directed at the fort of Maudlyn and its western neighbour, Little Pennycomequick. Colonel John Birch's foot (about 800 men) were responsible for the defence of Maudlyn when, at about 2am, Royalist guns opened fire. The Royalists advanced, spearheaded by the New Cornish Tertia, in three bodies, supported by two more divisions of foot, each 1,500 strong. Birch and most of his regiment were in reserve but the Colonel immediately set off for Maudlyn with eight companies 'in as good order as that black and dark night would permit'. He found that the attackers had already been repulsed, and according to one Parliamentarian account no less than thirty of the attackers had been killed in one discharge by a gun fired by the captain of the fort.

Birch noticed that the guns of Little Pennycomequick Fort had fallen silent and, suspecting the worst, led his troops in that direction. When the Parliamentarians had come within pike-length, those within the fort called: 'Stand, who are you for?' – 'For the Parliament!' Birch replied and the Royalists, who had indeed taken the fort, opened fire. Telling his men that it was 'safer to go on than retreat', Birch stormed the ramparts and retook the fort, killing or capturing twenty Royalists, among them a Colonel Arundell, whose sword Birch kept for himself.

Elsewhere the Royalist attack petered out and its failure became the subject of heated recrimination in Grenville's camp. On 17 January, in his own terse account, Grenville wrote:

> I have lately in the night attempted to force Plymouth works and took one of them nigh the Maudlyn work, and had my seconds performed their parts Plymouth in all probability had now certainly been ours.[109]

This was probably wishful thinking on Grenville's part, but according to the Parliamentarians the dispute between Sir Richard and his commanders came to a head at a Council of War in Plympton. Grenville reportedly ordered Colonel Phillip Champernown, commanding Prince Maurice's Regiment of Foot, to renew the assault. On the latter's refusal, the dispute escalated into an exchange of pistol shots, in which Grenville

> fired his own pistol upon the colonel and slew him dead upon the place, which the Colonel's brother seeing, fired off his pistol upon Grenville and missed him, whereat Grenville drew his sword and ran him through.[110]

It seems a pity to spoil a good story, but accounts of Champernown's death were exaggerated. He lived until 1684.

Further smaller attacks mounted by Grenville in the course of February achieved no success, and it was obvious that the defences of Plymouth were too strong for his available forces to take. By now the town's war effort had been taken in hand by the Plymouth Committee of Defence, including among its members the mayor, ex-mayors and other leading citizens, charged with financing the defences, collecting funds from all available sources, and administering payments. Financial shortages remained, with payments frequently having to be postponed until the arrival of the next shipment of money from London. However, the shortage of munitions had by now been eased, with supplies arriving regularly by sea from October 1644. The frosts and rains of winter had caused significant damage to the earthen defences, and between February and May 1645 much of the Committee's average monthly expenditure of £3,000 went on their repair.

At the end of February Grenville received orders from Prince Rupert to assist in the siege of Taunton. He did not obey until later in March, and then only after receiving a direct command from the King, claiming that, despite ample evidence to the contrary, Plymouth had been so reduced

> by a strict blockeering [i.e. blockading – ed.] that the enemy horse were almost starved and lost and their foot grown almost to desperation, in such sort that if the said army had been suffered to remain but two months longer before that town, very probably Plymouth had been thereby reduced to obedience.[111]

To maintain the blockade Grenville left behind 400 horse and 1,200 foot, of whom John Digby eventually resumed command, but the direct military threat to Plymouth was almost at an end. A stalemate lasted for most of the summer, punctuated by occasional minor skirmishes, whilst the defences of Plymouth were steadily strengthened, and the navy continued to bring in men and supplies.

The main danger to Plymouth came from within, with a new outbreak of plague. In October 1645 at least 136 people died, in the following month 107 and 140 in December. But by now the Royalist cause was on the point of collapse and on 12 January 1646 Digby – faced by the approaching New Model Army – raised the siege for the final time and retreated into Cornwall.

Plymouth's war was over at last. It had endured the longest siege and blockade of the Civil War but the cost had been enormous. In all, perhaps 6,000 townspeople and refugees had died in those years, together with 2,000 soldiers. Plymouth was left a depopulated and impoverished place, which would take years to recover.

Chapter Seven

Women Under Siege: Lathom House 1644–1645

Civil war rarely differentiates between soldier and civilian, man, woman or child. All are caught up in its struggle. This was the case for the hundreds of women who were involved in the sieges of the English Civil War. When a town became a garrison – and still more if it were besieged – the women within were in as great danger as their menfolk and often found themselves in the forefront of the fighting. Women were frequently involved in construction and repair work on the defences, or toiled under fire to repair breaches caused by enemy attack. At Chester during the major Parliamentarian assault of 9 October 1645, its Governor, Lord John Byron, described how:

> I must not forget the great courage and gallantry the Chester women expressed that day, who all the time the cannon played upon the new breach . . . carried both earth and feather beds, and other materials incessantly, and made up the breach in the very mouth of the cannon. And though eight or ten of them, at the least, were killed and spoiled with great shot, yet the rest were nothing at all dismayed, but followed on their work, with as great alacrity and as little fear as if they had been going to milk their cows.[112]

In many places, among them Royalist Chester and Parliamentarian Gloucester, women had a major role in spotting and extinguishing incendiary shells and fire arrows fired into the towns. In some situations, such as the siege of Lyme and the defence of Basing House in September 1645, women were alleged to have taken an active part in the fighting. This was probably through desperation and fear of the consequences of enemy victory rather than out of political or religious commitment. Indeed, some of the women who had toiled under the enemy guns at Chester were almost certainly actively involved later in the rioting that helped force Byron to surrender, for, as he complained:

> multitudes of women (who are ever first employed in seditious actions upon the privilege of their sex) daily flocked about my house

with great clamours asking whether I intended they should eat their children since they had nothing else left to sustain themselves withal.[113]

Also actively involved in the sieges of the war, and as a result often the stuff of popular legend, were those women – mainly, though not solely, Royalist – who found themselves in the role of 'chatelaine' in besieged garrisons. Despite the claims of contemporary propagandists, some of these heroines found themselves in such situations from choice rather than circumstance, and usually they had the advice of experienced officers to guide them. The presence of a female of high social standing in at least nominal command of a garrison often seems to resulted in the efforts of the besiegers being half-hearted and ineffective. In 1643 the Parliamentarian Lady Brilliana Harley and her garrison at Brampton Bryan Castle in Herefordshire had little difficulty in seeing off a siege by local Royalists, whilst the Royalist Lady Mary Bankes and her daughters, hurling missiles from the battlements at their attackers, withstood the notably inept efforts of the Parliamentarians under Sir Walter Earle.

As the war became more bitter, a number of the 'chatelaines', notably the Countess of Derby and Lady Bankes, withdrew to more peaceful accommodation elsewhere, leaving experienced soldiers to command their garrisons. An exception was Lady Helen Neale, defender of Hawarden Castle in 1645. Unusually among the chatelaines, Lady Helen was not defending her husband's estates. Sir William Neale, a younger son of a relatively minor Northamptonshire gentry family, had been scoutmaster to Prince Rupert before the latter appointed him Governor of Hawarden, probably in February 1644. As with other 'landless' commanders, his charge provided accommodation for his wife and family, and, as a result, in her husband's absence Lady Helen found herself nominally in charge of its defence, with the assistance of the Deputy Governor, Captain Thomas Whitley, when Parliamentarian forces unexpectedly laid siege to Hawarden in April 1645. Despite threats of mining, Lady Helen assured her husband by letter that

> though my mind is upon the rack betwixt hope and despair, I am proposed (God blessing me) to hold out as long as there is meat for man, for none of these eminent dangers shall ever frighten me from my loyalty, but in life and death I will be the king's faithful subject and thy constant loving wife.[114]

Lady Neale's ordeal was soon ended when the mine failed to explode, and Hawarden was relieved by the approach of the main Royalist field army.

The First Siege of Lathom House

The siege of Lathom House and the defiant stand of Charlotte de la Tremoille, Countess of Derby and a daughter of Henri of Navarre, is one of the celebrated episodes of the English Civil War. So much so, indeed, that the reality of Lathom being a strategically fairly unimportant garrison, and its attackers poorly trained and motivated, are often overlooked.

In April 1643 the fluctuating Civil War in Lancashire swung firmly in favour of the Parliamentarians following their decisive victory over James Stanley, 7th Earl of Derby, and his Lancashire Royalists at the battle of Sabden Brook. In June Derby departed for the Isle of Man, leaving his wife, Charlotte, and his children behind in his principal residence and stronghold, Lathom House, just to the east of the town of Ormskirk. Derby's departure dashed any hopes of a Royalist recovery in Lancashire. Remaining Cavalier garrisons quickly fell, and by the end of June only Greenhaugh Castle and Lathom House still held out.

For various reasons, including fears of Royalist incursions from Yorkshire, and dissension among their own leadership, the Lancashire Parliamentarians were slow to move against Lathom, a rallying point for Royalist die-hards. The garrison kept a deliberately low profile for some months, and it was not until the winter of 1643/44 that necessity drove them to begin a series of raids aimed at obtaining supplies and real or alleged Parliamentarian supporters to hold for ransom.

At the end of January 1644, with the arrival in Lancashire of the Parliamentarian commander Sir Thomas Fairfax, fresh from his victory at Nantwich, action commenced against Lathom.

The Setting

Little is known about Lathom House. Even its whereabouts is in dispute, with two possible locations being suggested. One is in an area of woodland, known as Spa Roughs, which lies about 800 yards south-east of the eighteenth-century Lathom House. There are extensive remains of what may be a moat, surrounded by low hills. However, other archaeological and topographical evidence, including musket shot and some human remains, point with some degree of certainty to the House of the siege having been on or very close to the site of eighteenth-century Lathom House, itself demolished in modern times to make way for scientific laboratories.[115] The most detailed contemporary description of Lathom House is that given by Lady Derby's chaplain, Bishop Rutter, who was present during the siege:

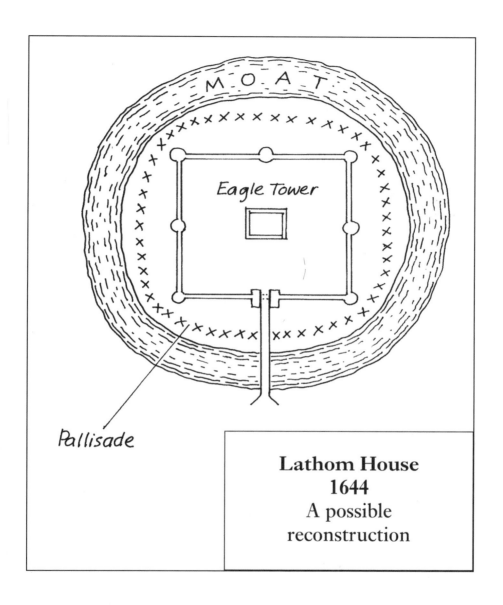

MOAT

Eagle Tower

Pallisade

**Lathom House
1644
A possible
reconstruction**

Lathom House stands upon a flat, a moorish [*sic*], spongey and spuminous ground, was encompassed with a strong wall of two yards thick; upon the walls were nine towers, flanking each other, and in every tower were six pieces of ordnance, that played three in one way and three the other. Without the wall was a moat eight yards wide, and two yards deep; upon the back of the moat between the walls and the graf was a strong row of palisades around; besides all these there was a strong tower, called the Eagle Tower, in the midst of the house, surmounting all the rest; and the gatehouse was also two high and strong buildings, with a strong tower on each side of it and in the entrance to the first court . . . if nature herself had found it for a stronghold or place of security, for before the house, to the south or south-west, is a rising ground so near it, as to over-look the top of it, from which it falls so quickly that you can scarce at the distance of a carbine shot, see the house over the height, so that all batteries placed there, are so far below it, as to be of little service when engaged against it . . . only let us observe for the present, that the uncommon situation of it may be compared to the palm of a man's hand, flat in the middle and covered with a rising ground about it, and so near to it that the enemy in a two years' siege, were never able to raise a battery against it so as to make a breach in the wall practicable to enter the house by way of storm.[116]

Lathom had medieval origins, added to somewhat haphazardly, with a series of courtyards surrounded by a mixture of stone and timber buildings.

Preparations

As attack loomed, the garrison of Lathom looked to their defences. There is conflicting evidence concerning how much combat experience the 300 men of the garrison had. Some had certainly seen action in Derby's rather undistinguished forces during the fighting in Lancashire. Lady Derby was nominally in command, and her resolute and defiant attitude, as well as her autocratic nature, was certainly a major factor in Lathom's resistance, although her actual involvement has been exaggerated in contemporary Royalist accounts and later popular legend.

Operational command rested with the officers of the garrison. Their senior was the Major of the House, Captain William Farmer, a Scottish professional soldier. The other captains – Henry Ogle, Molyneux Radcliffe, Edward Chisenall, Edward Rawsthorne, Thomas Charnock and Richard Foxe – were rather a mixed bunch, though Ogle and Radcliffe had previous military experience. Most of the others had probably served in Derby's forces. The garrison was divided equally among them, so that each officer led an under-strength company of fifty men. Half were on duty each night, and during the day sixteen marksmen were stationed in the Eagle Tower and the gatehouse towers. The garrison seems generally to have been well-provisioned, although gunpowder stocks were rather low.

The Countess of Derby was supplied with intelligence by the local population so was well prepared when, on 28 February 1644, a besieging force led by Sir Thomas Fairfax and a mutually antagonistic group of Lancashire Parliamentarians, Colonels Egerton, Alexander Rigby, Ralph Assheton and Holcroft arrived on the scene. The Parliamentarian troops were a mixed bag. Fairfax's own Yorkshire horse were only at Lathom for a short time, and do not seem to have played an active part in operations there. So far as the remainder were concerned, the usual practice seems to have been to draw levies for a fixed period from each of the Lancashire Hundreds. In theory the available force totalled 2,000–3,000 men, although there can rarely have been so many present at any particular time. The besieging forces were divided into brigades, or 'Tertias' each of 700–800 men, which were each on duty every third night, whilst the remainder were quartered in nearby villages. Each Hundred supplied troops in turn for about a fortnight at a time, the costs being borne by the place of origin of each company. Many of the more experienced Lancashire forces were employed in guarding the eastern borders of the county against Royalist incursions from Yorkshire, and many of the soldiers involved in the siege, for example those from Fylde Hundred, were raw recruits.

The Parliamentarians employed several artillery pieces. They included one demi-cannon, one culverin, three sakers, and (for part of the time) a mortar. The siege works erected around Lathom during its first siege were not particularly formidable, not much more than an open trench, forming a front line about 60 yards from the House, with, about 40 yards further back, another surrounding trench protected by a ditch and then a third defended with a rampart. During the course of the siege around eight sconces, protected with palisades and ditches, were also constructed.

The Siege Begins

From 27 February Parliamentarian troops began to take up positions in a 3-mile radius around Lathom. Several days passed in negotiations regarding terms for a Royalist surrender. It is unlikely that either side expected any result from these discussions, but it was in the Royalists' interest to spin out talks, whilst the Parliamentarian leaders were apparently divided in their strategy: some favouring a distant blockade by detachments of troops, others preferring a close siege. They were also encouraged by reports, apparently 'planted' by Lady Derby's chaplain, Samuel Rutter, that the garrison's provisions were running low.

Lady Derby seems to have taken full advantage of the divided counsels of her opponents by humiliating and embarrassing them in negotiations as much as possible, and adopting various stratagems to impress the enemy with the determination of the garrison to resist. Fairfax and his men may have already departed for Yorkshire when on 12 March the Parliamentarians made their final offer, by which the garrison would be allowed to depart with all their arms and possessions – terms that were curtly rejected.

In the event it was the Royalists who struck first. On the evening of 12 March they launched a large-scale sortie, led by Major Farmer, 'a faithful and gallant soldier', leading 100 foot:

> with Lieutenant Brettough ready to second him in any service, and some 12 horse, our whole cavalry commanded by Lieutenant Kay, sallied out upon the enemy, and because the sequel of any business dependeth upon the beginning, [Major Farmer] decided to do something which might remember the enemy there were soldiers within.[117]

The Royalists quietly approached the Parliamentarian siegeworks, which were still probably fairly rudimentary,

> and then firing upon them in their trenches, they quickly left their holes, when Lieutenant Kay, having wheeled about with his horse, from another gate, fell upon them in their flight with much execution, they slew about 30 men, took 40 arms, one drum and six prisoners.[118]

Before their numerically superior opponents could recover, the Royalists, having lost no more than two men, fell back into the House, their retreat covered by the musketeers of Captains Ogle and Rawsthorne. This sudden nocturnal onslaught seems to have had a lasting impact on the already shaky morale of the Parliamentarian soldiers, and was the first in a series of actions by the garrison designed to keep their opponents off-balance. The next few days passed relatively quietly, but on the night of 17 March the Royalists decided to again test the alertness of the besiegers. Captain Chisenall,

> a man of known courage and resolution, Lieutenant Brettough and Lieutenant Heape, with 30 musketeers issued out of the back gate to surprise the enemy in their new trenches, but they discovering some of the light matches ran faster than the Captain or his soldiers could pursue, securing their flight in a wood close by, where not willing to engage his soldiers in unnecessary dangers, he left 'em only killing two or three, and chasing the rest in flight.[119]

Recognising that there was little chance of a quick resolution to the siege, the attackers set to work to construct regular siegeworks, under the direction of Major Thomas Morgan, ' a short peremptory man', a Welsh engineer of some distinction, who had been left by Fairfax. Large numbers of local people were brought up to act as a labour force. They suffered a number of casualties from the fire of the Royalists, one of whom wrote that

> It moved both wonder and pity to see multitudes of poor people so enslav'd to the reformers' tyranny that they would stand the musket and lose their lives to serve nothing.[120]

Some work was carried out at night, so that the

> enemies' [*sic*] night works, which were begun about musket shot from the house, in a stooping declining ground, that their pioneers by the nature of the place might be secured from our ordnance as on the tower and so in an orb or ring work cast up, which grew every day by the multitude of country people forced into service.[121]

The bulk of the Parliamentarian troops were evidently fairly ineffective, and unwilling to come to close quarters with the Royalists, though ready enough to aimlessly fire off their muskets from a safe distance. One Parliamentarian present at the siege wrote:

> There was needlessly spent against it [Lathom House] in shot and powder an infinite quantity. Some was always shooting at nothing they could see but the walls.[122]

This practice was encouraged by the Royalists, who 'gave many Alarms in the Night tyme to the Guards which was the occasion that much powder and shot was wasted'.[123]

By the night of 19 March the Parliamentarian siegeworks had been pushed forward sufficiently to bring some of their guns into action. A 24-pound demi-cannon was emplaced, and next day fired 3 shots. They made little impact on Lathom's thick walls and so the gun shot high in an attempt to hit the Eagle Tower 'or please the women who came to see the spectacle'.[124] That night, under cover of a feint sally, a Royalist messenger slipped out of Lathom to carry news of its plight to the nearest Royalist garrison at Chester. The Earl of Derby had already returned there from the Isle of Man, and began bombarding Prince Rupert, who was in command on the Welsh Border, with urgent pleas for assistance for Lathom and his wife, who was a cousin of the Prince:

> Sir [ran one of his letters], I have received many advertisements from my wife of her great distress and imminent danger, unless she

be relieved by Your Highness, on whom she doth more rely than any other whatsoever . . . I would have waited on Your Highness this time, but that I hourly receive little letters from her, who haply, a few days hence, may never send me more.[125]

However, Rupert and Lord Byron, commanding at Chester, were unimpressed by this purple prose, as indeed was King Charles, whose Secretary of State wrote to Rupert, telling him that he should not hazard other plans by being diverted to Lathom 'since I do not hear otherwise than by my Lord of Derby's servant that the place is yet much distressed.'[126] The reality was that with virtually all of the rest of Lancashire in enemy hands, any attempt to relieve Lathom would be a major undertaking which could only be justified as part of a wider strategy.

The Bombardment

The garrison had not so far been seriously threatened by the actions of the besiegers, but from 25 March the rate of their bombardment increased. That day seven shots were fired by the demi-cannon and a culverin, one of which smashed the main gates, which were hastily barricaded with mattresses. This initial bombardment set the pattern for the next few days. One of the garrison was killed by a musket shot when he left the shelter of the battlements, and a cannon shot aimed to 'dismount one of our ordnance upon the great gates, struck the battlements, upon one of our marksmen ready to discharge at the cannonier, and crushed him to death.'[127] The Parliamentarians now added chain shot and iron bars to their projectiles, with the worst of Lathom's ordeals still to come.

The purpose of the circular earthwork 'in the form of a full moon, two yards and a half of rampier above the ditch', which had been dug, giving a 'full prospect of the whole building', about half a musket shot from the south-west corner of the House, became apparent on 2 April when a mortar, which had been brought from London and which was known to the Royalists as 'Sir William Brereton's Jewel', opened fire. Its effect was terrifying, as it lobbed 3 great stones, each 13 inches in diameter and weighing 80 pounds, into Lathom, one narrowly missing a room where Lady Derby and her officers sat at dinner. On 6 April the mortar fired an explosive 'granado', which fortunately overshot the House, but forced Major Farmer to station men equipped with wet hides at strategic points in case of fire.

On 10 April the increasing bombardment caused the Royalists to launch another major sally led by Farmer, Captain Molyneux Radcliffe and Lieutenants Worrel and Penketh, with 140 men, who sallied out of the

Fortifications were constructed according to the theories of various contemporary military writers, or from practical experience. They were constructed from plans drawn up by military engineers. Note the storm poles projecting from the face of the partially completed defences.

A cannon royal. Heavy siege guns could be highly effective, but were slow and cumbersome to transport, had a slow rate of fire, and consumed huge quantities of often scarce and expensive gunpowder. Its wicker gun platform was intended to absorb the effects of the gun's recoil.

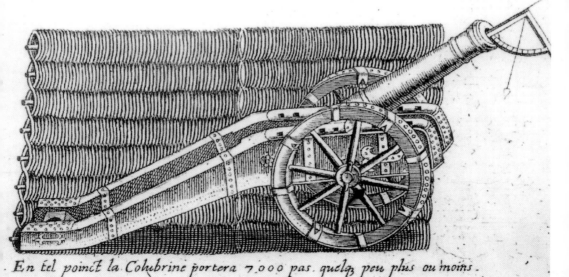

Tract. 2 dial. 20.

Quelle sera de plus grande portée la Colubrine ou le Canon.

Welches stuck am weitesten trägt die Colubrina oder die Carthaune

En tel poinct la Colubrine portera 7.000 pas. quelq; peu plus ou moins.

In solcher erhöhung trägt die Colubrina vngefehrlich 7000 schritt.

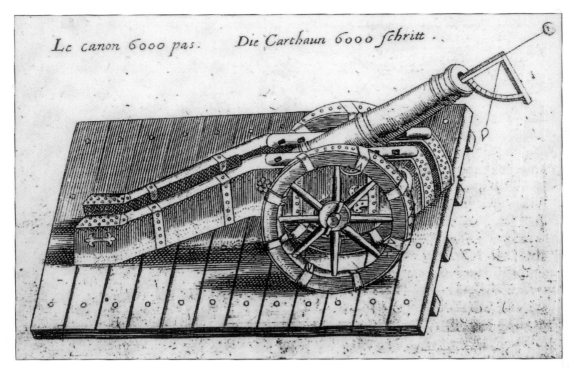

Le canon 6000 pas. Die Carthaun 6000 schritt.

A demi-cannon. Slightly lighter than the full cannon, and the most commonly used siege piece in the English Civil War. It has a wooden firing platform.

A battery in action. Gunners are firing, loading and swabbing out their pieces.

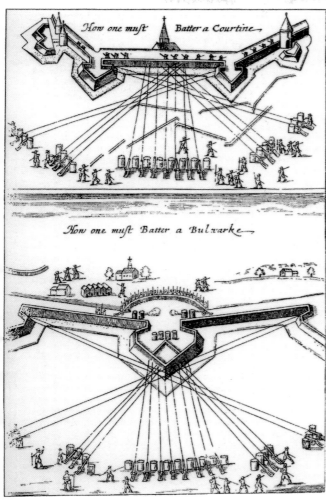

How one must Batter a Courtine

How one must Batter a Bulwarke

Guns had to be positioned carefully in order to combine their fire most effectively.

Garrison troops were notorious for plundering, as satirised in this contemporary engraving.

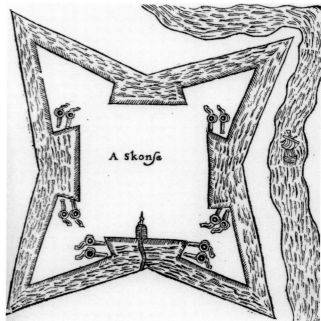

A skonse

A sconce. These earthen fortifications were a common feature of Civil War defences, and were often linked by ramparts or trenches.

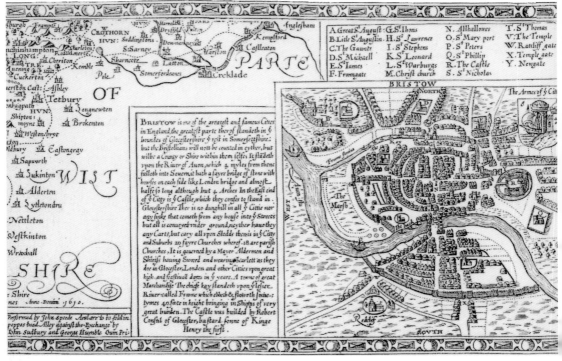

Bristol in 1610. Note the protection afforded to much of the town by its rivers, and the medieval walls still standing on its southern side. The castle (centre right) was still defensible.

Storming. Taking a fortification by storm was often the option of last resort, but more popular if time was short or a defending garrison was thought to be weak or poorly motivated. Note the 'granadoes' being thrown by the attackers.

Beeston Castle. Positioned high on a rocky outcrop, Beeston was reasonably secure from bombardment, mining or assault. During the war it fell only to surprise attack or from starvation.

Sir Thomas Fairfax. His appeal to Prince Rupert during the Second Siege of Bristol to avoid unnecessary bloodshed and destruction may have influenced the Prince's surrender.

Plymouth. Another garrison partly protected by water, and capable of being supplied by sea, Plymouth's defences were progressively strengthened and extended during the course of the war.

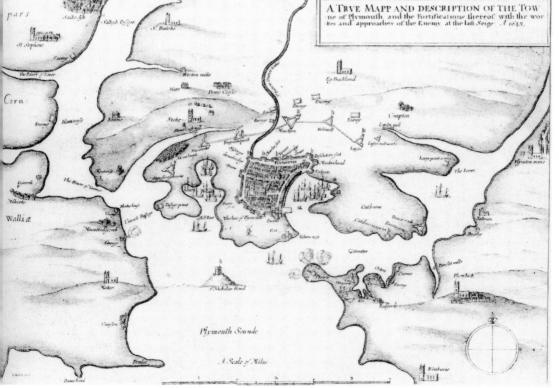

A TRVE MAPP AND DESCRIPTION OF THE TOWne of Plymouth and the Fortifications thereof with the workes and approaches of the Enemy at the last Seige A 1643.

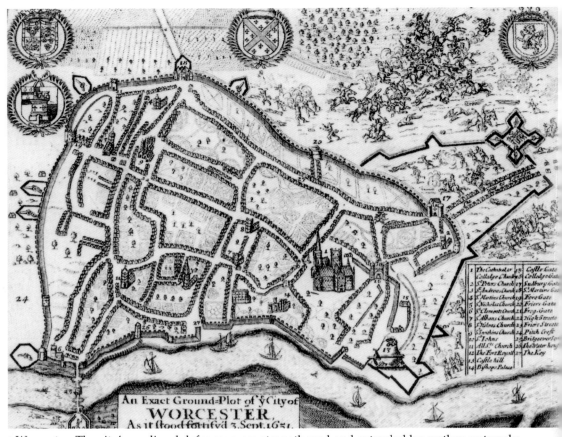

An Exact Ground-Plot of ỹ City of
WORCESTER.
As it stood fortifyd 3. Sept. 1651.

1	The Cathedrall	15	Castle Gate
2	Collolge Church	16	Collolge Gate
3	St Peters Church	17	Salsbury Gate
4	St Andros Church	18	St Martins Gate
5	St Martins Church	19	Fore Gate
6	St Nicholas Church	20	Friers Gate
7	St Clements Church	21	Frog Gate
8	St Albans Church	22	High Streete
9	St Helens Church	23	Frier Streete
10	St Swithins Church	24	Pitch Croft
11	St Johns	25	Bridgewardon
12	All Sts Church	26	The Water heng
13	The Fort Royall	27	The Key
14	Castle hill		
14	Byshops Palace		

Worcester. The city's medieval defences were strengthened and extended by earthen outworks, including the massive 'Fort Royal' (far right).

Prince Maurice, younger brother of Rupert, and somewhat over-shadowed by him, Maurice was a capable cavalry commander and administrator, although, partly because of ill-health and inadequate resources, he met with little success in siege operations.

Thomas Mytton. A pre-war friend of Salusbury, and commander of the Shropshire Parliamentarian forces, Mytton led the troops charged with capturing the Royalist-held castles of North Wales.

Sold by P Stent

Major Gen:
Mitton

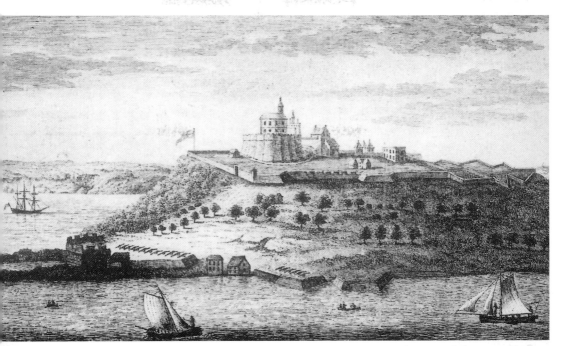

Pendennis Castle. One of the coastal fortifications built by Henry VIII, Pendennis's defences were extended on its landward side, and its position would render any assault costly.

Denbigh town and castle in 1610. The town had originally been situated in what was now the Outer Ward of the castle. The later expanded area had no defences.

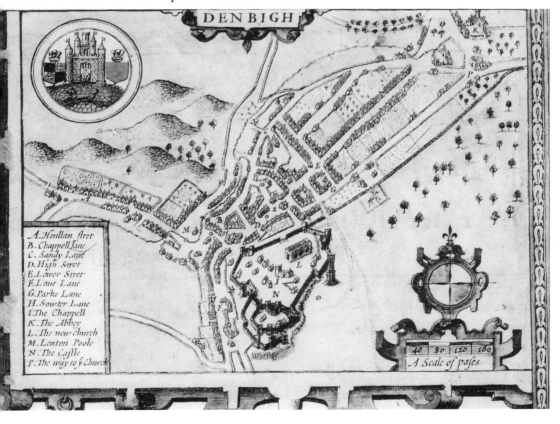

DENBIGH

A. Henllan street
B. Chappell Lane
C. Sandy Lane
D. High Street
E. Lower Street
F. Loue Lane
G. Parke Lane
H. Sowter Lane
I. The Chappell
K. The Abbey
L. The new church
M. Lenton Poole
N. The Castle
P. The way to ye Church

A Scale of pases

E. B. THE NEW. C. THE TOWER THAT IS HALFE BAT TERED DOVNE. D. THE KINGES BREAST WORKS. E. THE PARLI

Basing House. The New House is on the left, the Old House on the right. Note the brick perimeter walls, supplemented by earthen outer works.

Sir Arthur Aston. A Roman Catholic professional soldier who had fought for the King during the Civil War, when he had been Governor of Reading and Oxford.

Colonel John Hewson. A prominent supporter of Cromwell, whose politically motivated regiment spearheaded the assaults at Basing and Drogheda.

postern gate and 'beat the enemy from all works, nailed up all cannon, killed 50, took 60 arms, one colour and three drums . . . ' Captain Radcliffe, spearheading the assult

> with three soldiers, the rest of his squadron being scattered with execution of the enemy, he cleared two sconces, and slew seven men with his own hand. [Lieutenant Worrel] ingaging himself in another work among 50 of the enemy, bore the fury of all, till Major Farmer relieved him, who to the wonder of all, came off without any dangerous wound . . . The sally port was this day warded by Captain Chisenall who with fresh men stood ready for succour by ours if they had been put to the extremity, but they bravely marched round the works and came in at the great gates, where Captain Ogle with a party of musketeers kept open the passage. Captain Rawsthorn had the charge of the musketeers upon the walls, which he placed to the best advantage to vex the enemy in their flight. Captain Fox by a colour from the Eagle Tower gave signal when to march and when to retreat according to the motions of the enemy, which he observed at a distance. In all this service, we had but one man mortally wounded, and we took only one prisoner, an officer, for intelligence.[128]

Previously, prisoners had been handed back by the Royalists on the understanding that they would later be exchanged in the usual way for Royalist captives. But the King's men claimed that the Parliamentarians had breached this understanding

> and thus occasioned a greater slaughter than either her Ladyship or the Captains desired, because we were in no condition to keep prisoners, and knew that commanders would never release 'em but upon base or dishonourable conditions.[129]

The account of the skirmish given in the Royalist *Mercurius Aulicus* added several details, claiming that the garrison had killed forty-five of the enemy, captured two guns and the drum and colours of Colonel John Moore, Parliamentarian governor of Liverpool. In more peaceful times, Moore had frequently been a guest at Lathom, 'and therefore the brave Lady caused his Colours to be nailed on the top of the highest Tower of the House that all may see the ingratitude of a Rebel.'[130] The Royalists seem to have held parts of the siegeworks for up to an hour, although attempts to spike the enemy guns were not very effective.

One result of this affair was that Colonel Egerton was replaced as overall commander of the siege by Alexander Rigby, a lawyer who was particularly disliked by the Royalists, who accused him of harshness and cruelty. Rigby made his headquarters at Ormskirk and pressed on with the bombardment of Lathom. The latest sortie by the garrison had thoroughly unsettled the besiegers and the night following was 'with them one continual alarm, nothing but shouts and cries amongst them, as if the cavaliers had still been upon them.'[131]

By 12 April the Parliamentarians had at least two guns, the mortar and a saker, back in action, and a shot from the latter entered Lady Derby's own room. Next day

> their demi-cannon opened again, but spoke but once very low, some of the steel nails yet sticking in her teeth, and the gunners also suspecting poison in her belly.[132]

More firing on the 15th reached a climax on the 16th, when

> about 11 o'clock they played their mortar piece with stone, and perceiving it struck within the body of the house, they cast a granado at the same level, which fell into an old court, striking above half a yard into the earth, yet rose again with such violence in the bursting, that though its strength was much lessened, and deadened with earth, it shook down the glass, clay and weaker buildings near it, leaving only the carcass of the walls standing about it, yet without hurt of any person, saving that two women in a near chamber had their hands scorched to put them in mind thereafter that they were at the siege of Lathom.[133]

The effects of the mortar were beginning seriously to affect the morale of the defenders, despite the example of their officers, who made their own quarters in the most vulnerable rooms. The Royalists received some compensation when one of the enemy engineers was shot whilst inspecting the siegeworks, but this did nothing to lessen the attack. On the 20th the demi-cannon and the culverin fired thirty shots at the postern tower, part of which lay beyond the moat and palisade. However, it was largely protected by rising ground, so that only the battlements and part of the wall were damaged, and repaired the same night whilst one of the gunners was killed by a marksman firing from the Eagle Tower.

On the night of 22 April, Easter Monday

> too dark for action, the captains sent out 2 or 3 firelocks, which struck the whole night into alarms, so that to their musket they added one mortar piece, and 2 cannon with chain and small shot.[134]

But such minor exploits, however temporarily encouraging, did nothing to check the enemy bombardment, which was having increasingly serious effects. On 25 April a final summons from Rigby was presented, allowing Lady Derby to stage a morale-boosting piece of theatre:

> On Thursday he sends his last message, as he calls it, a furious summons to her ladyship to yield up Lathom House, and all the persons, goods, and arms within it, into his hands, to receive the mercy of the parliament, and to return her final answer the next day before two o'clock. Her ladyship having read this, with a brave indignation calls for the drum, and tells him that, 'a due reward for his pains is to be hanged up at her gates; but' says she, 'thou art but the foolish instrument of a traitor's pride; carry this answer back to Rigby' (with a noble scorn tearing the paper in his sight), 'and tell that insolent rebel, he shall neither have persons, goods, nor house; when our strength and provision is spent, we shall find a fire more merciful than Rigby's, and then, if the providence of God prevent it not, my goods and house shall burn in his sight; and myself, children, and soldiers, rather than fall into his hands, will seal our religion and loyalty in the same flame,' which being spoken aloud in her soldiers' hearing they broke into shouts and acclamations of joy, all closing with this general voice, 'we shall die for his majesty and your honour – God save the king!'

But the garrison were much less confident than they appeared:

> The mortar piece was that that troubled us all. The little ladies had stomach to digest cannon, but the stoutest soldiers had no hearts for granadoes, and might they not at once free themselves from this continual expectation of death?[135]

A Parliamentarian writer, Edward Robinson, who was present, felt that his side made a grave mistake in not making greater use of the mortar:

> The mortar piece if it had been applied in shooting as it might have been, the House had been yielded in a short time. It was but twice shot off with Granadoes which made a great rustle in the House that they could not tell where to abide safe. Especial[ly] when those Bullets made of free stone which weighed eight pound apiece they when shot forth would fly as high into the air that almost a man could not see them, and then the falling was so ponderous that they break down all where they lighted . . . if the Leaguer had continued

to shoot it two or three more she had yielded up the House. But whereof it was not continued was not known to the Soldiers.[136]

The most likely reason for the besiegers not making greater use of the mortar was shortage of gunpowder or ammunition. They had evidently been forced to fire large stones because of a lack of explosive or incendiary shells. For their part, the Royalists felt that their

> present condition was either to kill or be killed . . . either sheepishly to receive death, when they would send it upon our heads, or manfully return it upon their own. At last it was resolved, notwithstanding a battery and ordnance planted against every passage, to sally out the next morning, and adventure for all. All things prepared about 4 o'clock next morning [26 April] Captain Chisenall, and Captain Foxe, Lieutenant Brettough, Lieutenant Penketh, Lieutenant Walthew, and Lieutenant Worrall, are designed for the service. Captain Ogle had the main guard, to secure a retreat, at the southern gate; Captain Rawsthorne has the charge of the sally gate, to secure our retreat upon the east side; Captain Radcliffe has the care of the marksmen and musketeers on the walls, to attend the approach or the flight of the enemy. Major Farmer, with a reserve of fresh men, stands ready at the parade to relieve either Captain in state of necessity. All things thus disposed, Captains Chisnall and 2 Lieutenants issues out at the eastern gate, and before he was discovered, got under their cannon, marching straight upon the sconces, where they had planted their great gun. It cost him a light skirmish to gain the fort, at last he entered; many slain, some prisoners and some escaping.[137]

The capture of this battery secured the Royalist retreat, and Captain Foxe and his men advanced along the trenches from the east to the south-west corner:

> till he came to the work which secured the mortar piece, which being guarded with 50 men, he found sharp service, forcing his way through musket and cannon, and beating the enemy out of the sconce with stones, his musket, by reason of the high work, being unserviceable. After a quarter of an hour he got the trench, and scaled the rampier, where many of the enemy fled, the rest were slain. The sconce thus won, was made good by a squadron of musketeers, which much annoyed the enemy, attempting to come up again.[138]

Most of the siegeworks were evidently now deserted, and whilst some of the garrison began levelling the defences, others 'with ropes lifting the mortar piece to a low drag [sledge] by strength of men drew it into the house'.[139] Captain Ogle's men held off an attempted counter-attack. Attempts to bring off other enemy guns proved impossible: 'however our men took time to poison all the cannon round, if anything will do this feat'.[140] The whole action was said to have lasted for an hour. The Royalists claimed to have lost only two men, whilst enemy losses were unknown, although marksmen on the walls of Lathom inflicted further casualties as the enemy fled. Five prisoners were taken including an assistant engineer 'who discovered to us the nature of their trench in which they had laboured two months, to draw away our water [from the moat]'.

> But now neither ditches nor nought else troubled our soldiers, their grand terror, the mortar-piece, which had frighted 'em from their meat and sleep, like a dead lion quietly lying among them: every one had his eye and his foot upon him, shouting and rejoicing as merrily as they had used to do with their ale and bagpipes. Indeed every one had this apprehension of the service, that the main work was done, and what was yet behind but a mere pastime.[141]

With the loss of the mortar the threat to the garrison was much reduced: under cover of darkness the Parliamentarians removed most of their remaining guns.

The siege was not yet over, but the Parliamentarians seem to have lost most of what little enthusiasm they had ever had for the task. A futile attempt was made to cut off the springs supplying Lathom's well with water, and Rigby's men had no more success with a trench, intended to drain the moat, which had thwarted any plan to take Lathom by assault. Local people were conscripted to do the digging, but their lack of enthusiasm, and the suspected treachery of Browne, an engineer, resulted in the trench never being completed. Parliamentarian morale was plummeting. Rigby wrote to the Lancashire Committee in Manchester:

> We are obliged to repel them five or six times in a night. These constant alarms the number of the garrison and our great losses, compel our men to mount guard every other night or even two nights in succession. For my part I am spent with anxiety and fatigue.[142]

The Royalist marksmen in the Eagle Tower and elsewhere continued to take their toll:

> They were so observant in marking the loopholes in the works that
> when they saw . . . that these were filled that they could not see
> through them they would be sure to shoot through them. Thereby
> they killed many . . . [143]

The latter stages of the siege saw little real action. The Parliamentarians
seem to have no clear plan beyond hoping that starvation would do their
work for them. But their blockade was so loose that it was frequently possible
for messengers and small quantities of supplies to slip into Lathom under
cover of darkness. Just how far the Royalists had seized the initiative was
illustrated by the nightly alarms which members of the garrison were able to
carry out:

> Sometimes they would steal a cord about some tree near the enemy,
> and bringing the end round, would make it terrible with many ranks
> and files of light matches: sometimes dogs and once a forlorn horse
> handsomely starred with match, but turned out of the gate,
> appeared in the dark night like a young constellation.

Parliamentarian gloom was deepened by rain, desertions and lack of pay.
The siege was now breaking down without much need of further action by
the Royalists. The heavy rain was causing the collapse of large sections of the
siegeworks, and although on 23 April the Committee in Manchester had
resolved to raise £4,627 a week, plus additional troops, to press the siege there
is no evidence to suggest that this had much effect.

Meanwhile, on 18 May, Prince Rupert with 2,000 horse and 5,000 foot left
Shrewsbury on the first stages of his march to reconquer Lancashire before
going to relieve York. Aware of this, Rigby, on 23 May, sent Lathom a final
summons to surrender. It was scornfully rejected and on the same night one
of Lady Derby's scouts killed a Parliamentarian sentry and got into Lathom
with news of Prince Rupert's approach. This effectively ended the first siege
of Lathom. Rigby – in what proved to be a fatal delay – remained before
Lathom until the night of 27 May, when he slipped away under cover of darkness, only to be routed by Rupert next day when he attempted to take refuge
in Bolton. His captured colours were sent to Lathom by the Prince as trophies
for Lady Derby.

The Second Siege

With the recovery by Rupert of most of south-west Lancashire, Royalist hopes
were high. Chisenall raised a regiment of foot, which accompanied the Prince
on his 'York March', whilst the noted Royalist engineer, Bernard de Gomme,

drew up plans for the strengthening of Lathom's defences, with 'bastions, counterscarps etc., and all the other outworks necessary for the better defence thereof upon another siege'.[144] Unfortunately, no details of these defences, which were evidently largely completed, appear to have survived, but they were formidable enough to deter any assault ever being made.

But the peaceful interlude proved brief: on 2 July Rupert was defeated on Marston Moor. Among the Royalist dead was Major William Farmer.

Edward Rawsthorne had been promoted to Colonel by Rupert, and with the departure during the summer for the Isle of Man of the Earl and Countess of Derby, was made Governor of Lathom. His garrison included most of the officers who had withstood the first siege and was later reinforced by various 'reformadoes' and elements from the garrison of Liverpool when the latter surrendered on 1 November.

Serious attempts by the Parliamentarians to reduce Lathom did not begin until January 1645, and even the Committee in Manchester only passed a lukewarm resolution that 'a second siege should be laid against the house to reduce it if God would, or at least wise stay their Robbing'.[145] It is clear there was little enthusiasm for the operation amongst the Lancashire Parliamentarian leadership, whose memories of the cost and difficulties of the first abortive siege were rendered more acute by the knowledge that the defences of Lathom were now considerably stronger and more extensive.

Command was given to Colonel Peter Egerton of Flixton, Lancashire. From the start he eschewed the close siege attempted by Rigby. Instead, 'a great Ditch was drawn round the House a good distance from it, as convenient as possible, and the whole Country bore their Charge'.[146] For some time, Egerton and about 4,000 men, their main headquarters 3 miles away at Ormskirk, imposed no more than a loose blockade. This was on several occasions penetrated by Royalist sorties, one of which surprised Egerton in his quarters – forcing him to flee in his shirt and slippers – and captured his store of ammunition.

Siege operations were hampered by the demands placed on the Lancashire Committee to provide troops for service elsewhere, and there were the usual problems of sickness and desertion among Egerton's dwindling forces. Constant skirmishing continued throughout the spring of 1645, until shortage of ammunition forced the Royalists to suspend offensive operations. The Lathom House Chaplain, Samuel Rutter, meanwhile maintained sporadic communications with the outside world by various ingenious expedients, including:

a hound dog which he observed frequently to go betwixt his master in Lathom House, and his mistress about three miles off, got private notice to the gentlewoman, that as often the dog came home, she should look about his neck, and she would find a thread with a little paper wrapt about it, which he requested she would send to his Majesty; and when any papers were sent to her to come into the house, directed that she would tie them in like manner about the dog's neck, and keep him a while hungered, then open the door and beat him out. And thus the poor dog, being beaten backward and forward, conveyed all intelligence into and from the house, for nine months together, till at last, leaping over the enemies' [*sic*] works in his way to the house, an angry ill-natured soldier shot him, but he got to the moat side near the gate with his despatches, and there died, by which Mr Rutter lost his useful servant the dog.[147]

For some time the Lathom garrison continued to hope for relief, but the battle of Naseby on 14 June put an end to any realistic possibility of this, and during the summer the Parliamentarians were tightening their grip on Lathom and its two outposts in the Park, New Park and the Lodge. In early July the latter – held by Irish soldiers from surrendered Liverpool – was bombarded and stormed in a 'very hot fight', and the Lodge, threatened with similar treatment, surrendered.[148]

The fall of Lathom's outposts enabled the Parliamentarians to draw closer to the house itself, although they still did not launch a direct attack. The series of disasters being encountered by the Royalist cause elsewhere made such costly action in any case unnecessary. Indeed, following his defeat at Rowton Heath, near Chester, in September, the King gave the Lathom garrison leave to seek terms, 'since it was not in his power to relieve them'.[149]

The siege had still a little longer to run, although the defenders were no longer able to make sallies to bring in supplies; they were able at least to keep warm when they discovered a seam of coal just below the surface of the ground within the defences, and boredom was the soldiers' chief enemy, which they attempted to relieve by the time-honoured expedient of gambling:

> There was amongst the soldiers about fifty pounds in money, but of no use at all to them but to play at span-counter with; they lent to one another by handfuls, never telling or counting any; one day one soldier had all, and the next another, till at last all their sport was spoiled, the enemy at the gate stript them of every penny, and turned them out to the wide world.[150]

As with many another garrison, starvation and hopelessness of relief sealed Lathom's fate. Details of the fairly prolonged surrender negotiations are confused and sometimes contradictory, but terms seem eventually to have been agreed on 2 December. The officers were allowed to retain their swords, but the soldiers were disarmed, and those who wished – around ninety – were given safe conduct to the Royalist garrison at Conwy. The remainder, about 120 men, discharged themselves and went home.

The fate of Lathom House itself was devastating. Edward Robinson wrote that:

> Much of that famous house (like a little Town in itself) was pulled down and cast into the Moat that is about it, so that it is nothing in comparison of what it was.[151]

Seacombe is equally descriptive of the destruction:

> the house was yielded up to a merciless enemy, and all the rich goods therein, became a booty to them. The rich silk hangings of the beds, etc, were torn to pieces, and made sashes of; the towers and all the strong works razed to the ground and demolished, and all the buildings within it, leaving only standing two or three little timber buildings; as a monument of their fury and malice.[152]

Thus passed what Robinson, with a note of regret, described as 'The Glory of the County', adding prophetically: 'when it will be repaired again is doubtful'.[153]

Chapter Eight

The Die-Hards:
Worcester and Pendennis 1646

On 21 March 1646 the last remaining Royalist field army surrendered at Stow-on-the-Wold. Its commander, Jacob, Lord Astley, sat down on a drum amidst his captors and commented: 'You have done your work, boys, and may go play, unless you fall out among yourselves.'[154]

But across the British Isles numerous garrisons still bid defiance in the name of King Charles. Why, in a seemingly hopeless military situation, did these die-hard Royalists continue to fight on?

In some cases, such as Pendennis in Cornwall and the coastal strongholds of North Wales, their defenders desperately hoped for foreign armies – whether French, Irish Confederate or mercenary – to arrive and rekindle the Royalist cause. In others, such as inland Denbigh – a place without any remaining strategic significance – garrisons were unwilling to surrender without direct permission from the monarch. Others had more selfish reasons. At Dudley Castle, the unpopular Sir Thomas Leveson was unwilling to quit the protection of his fortress until the Parliamentarians guaranteed his safety from a vengeful local populace. Sir Michael Woodhouse, governor of Ludlow, required a guarantee of immunity from prosecution for various actions during the war, notably the massacre at Hopton Castle.[155]

'The Faithful City'

A notable episode of this kind took place in the city of Worcester. In post-Restoration Royalist mythology, Worcester was given the title of 'Faithful City', as a tribute to its supposed unswerving loyalty to the King during the Civil Wars. In reality, such devotion had never been total or unconditional.

In 1642, like most English cities, the population of Worcester included significant pro-Parliament and neutralist elements. Munitions, including cannon bought in the summer of 1642, were described as being 'for the defence of the city', without specifying against whom. The pro-Parliamentarian citizens had the upper hand for much of the year and raised a City Regiment

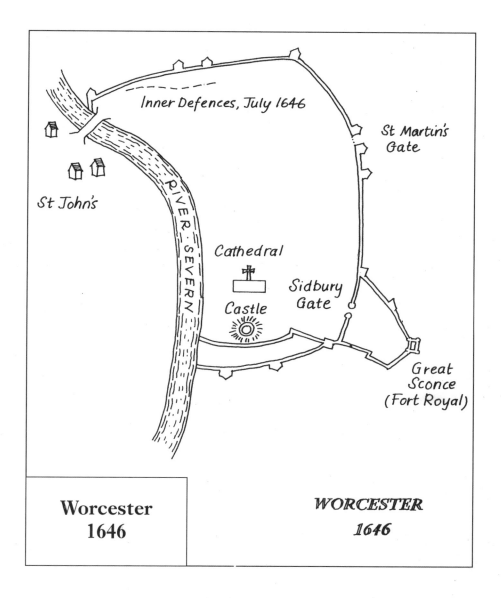

Inner Defences, July 1646

St Martin's Gate

St John's

RIVER SEVERN

Cathedral

Sidbury
Gate

Castle

Great
Sconce
(Fort Royal)

**Worcester
1646**

*WORCESTER
1646*

with the permission and active support of Parliament. In September 1642 Worcester was occupied by Parliamentarian troops, who inflicted considerable damage, notably in the cathedral. However, the fortunes of war meant that the Parliamentarian occupation of Worcester was brief, and by early November the last of their troops had gone. Worcester would be under Royalist control for the remainder of the war.

The city had considerable importance for the King's war effort. It was a major crossing point of the River Severn, and became an important centre for gunpowder production, as well as being a clearing house for troops and munitions. Weapons, ammunition and supplies from the forges of the North West Midlands were carried by barge down the Severn to Worcester, and it was a role of the Worcester garrison to escort the convoys carrying this material across the contested lands of the Cotswolds towards Oxford.

Worcestershire was never unchallenged Royalist territory, being subject to Parliamentarian raids, as well as the demands of the opposing armies. For these reasons the defences of Worcester had to be given high priority. Its original fortifications consisted of its medieval walls, and these were now strengthened by an earth backing 6–9 feet thick. In front of the walls were ditches up to 36 feet wide and 10 feet deep. Additional outworks and bastions were constructed and some of the suburbs cleared. This process was hastened after May 1643, when Worcester was besieged for two days by the Parliamentarian army of Sir William Waller. The remaining suburbs were now burnt, and a small fort constructed to defend the eastern approaches to the city.

Around the same time a Town Regiment was raised, 'for the guard and securing of the city'. Its colonel, Martin Sandys, was a leading Royalist resident of the city, and most of the City Council were among its officers. The strength of the regiment varied according to the degree of threat to the city. In March 1645 it was 1,800 strong, possibly then comprising all the able-bodied men in the city. Serving in the regiment was probably seen as preferable to being conscripted for service in the field armies, especially as it was a part-time unit, only its officers were paid, the rank and file being excused part of their tax assessment. The Regiment was normally only employed locally, although high rates of absenteeism and a generally half-hearted attitude suggest that the Worcester Regiment was never as highly motivated as similar units elsewhere. The garrison was augmented from time to time by various other units.

In the spring of 1646, Worcester's Governor was Colonel Henry Washington. Washington was brother-in-law to a Worcestershire man, and had married the widow of leading local Royalist, Sir Samuel Sandys. He was a professional soldier, who had served on the Continent in the Thirty Years War, and fought in the King's ranks from the start of the Civil War, seeing action at Edgehill, Lichfield, Bristol, Gloucester and the First Battle of Newbury. Washington was probably too much the hard-bitten soldier and outsider to win the affections of most local Royalist gentry, but he proved an extremely competent fighting commander, contending on the whole successfully with the problems of lukewarm citizen soldiers, and long-standing feuds over pay and supplies between the men of the local regiments of Samuel Sandys and Sir William Russell, some of whom occasionally came to blows.

The defeat at Stow-on-the-Wold, in which some troops from the Worcester garrison were involved, served notice that the city would soon come under attack. In February Washington spent £224 16s 8d on 'iron guns, and bullets and granadoes'.[156] On 26 March, fresh from his victory at Stow, Colonel Thomas Morgan, Parliamentarian Governor of Gloucester, summoned Washington to surrender. His call rejected, Morgan drew off again, but Washington knew he had gained only a temporary respite. His troops made far-ranging forays to bring in supplies, and on 30 March began pulling down what remained of the suburbs, clearing houses and demolishing St Thomas's Hospital. Over 1,000 loads of kindling were brought into the town from Strawley Wood.

For the moment, the Royalist capital of Oxford had priority for the Parliamentarians, although in May, troops of the New Model Army under Colonel Edward Whalley were detached to 'straiten the garrison of Worcester until such time as the army was at liberty to march against it'.[157]

On 16 May Sir Thomas Fairfax wrote to Washington, asking for his surrender. The Governor responded:

> It is acknowledged by your books [news sheets] and by report out of your own quarters that the King is in some of your armies. That granted, it may be easy for you to procure His Majesty's commands for the disposal of this garrison, till then I shall make good the trust reposed in me. As for conditions, if I shall be necessitated I shall make the best I can. The worst I know and fear not. If I had, the profession of a soldier had not been begun, or so long continued, by your excellency's humble servant . . .[158]

Washington was, of course, partly playing for time, but he had another motive for prolonging his defence, not perhaps suitable for mention in a letter to Parliament's principal commander. As a professional soldier, he had an eye to future employment after the Civil War drew to what he knew must be its imminent conclusion. As he put it: 'I owe so much to my Reputation, which I gained and must hereafter add and maintain abroad, when these wars shall cease, as not to be persuaded to the least unworthy action.' Unfortunately, it would be the citizens of Worcester who would pay the price for his ambition.

When the siege began it was estimated that there were 5,676 civilians in Worcester. The garrison totalled 1,507 men, including 400 currently listed in the City Regiment (regarded by Washington as of dubious value) and his own, Samuel Sandys and Sir William Russell's Regiments of Foot (all badly under-strength) and 224 cavalry, including a large number of 'reformadoes' and, it was alleged, 'Irish'. The garrison also had twenty-eight guns, including six lighter drakes and some 'sling-pieces'. They were manned by fifty-eight gunners and their assistants, headed by the distinguished mathematician and gunnery expert, Nathaniel Nye. On 23 May the city was assessed for the sum of £240 per week to pay the troops. In practice there proved to be difficulty in raising it, and from an early stage 'many foot have run out of the city for want of pay'.[159]

There was considerable resentment felt by the citizens towards the garrison officers, gentry and 'Irish', who were in many cases correctly suspected of prolonging the siege for their own ends. They were also undisciplined and the civilians feared their excesses. As early as February the sum of £20 had been paid to the 'reformadoes' in an attempt to keep the peace. The City Regiment had now disintegrated to the point that it was fit only for sentry duty, and despite the new assessment, rates of pay for the regular troops gradually fell from 3 shillings a week at the start of the siege to 2 shillings 6 pence in July.

The besieging forces varied in size, gradually increasing as the siege went on until 2,500–5,000 of the New Model Army and considerable numbers of local militia were involved.

On 21 May Whalley began to deploy on the high ground to the north-east of the city. On the 24th Washington made a sortie and fell on the Parliamentarian foot near Roger's Hill, claiming to have killed or wounded forty of them:

> About 7 at night a strong sally with 50 horse fell on their foot that lined the hedges and were stationed about Roger's Hill, beat their guard there back, and killed and hurt at least 40; 2 of ours killed and 3 hurt, 3 taken.[160]

On the same day Whalley sent a new summons, directed at the citizens of Worcester, and warning them:

> Our soldiers would fain be trading with you; you will find them but ill customers. A month's pay to the whole Army both of Horse and Foot will scarce keep them out of your shops and homes.[161]

The Mayor and Aldermen remained defiant, and when they were refused permission to send a messenger to the King in order to ascertain his views, the Mayor, William Evetts, replied to Whalley's drummer

> that he should forbear bringing any such summons, that he will draw out and fight with them, if they will, and leave men enough to man the City beside.[162]

No doubt as a result of Washington's sally, on 25 May Whalley began constructing defences for his main camp on Roger's Hill and around Wheeler's Hill, and by 3 June the siegeworks extended from Windmill Hill on the south side of the city to Barbourne on the north and then across the fields to the River Severn. On 28 May some drunken Parliamentarian soldiers managed to burn down their own huts. However, the fall of Ludlow released more troops for the besieging forces and large numbers of countrymen were being conscripted to work on the siege lines, guarded by 500 foot and 200 horse.

In Worcester, on 5 June, the City Council requisitioned all shovels, spades, mattocks and horses, and buildings adjacent to the city walls were cleared to allow for the speedy movement of troops.

On 9 June, tightening his grip, Whalley sent 1,500 men to occupy the suburb of Henwick, whilst next day, unbeknown to the defenders of Worcester, King Charles – effectively a prisoner of the Scots in Newcastle – issued a general order to his remaining garrisons to surrender. On the 11th the Parliamentarian guns commenced a desultory bombardment of the eastern and western sides of Worcester, doing no notable damage.

Next day the Parliamentarians moved into the suburb of St Johns, placing musketeers in some of the houses. The Royalists responded at 11 o'clock that night by mounting a major sally with 500 foot and 200 horse. The Parliamentarians had barricaded the entrances to the village, but the attackers infiltrated via the back ways and drove the enemy out, forcing some to take refuge in St John's Church. The Royalists claimed to have killed 100 of their opponents and to have taken 10 prisoners, along with 3 colours, which they hung derisively on the bridge and the Cathedral tower. The Parliamentarians claimed, not improbably, that many of the attackers were drunk.

Among the Parliamentarian dead was an officer. A truce was arranged to allow his comrades to carry away his body, during which there was some fraternisation between the opposing sides. Washington and some of his officers spent two hours drinking wine with their Parliamentarian counterparts, although Edward Whalley himself refused to join them. It was probably also at this time that some of the common soldiers indulged in some not particularly sparkling repartee, with the Parliamentarians calling out: 'Papists!', 'Russell's Apes!' and 'Where is your tottering King?' The Royalists replied with 'Traitors!', 'Go and preach in a crab tree!' and 'Where are the Scots you hired to fight against the King?'

Drunkenness and lack of discipline was a constant, and indeed growing, problem among the garrison. Henry Townsend confided to his diary: 'From the plundering of soldiers, their Insolency, Cruelty, Atheism, Blasphemy and Rule over us, *Libera nos Domine*.'[163]

The Parliamentarian batteries continued their bombardment, concentrating on the St Martin's area and Friars' Gate, although the amount of damage was lessened by the fact that thatched roofs had been banned in the town since the fifteenth century. On 14 June the Parliamentarians improved the communications linking their forces on either bank of the River Severn by completing a bridge of boats wide enough for eight men to cross abreast at the upper end of Pitchcroft, defended by a half-moon battery on Pitchcroft itself.

Worcester was not yet completely isolated, the south side of the city still being open, allowing the defenders to bring in cattle and fodder, and this was not blocked until 23 June. In the meantime periodic sallies by the garrison continued. On 16 June one of the more notorious of Washington's officers, Captain William Hodgkins (known as 'Wicked Will'), raided St Johns with sixteen horse. He was described as being 'so drunk that he fell twice by the way' and was brought back into the city asleep in a boat.

The Parliamentarians attempted to lower the morale of Worcester's defenders by psychological warfare. On the evening of 16 June their troops fired three celebratory volleys – supposedly to mark the surrender of Oxford – although this did not actually take place until a few days later. On 17 June the besiegers' batteries fired thirteen shots at St Martin's Church and the Cross Inn. But on another occasion, presumably to atone for his earlier lack of courtesy, Whalley sent Washington a buck he had killed when hunting. The garrison, meanwhile, were hard at work preparing some last-ditch defences. A second defensive line was constructed running between Foregate Street and St Clement's Church, with Washington rejecting another summons to surrender and continuing his sallies.

However, on 25 June Prince Maurice's Secretary was allowed through the siege lines with confirmation of the surrender of Oxford. Next day a Council of War was called in Worcester. The first reaction of those present to the news of the fall of the Royalist capital was annoyance that the King's Council there had not attempted to include Worcester in the articles agreed for surrender. It was soon apparent that there were differences of opinion between the military and civilian leadership. The reformadoes, and not unnaturally the Irish, wanted to fight on, and they were supported by Washington, who asked his fellow councillors: 'if they would live and die with him upon the walls, and fight it out to the last man'? He then attempted to rush out and fire a defiant gun from the walls, and a scuffle followed before the Governor was restrained by the Bishop of Worcester and some of the civilians.[164]

It was eventually agreed that a committee – formed of six soldiers, six of the gentry and six citizens – should discuss surrender terms with the besiegers. A truce was agreed on 27 June and Washington was among those who went out to negotiate. However, he was evidently somewhat distracted by encountering another of his former comrades-in-arms, Colonel William Dingley, with whom he settled down to a drinking session lasting until ten in the evening. This camaraderie occasioned some alarm among the citizens and rank and file soldiery, who feared that 'they were to be sacrificed to the will and pleasure of soldiers of fortune'.[165]

The talks dragged on for two days, the Royalists holding out for an amnesty for all those within the city and one month's pay for the troops. It was probably in an attempt to ensure that Washington stood up for their interests that, on 29 June, the City Council presented him with £100, 'whereof £50 ready, for his especial care and love towards the City, towards the maintenance of his table'.[166] Henry Townsend felt that

> it is wisely and lovingly done of them. For there was no Governor more complied with them. And laid less pressure upon them . . . Besides it being done freely, it engageth him the more to preserve them.[167]

However, on 30 June, regarding the Royalist demands as unacceptable, Whalley called off further talks, declaring the truce to be over. He informed the defenders that

> the kingdom is at great layings out after you and your city, and much increased by the addition of forces, I intend to be a good husband for you, and not to lose time, which may be improved by the reducing Worcester, therefore give you notice the cessation is at an end.[168]

Washington responded defiantly with a single cannon shot followed by a more general bombardment of the Parliamentarian-held suburbs.

The siege dragged on into July, with the Royalists still making occasional sallies. But conditions inside Worcester were deteriorating. Washington remained determined to resist, on one occasion angrily firing back an 18-pound shot that had hit the Bishop's palace. He led a number of determined raids on the besiegers, on one occasion attempting to surprise Parliamentarian Colonel Betsworth in his quarters at Kempsey.

But the citizens were growing increasingly discontented, and at times mutinous. They were expected to work at repairing and strengthening the defences, which exposed them to considerable danger. On 11 June a boy had been shot dead whilst collecting peapods outside the walls, and two days later a man and his wife were killed by a cannon shot whilst in bed. The city's bakers threatened to strike for more pay: Washington's response was to whip Smith the baker and threaten to hang him over the walls. This did not deter further trouble, however, and on 13 July Townsend complained that the 'Workmen, carpenters and masons expect money now for their work, as though there were no sieges, nor that their estates were not concerned in it if the City were taken by Storm.'[169] The Council members had to meet their demands out of their own pockets.

In the meantime, Colonel Edward Whalley had been replaced in command of the siege by Colonel Thomas Rainsborough, who increased the pressure on Worcester by placing two sakers on Red Hill Cross, which scored numerous hits on the defences. The garrison completed the earthen lining of the city walls, and mounted two sling-guns and another piece on the Cathedral tower, 'to gall the besiegers'. The Royalists also thwarted an enemy attempt to construct a new siegework at Wall's Furlong, during which 'our men wifted [i.e. flourished – ed.] all their light matches over their heads, which made a great show of light, and withal gave a cheerful and courageous shout'.[170]

Nevertheless, food supplies in Worcester were growing desperately short and the Parliamentarians refused a request that children be allowed to leave the city. Civilian pressure forced Washington to open up the last remaining food stores, making surrender only a matter of time. The majority of citizens no longer favoured further hopeless resistance, Townsend rather heartlessly describing them as 'besotted and stupid concerning their own preservation', and they were thought likely to betray the city in case of an enemy assault. As for the military, Townsend complained that 'soldiers take the insolency to pull down men's back houses upon pretence of fuel, and to sell it for liquor . . . So wicked are the Irish soldiers chiefly, and given to spoil and ruin.'[171]

Matters came to a head when the Council and a deputation of women called on Washington to surrender, and Townsend admitted that

> the city began to grow so mutinous that many gave out, they will throw the soldiers over the wall or club them if they should oppose the treaty, being now as all quiet people are weary of war, desiring their trading may go on.[172]

On 16 July Washington informed Rainsborough that 'in conformity to His Majesty's Command, we do not decline the rendering of the City upon honourable and equal conditions.'[173] A further truce followed, during which Parliamentarian soldiers bathed in the river Severn, taking the opportunity to fraternise with their opponents and spread dissention between the soldiers and citizens.

On 18 July Rainsborough offered his final terms, threatening that if they were not accepted, Worcester would be stormed. With only sufficient powder for one day of fighting, and food for two weeks, and with some of his soldiers already slipping away to enlist in foreign service, Washington had no option but to agree. The City Council felt they had been let down by the King:

> Never poor Gentlemen and City held out more loyal and never any so ill-rewarded as being neither remembered by the King or the Council at Oxford in the Treaty.[174]

On 23 July, following a service in the Cathedral, the garrison of Worcester marched out of the city to surrender on Rainbow Hill. Ironically, the King had written to Washington on the same day, urging him to hold out for another month. For the citizens, the entry of the Parliamentarian forces was in some ways a relief. For Henry Washington and his 'reformadoes', foreign wars beckoned.

Pendennis

By March 1646 the last Royalist field army in South West England, commanded by Ralph, Lord Hopton, had been pushed back by the New Model Army into Western Cornwall. Further resistance was plainly hopeless and Hopton surrendered his Royalist force on 14 March.

But the war in the West was not quite at an end: a number of garrisons still remained and, as the Royalist cause declined, hope had lain with rumours of the imminent arrival of troops recruited on the Continent by Queen Henrietta Maria. Such reinforcements were illusory, but their faint possibility made Hopton and the Prince of Wales (himself seeking refuge in the Channel Islands) determined to maintain at least one mainland foothold where troops from abroad might land, and which would serve as a rallying point for local Royalists.

Pendennis Castle in Cornwall seemed a suitable choice. It was situated at the southern tip of a narrow, flat-topped promontory, dividing Falmouth Bay on the west from Carrick Roads and the River Fal to the east. Pendennis had been built between 1540 and 1550, one of a series of fortifications ordered by King Henry VIII as a defence against French invasion. Along with the smaller fort of St Mawes on the opposite side, the role of Pendennis was to guard and control the anchorage of Carrick Roads.

Pendennis was originally intended primarily as a gun platform, with three decks or stories to mount guns as well as an outer gun terrace. Its outer ramparts were mainly terraced into the hillside and covered an area of two acres. In the course of the first half of the seventeenth century the defensive area was extended by large-scale outworks on its northern side, which, furnished with additional ramparts, was known as the Hornwork. As well as the gun platforms, the area within the defences contained barracks, other living quarters and storehouses. Although by 1630 Pendennis's defences were relatively obsolete by Continental standards, they were maintained in a good state of repair. The permanent garrison totalled around fifty men, and in 1635 mounted fifty-five guns.

At the outbreak of the Civil War Pendennis's Governor was a leading Cornish Royalist, Sir Nicholas Slanning. Slanning was killed in the storming of Bristol in 1643 and replaced by Sir John Arundell of Trerice, by now approaching eighty years of age and known variously as 'Jack for the King' or 'Old Tilbury', having reputedly been present there when Queen Elizabeth I delivered her famous speech during the Armada campaign of 1588. It was from Pendennis, in 1644, that Queen Henrietta Maria had sailed to exile in France, whilst in the following year a frigate had lain at anchor beneath its guns in readiness to carry the Prince of Wales to safety in the event of Royalist defeat. During the winter of 1645–1646 Pendennis had served as Prince Charles's headquarters, until on 2 March he had set sail for temporary refuge in the Isles of Scilly.

Before surrendering, Hopton had made energetic efforts to strengthen his remaining garrisons: 200 men were sent to St Michael's Mount, and 860, including the remnants of Colonel Matthew Wise's Welsh infantry and Prince Rupert's Dragoons, to Pendennis. With them were despatched forty-five barrels of gunpowder, ammunition, fat and draught oxen. Hopton – who was himself leaving for France – appointed a Council of War to command Pendennis, consisting of Sir John Arundell, his son Colonel Richard Arundell, and a number of other experienced Royalist commanders.

Royalist hopes suffered a blow on 12 March when Captain Hannibal Bonithon, Governor of St Mawes, surrendered without firing a shot. His small fortress, mounting thirteen guns, was indefensible against landward attack, being overlooked by high ground. The Parliamentarians expected Pendennis to fall equally quickly and reported on 14 March that 120 musketeers had deserted from the Castle and surrendered. It was true that a number of the Welsh soldiers in particular had little enthusiasm for prolonging resistance, but Arundell's garrison of around 1,000 men included many veteran Royalist officers, and with provisions for 6 weeks, he had no intention of tamely submitting. On 16 March the Royalists made a major sally with the objective of burning the neighbouring hamlet of Smithwick and Arwenick House, in order to deny their shelter to the enemy. They succeeded at Arwenick but were chased out of Smithwick by the approaching Parliamentarians.

Fairfax stationed two regiments of foot at Pennycomequick in order to isolate Pendennis by land, and made his own headquarters in what remained of Arwenick House. As the Parliamentarians approached, a ship lying at anchor below Pendennis

> let fly at us, but their shot (by God's mercy) did us no harm, though the bullets flew very near us, and one grazed not far from me, which we found, and was a bullet of some 12 lb weight.[175]

As was customary, Sir Thomas Fairfax sent a drum to Arundell with a summons to surrender. The old Royalist was predictably defiant, particularly as he was

70 years old, and could not have many days to live, and therefore would not in his old years blemish his honour in surrendering thereof, and would rather be found buried in the ruins thereof, than commit so vile a treason.[176]

A Parliamentarian newsletter admitted that:

Questionless the place is very strong, as well by its natural situation (it being almost an Island, and seated on a rising hill) as by Art and great industry; and it is victualled (as they say) for nine to ten weeks, and they have in it about one thousand or twelve hundred men, all desperate persons, and good soldiers; and they have powder and shot great store, and at least eighty great Guns mounted, besides forty in the ship which lies on the North side of the Castle.[177]

Fairfax had no wish to incur the heavy casualties of an assault, and

resolved to block it up very close both by Land and Sea . . . if we draw a line thwart the narrow neck of land, a little on this side Arwinkle [sic] house, which is not above Musket shot over, Pendennis Castle will remain unto them but as a close and secure prison, and so in the end the belly will conquer them, without striking of a stroke.[178]

There were problems within Pendennis. Many of the soldiers who had been thrust into its garrison had arrived without shirts or shoes; and plans to extend the defences had to be abandoned when the troops refused to work without pay. The Council of War in Pendennis sent urgent requests to the Prince of Wales in Jersey, asking for clothing, medical supplies, beef, butter, oatmeal, herrings, sugar, spice, vinegar, wood, wine, biscuit, sea coals, needles, fish-hooks, 2,000 pounds of tobacco, munitions and 3 months' pay. Although Pendennis was not yet completely isolated by sea, a Parliamentarian naval squadron under Sir George Ayscue was operating in its vicinity, and soon after the siege began, struck a telling blow at the Royalists:

This last night one of the ships which came down with Sir George Ayscue, fell into the harbour of Falmouth, on St Mawes' side, and notwithstanding both the Block-house, and the Bulwark at the point of Pendennis shot very furiously at her, yet she came very safely into the harbour, and so passed upon the tide, to a place in the harbour called Maupasse passage, where a Frigate of Dunkirk had run herself aground and [which] came on purpose to assist Pendennis Castle. She had in her 26 pieces of Ordnance, and though our men entered her, yet she stood very stoutly to her defence, yet at last we mastered her, and took all the men out of her, and put in her about fifty men of our own, and so intend to make her a Man of war to serve the State . . . [179]

On 18 March Fairfax followed up this success by again summoning Arundell to surrender, giving him two hours to reply. Sir John remained unimpressed, replying:

Sir, the Castle was committed to my Government by His Majesty, who by our laws hath the command of the Castles and Forts of the Kingdom; and my age of seventy summons me hence shortly. Yet I shall desire no other testimony to follow my departure than my conscience to God and loyalty to His Majesty, whereto I am bound by all the obligations of nature, duty, and oath. I wonder you demand the Castle without authority from His Majesty, which if I should render, I brand myself and my posterity with the indelible character of Treason. And having taken less than two minutes' resolution, I resolve that I will here bury myself before I deliver up this Castle to such as fight against His Majesty, and that nothing you can threaten is formidable to me in respect of the loss of loyalty and conscience. [180]

On 26 March a Parliamentarian news letter explained:

Here are in this fort many very considerable men, and the most desperate persons and the violentist enemies that parliament hath in this Kingdom.

Soon after the rejection of his summons, Fairfax and most of his forces left to begin operations against Oxford. Colonel Robert Hammond was put in charge of operations against Pendennis. There was very little bombardment of the Castle, but some skirmishing, during which the Parliamentarian Colonel Richard Ingoldsby was killed: 'who with other Commanders going to view Pendennis Castle received a shot from the Enemy, who lay in ambush behind a mud-wall'. [181]

Despite this reverse, the general opinion among the Parliamentarians was that the defenders

are blades of the right stamp, and having within 200 Tuns of wine, spare not to be daily drunk, and this the Governor encourages, that their disorders take not over much hold of them, which are very great already. They are at sixpence per diem, nor will that hold long. [182]

Conditions within Pendennis were indeed beginning to cause some concern to the Royalist Council of War there, who, on 11 April, repeated their pleas to the Prince of Wales, telling him that the enemy siege lines now stretched across the neck of the peninsula 'from sea to sea', and that the garrison was in a bad state and short of clothing. Begging for relief from France, the Council asked for supplies sufficient to sustain 1,500 men for 6 months to be sent from Ireland, to include '20 gross' of tobacco paper.

The *Scottish Dove* of 8–15 April reported that a Royalist Captain Rivers had deserted along with a Lieutenant Colonel and fifty-two men. On 17 April Pendennis was summoned by Colonel Hammond, who told Arundell that 'it will be a sufficient honour to have held out the last garrison . . . betwixt Oxford and Land's End for the King'. Arundell remained defiant, telling Hammond:

> I hope you understood my answer to the demand of Sir Thomas Fairfax, that disloyalty and honour were inconsistent and yourself born an Englishman and His Majesty's sworn subject cannot think any man led with the spirit of honour and loyalty should desert the King though his condition were desperate and declining, and yield this Castle to the name of King and Parliament when the King is excluded, and his estate more ruinous thereby. How you satisfy your-self herein, God Almighty will one day reveal. I cannot think the peace of the Kingdom (which no man more passionately desires than myself) can be established by the ignominy, spoil and oppression of His Majesty. I place not honour in other men's opinions but the rules of Justice and Piety, which shall bear me though were the world against me . . . [183]

Two days later Arundell warned the Prince of Wales that the besiegers were being reinforced and that unless relieved Pendennis must soon surrender. Although the Prince of Wales's Council was aware of Arundell's needs, and was attempting to send by ship such provisions as they had available, the Parliamentarian blockade of Pendennis by sea was tightening. On 30 April Admiral William Batten, now in command of the Parliamentarian squadron, summoned Pendennis to surrender, offering its defenders safe passage to Weymouth or France, 'for here (God willing) I intend to spend the summer, what ever I do in the winter', but this plea also was rejected.[184]

On 7 June the Parliamentarian navy captured a vessel on its way to Pendennis with a large quantity of ammunition, clothing and other supplies. As a result, a Parliamentarian news letter, the *Weekly Account*, claimed, rather prematurely, that 'the Enemy within the Castle begins to droop'.[185]

On 27 June Colonel John Digby and other senior officers in Pendennis sent a desperate plea to the Prince of Wales:

We informed you of our condition nine weeks since, and have heard by chance only that the messenger came safe to you. It is now come to the last with us, and this place which [is] your and your Father's whole interest in the West must be necessarily so ruined within three weeks, and twice as many years will not be able to repair it. We urge nothing for ourselves, nor the rest of your loyal servants here who are now poorly clothed and sickly, fed upon bread and water. We hope the weight of the matter will move, and therefore lay by all eloquence about the deserts or sufferings of your highness's most humble servants.[186]

The picture painted by the Royalist commanders was in part confirmed in a Parliamentarian news letter, which reported:

The letters from Pendennis say, the soldiers run out daily which its possible may be a benefit to the Castle. The common report of the soldiers that come out, is that it cannot hold out above three weeks, they shoot continually both cannon and small shot, and yet few have been killed.[187]

The Royalists were becoming increasingly desperate, and it was reported that

About the latter end of July the Enemy made a sally by Boats to fetch in relief, but were forced back with loss.[188]

A further summons to surrender had been despatched to Arundell ten days earlier, but rejected as the garrison hoped that relief ships from St Malo might reach them when the wind turned favourable. Aware of these relief attempts, Captain Batten stationed ten boats and barges, 'well manned', on patrol outside the mouth of the harbour every night. One morning, just after the patrol was withdrawn:

a Shallop [i.e. a light river craft with sails and oars – ed.] got in by stealth, which caused great triumph in the Castle, but 'twas conceived (and Colonel Fortescue was so informed by good hands) that little Relief was in it, save a Hogshead or two of Wine.[189]

Nonetheless, the Parliamentarians were increasingly concerned to conclude the siege before winter, and in a fairly unprecedented move, an agent of the King of Spain was allowed to speak to the Royalist officers in a bid to recruit them into Spanish service in Flanders. The reply was:

That at present they were engaged, but should they once be free, next to their present Master they would serve His Majesty of Spain. This courtesy was taken well from Colonel Fortescue by the Enemy, and the Agent, and certainly anything belonging . . . to civility without involving danger in its consequence, was never denied by him.[190]

Meanwhile, the desperate Royalists kept bonfires burning at night as a signal to any relief ships, and, perhaps in an attempt to boost morale, fired off 200 cannon shot in 3 days, 'but without any great execution, only three of our men being slain thereby'.[191]

By early August Arundel was putting out peace feelers, and instructed four of his officers:

> to view all the horses within this Garrison and that they take partic-ular notice of all such horses, as are fit to be killed for beef, for provisions for the Garrison.[192]

Despite their increasingly desperate plight, there were still die-hard Royalists in Pendennis. Sir John Digby, supported by about 100 reformadoes, reportedly threatened to blow up the Castle and make a last desperate sortie if not granted favourable terms, until prevented by a mutiny among their men.

The usual haggling took place before agreement was reached and terms signed on 16 August. The defenders of Pendennis marched out:

> with flying Colours, Trumpets sounding, Drums beating, Matches lighted at both ends. Bullets in their Mouths, and every Soldier Twelve charges of Powder, with Bullets and Match proportionable, with all their own proper Goods, Bag and Baggage, with a safe convoy to Arwenneck Downs.[193]

Here the Royalists were to lay down their arms and be given passes to their homes. The officers and their families had vessels prepared to carry them to France, whilst the Welsh soldiers of Colonel Wise were shipped back to South Wales.

About 800 men marched out of Pendennis, with 400 others too sick to leave, who would receive care until fit. Little food remained in the Castle, although there were still considerable quantities of arms and ammunition.

Thus fell the last Royalist garrison in mainland England.

Chapter Nine

Castles and Cannon: The Sieges of Goodrich and Denbigh 1646

Goodrich Castle, on the banks of the River Wye in Herefordshire, was an excellent example of those strongholds whose garrisons – active partisans of King or Parliament – were a plague and terror to their neighbours.

There had been a castle at Goodrich since the eleventh century, but it had been largely rebuilt and extended in the thirteenth by William de Valence, both as a residence and stronghold. It took the form of concentric curtain walls with massive round towers at each corner, a D-shaped barbican in front of its gatehouse, itself flanked by towers, and strongly defended by draw-bridge and two massive gates with portcullises. Within the walls were a Norman keep and various domestic buildings and living quarters clustered around a central courtyard. The outer ward was walled on its northern and western sides, with stables running along the western wall, and protected on the southern and eastern sides by a dry ditch cut into the rock. Goodrich had fallen into neglect during the long Tudor peace, although it had remained in better condition than many, and in 1631–1632 had undergone a programme of repair.

On the outbreak of Civil War in 1642 Goodrich was occupied by Parliamentarian forces under the Earl of Stamford. Local Royalist troops had found Goodrich's defences too strong to be breached, and the castle remained in Parliamentarian hands until evacuated by them at the end of the year. It was then occupied by the Royalists, who easily withstood a half-hearted attack by Sir William Waller in the spring of 1643. However, the Royalists' failure in the same summer to take Gloucester increased Goodrich's significance as a barrier to any attempt by the Parliamentarian forces at Gloucester to extend their area of control northwards. In late 1643 or early the following year Goodrich was strengthened under the command of the Sheriff of Herefordshire, Henry Lingen, who maintained there a garrison averaging around 100 men. Lingen quickly made his presence felt over the surrounding

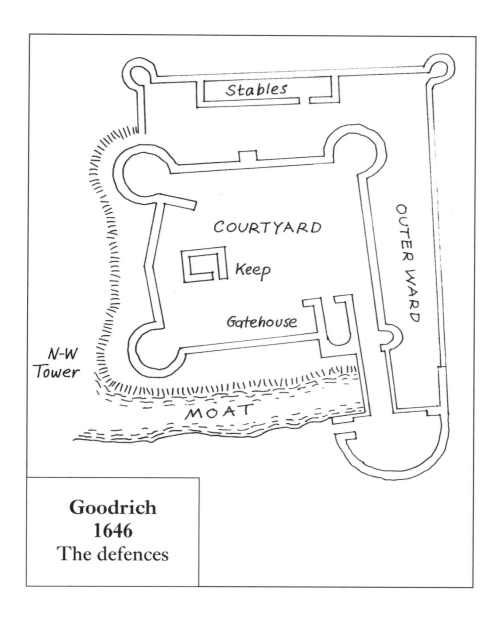

Stables

COURTYARD

Keep

Gatehouse

OUTER WARD

N-W
Tower

MOAT

**Goodrich
1646
The defences**

countryside. Even in the late nineteenth century a historian noted that: 'The country is still possessed with vague rumours of them',[194] for it was said of Lingen that 'his regiment never slept'.[195]

The fall of Hereford to the Parliamentarians in December 1645 meant that the area around Goodrich was now in the front line of the war. Sir Henry

Lingen (knighted by the King that summer) had been in Hereford at the time of its capture, but had escaped and made his way to Goodrich, which now became his headquarters. He faced a critical situation, with Raglan Castle in Monmouthshire the only remaining nearby Royalist garrison of note. However Lingen could gain some comfort from the knowledge that most of his men were 'die-hard' Cavaliers, including 'reformadoes' and veterans of other garrisons, whose spirit was typified by the fact that even the garrison cook had engraved on the handle of a pan: 'C.V.R. LOYAL TO HIS MAGISTEIE'.[196]

The garrison of Goodrich included around fifty cavalry, who raided over a wide area, carrying off sheep, cattle, timber and sometimes household furniture and personal possessions. In January 1646 Lingen attempted to cut off a party of enemy troops on their way from Newnham to Hereford, and the latter's Parliamentarian Governor, Colonel John Birch, complained that no messengers could travel safely between Hereford and Gloucester, and that he could not detach men to begin operations against the important Royalist garrisons at Ludlow and Worcester without risking the Goodrich horse raiding up to the gates of Hereford. It meant that Birch was effectively tied down until Goodrich could be taken or contained.

The Parliamentarian commander made his first move on 9 March. Taking advantage of a dark night and information regarding the height of one of the walls of the outer ward enclosing the area where the stables were located, Birch launched a daring raid. He made a stealthy approach with 100 firelocks, who used scaling ladders to climb the wall. They killed a captain and five soldiers presumably on guard duty, and turned loose about eighty horses before setting fire to the stables. The Parliamentarians then attacked the guards the Royalists had placed at the building housing the boat used as a ferry across the Wye, about 20 yards from the castle. According to Colonel Birch:

> I marched out of Hereford Monday night last with 500 horse and foot under cover until I came within Pistol shot of Goodrich, a little before day: then fell on with 100 firelocks for the Forlorn, and entered over the Wall near the end of their stable, the wall was very high, yet got over.

The defenders held out for two hours, until a wall of the boathouse was undermined, when those within, a major and fifteen 'gentlemen' and common soldiers, surrendered. Lingen had lost all his mounts, apart from the horses belonging to a small party of troopers absent from Goodrich at the time of Birch's raid.

However, the resolute Royalist commander was not deterred for long, and a few days later placed an ambush at nearby Old Gore in a bid to catch Birch and Colonel Kyrile, Governor of Monmouth, who were on their way to Gloucester, escorted by a dozen troopers. As the Royalists burst out of cover, Birch kept his nerve and ordered his men: 'Do as I Do!' and charged the Royalists, killing or capturing all but two of them.

Over the next few weeks Lingen succeeded in replacing most of his lost horses, and whilst Birch was absent on the Stow-on-the-Wold campaign, Lingen made a daring attempt to regain Hereford, still garrisoned by 700 foot and 50 horse. The Royalists were counting on the support of a popular uprising within the town, and at the head of thirty horse, Lingen charged the guards at one of the city gates, killing four of them. But the hoped-for rebellion within Hereford failed to occur and Lingen was forced to withdraw.

Once Birch returned to Hereford, the Goodrich garrison knew that it would soon be their turn to come under attack. For some time Lingen had been making preparations for the coming siege. On 3 March he had sent a letter to Mr Grubb of nearby Pengethley:

> I shall desire you to send your three teams loaded with boards thither presently and that they may be of your Longest size of Boards, for I am informed that you have very Longe ones, I pray you send them away presently for I must make use of them presently . . .[197]

Birch apparently began operations against Goodrich on 1 June, ordering the construction of emplacements to house his siege guns. He did not summon Lingen to surrender until 13 June, telling him:

> Before this, I question not but you expected what I have now sent unto you, which I did the rather forbear, being informed of your strong confidence of a speedy relief, and no less in your own ability to prevent such near approaches as are and may be made upon you . . .[198]

Though told by Birch of the recent surrender of Oxford, Lingen remained defiant:

> The King placed me in it [Goodrich] by his commission, to keep it for him and to his use, and until I shall receive an immediate order to the contrary, I shall do it to the uttermost of my power; otherwise I conceive I should not discharge the part of a soldier and an honest man, which I hope to carry with me to my grave . . .[199]

Five days later Birch reported to the Speaker of the House of Commons:

> they within resolve to stand it out, as you may perceive by their
> answer: they are excepted [from pardon] persons, and Papists very
> desperate: they never left sallying whilst they had one horse to sally
> out with, having lost in all, upon their sallies, above one hundred. I
> am approached within the reach of their stones, which they throw
> abundantly, and am now almost ready to play upon them with a
> mortar piece, which I have cast here, carrying a shell of above two
> hundred weight: and have planted my battery, and am going on with
> my mines; for effecting of all which, a considerable quantity of
> powder will be speedily necessary. I therefore humbly entreat your
> honour will be pleased to move the honourable house for eighty
> barrels, which will much forward the service . . .[200]

The mortar referred to by Birch was cast in the Forest of Dean, and may be
the one which was nicknamed 'Roaring Meg', and which, after various
vicissitudes, is now on display at Goodrich.

To tighten pressure on the defenders of Goodrich, Birch cut the pipes
carrying water to the castle from a nearby spring, close by which he sited one
of his batteries. Though probably short of water, the defenders of Goodrich
held out with determination, despite undergoing six weeks of bombardment,
during which twenty-two granadoes were fired at the castle from the mortar,
nineteen of which were aimed by Birch himself. Every room in the Castle was
damaged, and most of the interior buildings destroyed. Lingen replied as best
he could with two small 'hammer-pieces'. Birch now began mining operations
aimed at the North West Tower, which was already suffering significant
damage from his mortar fire. The miners had to cut their way 10 yards
through solid rock and Lingen responded with a countermine.

A new Parliamentarian battery was established under cover of darkness,
and its fire caused the collapse of much of the North West Tower. This not
only blocked Lingen's countermine, but also opened an assailable breach in
the castle defences. Birch had drawn up his troops and was preparing to
launch an assault when the Royalists:

> perceiving in what posture we were in, and seeing how they were on
> all sides surprised, their hearts began to fail them, so that they took
> a most fearful Alarm; and (whether by Council of War, or other-
> wise), they speedily took their condition into consideration, and
> (perceiving that we would not baulk with them) being unwilling to
> endure a storm (which was much the more terrible to them, because
> of divers Gentry amongst them) they desired a Parley, but my

Colonel would not grant that, though much importuned for it: insomuch that when they saw we would not admit of any delay, they took in their Standard Colours, and held out their white Flag of truce, and begged that they might but march out Honourably to their own homes, and some to Garrisons. But nothing would be agreed more than quarter for their lives.[201]

The same day, 31 July 1646, Lingen, with around 50 gentlemen and 120 soldiers, marched out of Goodrich to the music of a now lost tune called 'Sir Henry Lingen's Fancy', to render themselves as prisoners-of-war. Despite the fury of the bombardment, only one Royalist fatality, Miles Lockhard, a gentleman-volunteer, is recorded.

If Goodrich is an example of medieval defences succumbing to the power of artillery, our next example proved much more defiant.

An 'Impregnable Rock': the Siege of Denbigh 1646

The capture of Chester (3 February 1646) opened the road into North Wales for the Parliamentarians. For most of the war North Wales had been predominantly Royalist in sympathy, and had mostly remained firmly under the King's control. It had also been a major source of recruits for the Royalist forces, and although by early 1646 North Wales was war-weary and its resources of manpower exhausted, it remained vital to the faltering Cavaliers as a landing place for troops the King still hoped the Irish Confederate rebels would send to assist him. For the same reason it was important to the Parliamentarians to bring the area under their control as soon as possible.

The key to North Wales still lay in its castles. Though in varying states of disrepair, the fortresses of the English medieval conquest remained formidable. All with Royalist garrisons, the castles of Caernarvon, Conwy, Rhuddlan, Flint, Holt, Ruthin, Denbigh and Harlech might prove difficult to reduce.

The Parliamentarian forces that advanced into North Wales in the spring of 1646 had the primary task of taking or neutralising the coastal fortresses, under whose protection troops from Ireland might disembark. The inland castles were less urgent, and at a time when the Civil War had been to all intents and purposes won by Parliament, there was natural reluctance to incur the heavy expenditure in men and material storming them would involve. The first objective of the Parliamentarian forces under the command of Colonel Thomas Mytton, formerly Parliament's commander in Shropshire, was Caernarvon. This fell in June, and with Conwy defiant but blockaded, Mytton was able to turn his attention to the lesser fortresses. The strongest of

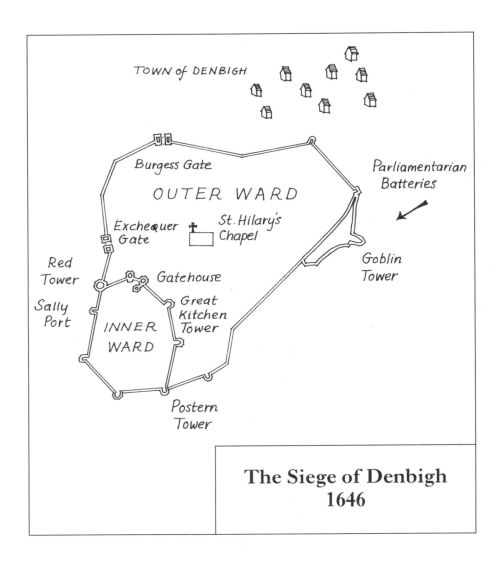

TOWN of DENBIGH

Burgess Gate

OUTER WARD

Exchequer
Gate

St. Hilary's
Chapel

Parliamentarian
Batteries

Red
Tower

Gatehouse

Goblin
Tower

Sally
Port

Great
Kitchen
Tower

INNER
WARD

Postern
Tower

**The Siege of Denbigh
1646**

these was the castle at Denbigh. Situated on a rocky crag, the castle dominated the town nestling below it, and much of the fertile Vale of Clwyd to the
east.

Denbigh Castle had its origins in a fortress of the Welsh princes, but was
totally rebuilt and extended after the Edwardian Conquest of Wales by Henry
de Lacy, Earl of Lincoln. The basic layout of the castle consisted of a curtain
wall with hexagonal or octagonal walls, and a great gatehouse, possibly never
fully completed, situated on the highest point of the hill, and built around an

inner ward or bailey, which contained the usual living quarters and store-houses for its garrison. Built in association with the castle itself were the town walls, surrounding the Edwardian settlement, strengthened by four towers, the most important being the great hexagonal Goblin Tower, containing a well, at the south-eastern angle of the defences. The walls were entered through two twin-towered gateways. In the late fourteenth century the castle was strengthened with additional defences on its southern and western sides, consisting of a mantlet [i.e. a protective stone shelter – ed.] with sally port.

Even by the early fourteenth century the town of Denbigh had begun to expand beyond its walls and, with occasional setbacks such as the damage caused during the Glyn Dwr Revolt, this process had continued. By 1642 only a few houses, a church, and the uncompleted collegiate church of the Elizabethan Earl of Leicester still remained within the medieval town walls, and the area was now treated as the outer ward of the castle. A survey carried out in the reign of King Henry VIII said of Denbigh:

> The said castle is built upon a rock of stone, very stately and beau-tifully, in a very sweet air, seven miles from the sea, and near to the same castle are a few houses and a fair chapel . . .[202]

By 1561 only the Great Gatehouse and three towers were regarded as being in good repair, the remainder being in 'utter decay', although the former town walls were repaired in 1595.

Denbigh was in Royalist hands from the start of the war, and as virtually all the gentry of the surrounding area were loyal to the King, there was no immediate need to garrison the castle. But in November 1643 Parliamentarian forces launched a major incursion that quickly overran most of North East Wales, and Royalist collapse was only averted by the fortuitous landing of English troops from Ireland.

It was a result of this scare that, in November 1643, Denbigh Castle – in which a number of Royalist gentry of the area had taken refuge – was garrisoned for the King by William Salusbury of Bachymynd, situated between Denbigh and Ruthin. Born in 1566, Salusbury was known locally as Hen Hosannau Gleision ('Old Blue Stockings'), apparently a reference to his knowledge of traditional Welsh verse. Born in 1580, Salusbury was a member of a prominent Denbighshire Royalist family. His kinsman, Sir Thomas Salusbury of Llewny, just outside Denbigh, was one of the first to raise a foot regiment for the King in 1642. William was the youngest of three sons, and lacking other means of support enlisted as a volunteer with the English forces serving against Spain in the Low Countries, after which he took passage to India, presumably as a trader. He made a good deal of money there, though he lost a sizable amount of it when shipwrecked on his way home. Back in Wales, William made his living as a cattle dealer.

Both of William's older brothers died unexpectedly, so that he inherited the family estates in 1611, but his family had been extravagant, so that William had to raise £12,000 to clear their debts. In 1620–1622 Salusbury was MP for Merioneth, and aged sixty-two in 1642, was a man of some means. Salusbury was firmly high Anglican in his religious beliefs and the chapel he had built at Rhug, near his home, remains one of the finest examples of early seventeenth-century church architecture.

Salusbury carried out basic repairs to Denbigh Castle at his own expense, and commissioned a regiment of foot to garrison it. Sir Thomas Myddleton of Chirk Castle, one of the leaders of the Parliamentarian invasion of 1643, was related to Salusbury and wrote to him from Wrexham, as 'your old and true friend and kinsman', urging him to surrender Denbigh. Salusbury replied with the blunt honesty that was his hallmark:

> but to be plain – to betray so great a trust as the keeping of Denbigh castle, tho' upon ever so fair pretences, may be acceptable to them that desire it, but in my opinion, in itself is abominable: and must needs render him that shall do it villainous to God and all good men, and I will never account him my friend that should move me to it . . . This is my answer to you, and with God's help, the firm and constant resolution of him that is your kinsman, and would be your true friend, so far as truth and loyalty will give him leave.[203]

In the event, the Parliamentarian retreat following the arrival of the forces from Ireland meant Denbigh's defences were not yet to be put to the test. Over a year of relative tranquillity for Denbigh followed, during which Salusbury continued work on repairing the Castle's defences, using building material taken from the old town walls.

By early 1645 the tide of Royalist defeats, which had set in after the battle of Marston Moor, meant that the war was once again drawing closer to Denbigh. As the Parliamentarians under Sir William Brereton established their 'leaguer' of Chester, raiding parties spread out further into North Wales, and in April appeared briefly before Denbigh.

In September the King suffered a major defeat at Rowton Heath, near Chester, and headed for Denbigh to rally his broken forces. He remained in the castle for three days, during which time the redoubtable William Salusbury gave free vent to his own views, allegedly causing Charles to comment: 'Never did a prince hear so much truth at once.'[204]

Chester was now closely beleaguered, and Denbigh became a centre for Royalist relief attempts. This led on 1 November to the largest battle of the war in North Wales. Sir William Vaughan, entrusted by the King with assisting Chester, had mustered at Denbigh Green, just outside the town, a small force drawn from Royalist garrisons on the Welsh Border. They intended to rendezvous with reinforcements from North Wales, but before the latter arrived, Vaughan was attacked by a detachment from the Parliamentarian forces besieging Chester, led by Lieutenant General Michael Jones and Major General James Lothian. After a brisk dispute in the hedgerows, the Royalists were routed. Vaughan and his cavalry fled deeper into the mountains of North Wales, whilst his foot took refuge in Denbigh Castle. That night William Salusbury wrote to Vaughan:

> Sir, I wish you to be as free from danger as I hope we are secure and in good condition here. On your Foot being perceived under the Castle wall, I received them in, tho' I conceived I had no need of them in the defence of the place; yet having, I doubt not, provisions enough, their valour and good service withal meriting my compassion, I freely entertained them, I judge the enemy had a force, that came the other way over the Green, equal in number or thereabouts, to what you fought with. Mytton and the Foot, I am informed, quarter in the town, and most of the Horse in the country about.
>
> God bless us all!
> Your friend and servant,
> William Salusbury.[205]

The Parliamentarians quickly returned to their siege lines around Chester, and it was not until the spring of 1646 that Denbigh once again came under serious threat. Following the surrender of Chester many of its defenders chose to fight on in the North Wales garrisons, some of them coming to Denbigh, whose garrison had already been joined by die-hards from Beeston Castle and Lathom House, and in March around 100 men from recently surrendered Aberystwyth Castle, under Colonel Roger Whitley.

In March the Parliamentarians took Hawarden Castle, and moved against Ruthin, 6 miles up the Vale of Clwyd from Denbigh. Salusbury did what he could to disrupt enemy siege operations there by raids on their quarters. Early in April 150 'mounted firelocks' attacked Captain Richard Price's quarters at Rhewl, 2 miles from Ruthin. However, word of the intended attack had reached the enemy, and Parliamentarian horse under Colonel John Carter were placed on the alert that night.

The Royalists appear to have abandoned their enterprise, but as they were returning to Denbigh they were attacked in the rear by Carter's men, probably near the village of Llanrhaeadr. The Parliamentarians claimed to have killed seven of the enemy, although Salusbury admitted to the loss of only one. On 7 April, Colonel Thomas Mytton wrote to Salusbury, enclosing a list of prisoners, and telling him:

> I am heartily sorry that things do grow so high between us, and so are your friends at London. Sir, I beseech you to remember your country, yourself, and your posterity, and go no further in this way, to the undoing of the first and extreme hazarding of the others.[206]

Ruthin fell after three weeks' siege but, as the enemy closed in around him, Salusbury remained defiant. Despite being told by Mytton: 'Credit me, the King has no army left in the field in any place in England,' Salusbury responded:

> The Parliament (if I may so call it) I have no ways offended, unless (as before) in being loyal to my king, in observing his commands, as well by commission under his hand and seal, as also by word from his own mouth for the keeping of this place, his Majesty's own house; which (without regard to my own life, lands or posterity) with God's assistance, I will endeavour to make good for him to my last gasp. So I rest, your poor kinsman, and old play-fellow to serve you . . .[207]

The close friendship of earlier days did not prevent either Mytton or Salusbury from prosecuting these closing weeks of war vigorously. On 17 April Mytton began his advance from Ruthin to Denbigh, his march harassed by parties of Salusbury's men. A skirmish took place at the village of Llandyrnog, in which a Parliamentarian captain was killed. The Parliamentarians occupied those parts of Denbigh that lay outside the castle walls, and established an observation post in the tower of St Marcella's Church at Whitchurch, just beyond the town, where Mytton also had his headquarters. From here on 18 April Mytton formally demanded the surrender of Denbigh Castle, telling Salusbury of the hopelessness of his situation, and warning that if he remained defiant,

> the whole charge of the siege may, for the saving of this poor exhausted country from ruin, be maintained out of your . . . estates, which will certainly be prosecuted by him who rather desired to be unto you, as heretofore, your old friend and servant, Thomas Mytton.[208]

Salusbury remained inflexible:

I am sorry to see the ruin of my innocent native country for their loyalty to their king, and sensible to the effusion of Christian blood, but upon whose account that which is, or shall be spilt in your attempt to force this castle from me . . . I will leave it to the Highest Judge: and in answer to your summons, I will say no more than that with God's assistance, I do resolve to make good this place till I receive our king's command and warrant of my discharge – to whom, under God, we all are tied by common allegiance; and when I shall have need of relief, I shall undoubtedly expect it from my merciful God, who knows the justice of my cause.[209]

At the same time as they drew their lines around Denbigh, the Parliamentarians were also beginning their sieges of Holt, Caernarvon and Flint Castles. Some of the guns they had used against Chester, including an 18-pound culverin, were brought into play at Denbigh. At least one battery was deployed against the Goblin Tower, another was emplaced near Parliamentarian Sir Thomas Myddleton's residence of Galch Hill, aiming at another section of Denbigh's walls. To reply Salusbury had only one large gun.

The Parliamentarians evidently lacked sufficient heavy artillery to breach the castle walls, and in any case were reluctant, at this late stage of the war, to incur the casualties likely in any storming attempt. At the end of May several Parliamentarian officers wrote describing the current situation:

Our forces are so many that all the countries under our command will hardly afford us provision. We are put to use our utmost skill to get maintenance in this way; then you may judge how hard it is with us for want of pay, without which our soldiers, will not continue . . . to go on in their hard and difficult duty that hitherto they have undertaken; harder, we may boldly say, hath not been in any place since the wars, and, besides, many of our soldiers with us are auxiliaries from Lancashire, who are most unreasonable men if they are disappointed in their pay . . . Denbigh we laid siege to as soon as we took Ruthin, which now is six weeks hence. Its governor is a very wilful man, and hath very nigh 500 fighting men in it. It hath in its situation all the advantages for strength that any castle can have. There are many gentry in it and some riches . . . Their hearts are as hard as the very foundations of the castle itself, being an impregnable rock. There are mounts raised round about it, and approaches for battering of a tower called the Goblin's Tower; hoping thereby to deprive them of the benefit of a well in that tower, which, can we attain, we may then soon expect the castle, through want of water, they having but one well more, which is usually (as it is reported) dry in June or July every summer.[210]

It was clear that the siege was likely to be prolonged, and the local civilian population would suffer as much as the besieged from the depredations of the besiegers. A petition signed by forty-seven leading inhabitants of the locality – known rather unkindly to the Royalists as the 'Bumpkins' Petition' – was forwarded to Salusbury on 8 May, urging him to make terms. Salusbury replied:

> How I became interested in this place and command is very well known to the most of you; and with what moderation I have since managed it doth clearly appear by the exhausting of my own estate for the supply of this castle (but what hath been plundered from me by the Parliament forces) to avoid my pressure upon the country, who cannot in justice complain, at the practice of other garrisons, be impartially looked upon . . . neither can I discern how the country may be preserved, or your charge lessened by the surrender of this castle, since others of no less strength and consequence are continued in our king's obedience and command, will probably engage the same force, which will be maintained by the same means.[211]

Late in May Mytton moved on to take command of the siege of the key fortress of Caernarvon, leaving operations at Denbigh in the charge of Colonel John Carter. The garrison of Denbigh remained defiant, making a number of sallies, in one of which the Royalist Captain Edward Wynne of nearby Ystrad Hall was mortally wounded. On his death, his fellow officers of the garrison were permitted to carry the body as far as a small stream that crossed the road near Whitchurch. Here it was handed over to the Parliamentarians, who fired a volley of musketry in salute before taking the body to Llanrhaeadr church-yard for burial.

The fairly desultory Parliamentary bombardment of the Castle continued, with the Goblin's Tower the main target of batteries sited in what are now the grounds of Howell's School, where a number of shot, of from 8–32 pounds in weight, have been uncovered.

Early in June both Caernarvon and Beaumaris Castles surrendered to Mytton. The Parliamentarian commander told Salusbury of their fall on 24 June, when he again summoned him to surrender. But the intransigent Governor of Denbigh retorted that their fate:

doth nothing concern me; that must be upon their account who were therein entrusted by our king; now for the holding of this castle I do hold it, in its proper and due obedience to our king . . . for prevention of the loss of innocent Christian blood, of which I am very sensible, do you withdraw your forces from before this castle and country: I shall give you good assurance, that this garrison shall neither be hurtful, nor burdensome to the country.[212]

Salusbury asked permission to send two gentlemen to learn the King's wishes with regard to Denbigh:

till then, with God's leave, I shall cheerfully run the extremest hazards of war, as shall please god. Lastly, for your summons,— when I see the authority you have from our king, and his parliament, commanding me to deliver this place to your hands I shall with god's help, return you an honest and plain answer . . .[213]

And in a postscript:

What ruin shall befall this country, I refer it to the Supreme Judge, from whom no secrets are hid, so I rest, and so I am. There is a God that judgeth the earth.[214]

The siege of Denbigh dragged on into the summer. Neither side was anxious to initiate active operations, likely to result in needless casualties. The chief enemy of both besieged and besieger was the heat of summer, with both suffering from the effects of disease, and the Royalists from shortage of water.

On 30 August, in his first real sign of weakening, Salusbury repeated his request to be allowed to send two emissaries to the King. Mytton replied that Parliament had forbidden such a concession, and added the news that Flint Castle had now surrendered. However, next day, possibly with Mytton's tacit connivance, Salusbury managed to slip a messenger out through the siege lines, telling his opponent that, as he had been forbidden openly to approach the King:

I must apply myself to other means, in that particular, for my satis-faction, which will take up some time; and if I must quit the place, I confess I had rather you had the honour of it, than any other person in England, of your party; though give me leave to tell you, that the addition of a new force, [from the siege of Flint] be the consequence what it list, will but act to my honour which is all I have now left to care for.[215]

Salusbury's messenger reached the King at Newcastle upon Tyne, where Charles was now a prisoner of the Scots, and received the royal thanks to Salusbury:

> I heartily thank you for your loyal constancy, and assure you, that whensoever it shall please God to enable me to show my thankfulness to my friends, I will particularly remember you.[216]

The King also sent Salusbury his Royal Warrant of discharge, authorising him

> upon honourable conditions to quit, and surrender the Castle of Denbigh, entrusted to you by us, and to disband all the forces under your command; for which your so doing, this shall be your warrant.[217]

The articles of surrender for Denbigh were agreed and signed on 14 October, although it was not until the 26th that the Royalists actually marched out. Salusbury and his men were to be treated with respect, and allowed to return to their homes, their part in the war over. Salusbury himself is said to have flung the castle keys down angrily from the walls with a comment to the besiegers to the effect that 'they had gained the world, and might make it their dung hill'.[218]

In his message, the King had promised Salusbury – that 'upright and honourable man' – some reward for his loyalty when fortune favoured him again. That day never dawned, but just before his execution in 1649 Charles remembered 'Old Blue Stockings', sending him all he had – an embroidered crimson cap often worn by the King, which became a treasured token for the Salusbury family.

William Salusbury lived to see the Restoration, dying at his Rhug estate, where he had quietly spent his remaining days after the siege of Denbigh.

Chapter Ten

Siege and Blockade: Newark 1643–1646

Some garrisons were so strongly fortified and defended that bombardment, starvation and storm were unlikely to succeed – at least not quickly or at reasonable cost.

This was often the case with key strategic towns such as London, Oxford, Chester, Plymouth and Newark. The defences of London and Oxford – rival capitals of Parliament and King – eventually became so strong and so extensive that neither offered much prospect of speedy capture. After a tentative Royalist approach in the autumn of 1642 ended in a stand-off at Turnham Green, the King's forces never again mounted a serious threat to London. In its turn, Oxford remained unconquered until the closing months of the war, when the lack of a viable Royalist field army allowed Parliament to undertake the lengthy operations necessary to reduce it. Even then, the Royalist surrender was largely due to flagging morale.

Although the term 'leaguer' was often applied rather loosely to a variety of sieges, it more accurately describes the prolonged operations – usually a mixture of assault, bombardment and blockade – required to reduce extensive fortified complexes. The nature of the Civil War, with key strategic Royalist garrisons generally more vulnerable to attack than those of their opponents, meant that – with the exception of one or two coastal towns such as Plymouth – most 'leaguers' involved operations against Royalist garrisons, such as Chester and Newark-on-Trent.

In 1642 Newark, with a population of around 2,000–3,000, was a thriving market town, owing its role in the Civil War largely to its location. It was a major communications centre, linking roads across the River Trent to Leicester and Nottingham, and commanding the main route to the North from the Midlands and Southern England. To the Royalists, Newark was of vital importance in maintaining links between the Royalist-dominated North of England and the King's forces around Oxford. Through the town would pass the great convoys of munitions landed on the coast of North East England for the Royalist armies, whilst from Newark raiding cavalry scoured a wide swath of Parliamentarian territory, posing the threat of a major incursion into the Parliamentarian heartlands of the Eastern Association.

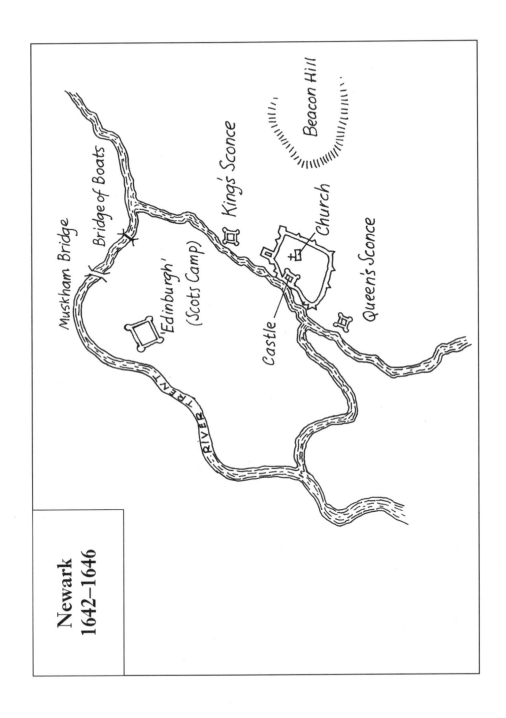

Newark
1642–1646

Muskham Bridge

Bridge of Boats

RIVER TRENT

'Edinburgh'
(Scots Camp)

Kings' Sconce

Castle

Church

Queen's Sconce

Beacon Hill

Newark – whose inhabitants seem to have been predominantly pro-Royalist – was occupied by troops of the Earl of Newcastle's Northern forces at the end of 1642. Like many other towns, Newark was not initially well fortified. Its Castle, dominating the crossing of the River Trent by the Great North Road, remained defensible, but the medieval walls of the town had been partly demolished, and the suburbs had, in any case, spread beyond them. The arms of the Trent enclosed an area to the west of town known as 'the Island', from which bridges led at Ketcham and Muskham.

The first task of Newark's new Royalist Governor – a Scottish professional soldier, Sir John Henderson – was to establish an outer line of earthen defences. These were not initially elaborate, apparently consisting of a simple ditch and embankment with irregular projections, not bastions, at intervals. A contemporary report said of them: 'Most pitiful works they were, very low and thin, and with a dry ditch most men might easily leap on the east and south.' [219] The Royalist intention was also to fortify and garrison the ring of villages (some 2 miles distant) around Newark, together with residences such as Wiverton and Shelford Manor. But work on this had scarcely begun when Newark faced its first attack. The initial garrison was fairly small, consisting of around 1,200 foot and 300 horse plus a few hundred armed townsmen. Henderson – a veteran of the Thirty Years War – was a hard drinker, a typical soldier of fortune, whose loyalty remained uncertain.

The first assault on Newark came in February 1643, and was mounted by another professional soldier, Major General Thomas Ballard, with a claimed 6,000 men (though probably fewer) drawn from Lincolnshire and the East Midlands, along with 6 light guns. Learning of Ballard's approach, Henderson attempted to disrupt his preparations by a night raid on the Parliamentarian quarters at Beckenham, but failed.

On 27 February Ballard's forces appeared before Newark. Henderson had drawn up around 1,000 cavalry on Beacon Hill, just outside the town, but heavily outnumbered, retreated within the defences, skirmishing as he went. Many critics claimed afterwards that Ballard's summons next day was rejected, with the response that the enemy must 'win it and wear it', and the Parliamentarians divided their troops into three bodies, sending one to besiege the outlying defences around a ruined house known as the Spital.

The Nottinghamshire and Derby Parliamentarian troops took up station to the south of Newark, probably around the village of Farndon, and a Council of War, held on Tuesday, 28 February, took the decision to storm the town, although Ballard himself reportedly displayed little enthusiasm for the idea.

Next day, the Parliamentarian guns fired about eighty shots into the town, though with little effect, and two brigades of Ballard's foot prepared to assault the Royalist defences. Storming parties advanced from the north and south, and on the northern side met with some initial success. The Lincolnshire troops took the Spital and, driving on, penetrated into the town itself.

What happened next was the subject of some dispute. Mrs Lucy Hutchinson, wife of Colonel John Hutchinson, Parliamentarian Governor of Nottingham and an opponent of Ballard, alleged that the Major General refused a request for horse to be committed to exploit the initial success, and then ordered the Lincolnshire men to withdraw. In another version, the Lincolnshire troops advanced into Newark as far as the cross in the centre of the town, but were then brought to a halt by the fire of Royalist musketeers and guns firing from the cover of buildings.

The attack on the southern side of Newark, mounted by the Nottingham and Derby forces, made little progress. Here the Parliamentarians – displaying common failings of raw troops – went to ground when they came under enemy fire, taking refuge in a ditch within pistol shot of the defences, from whence they maintained an ineffective fire on the Royalist positions.

The Lincolnshire troops had fallen back, but at around 3pm were prevailed upon to join the Nottingham and Derby men in a renewed assault. This move had been anticipated by Henderson, who had concentrated most of his troops at the threatened point. As a result the attackers were 'entertain[ed] with a hotter service than they expected' and after three hours 'began to wax weary of the work'.

At around 6pm, as the attack faltered, Henderson counter-attacked. According to Mrs Hutchinson:

> two hundred Lincolnshire men . . . first ran away, then Sir John Gell's [Derby] greycoats made their retreat after them. Major Hutchinson and Captain White all this while kept their trenches, and commanded their Nottingham men not to stir, who accordingly shot there, till all their powder was spent.[220]

Lucy Hutchinson alleged that Ballard ignored the pleas of the Nottinghamshire men for ammunition, so that they were

> forced, unwillingly, to retreat, which they did in such good order, the men first, and then their captains, that they lost not a man in coming off.[221]

The Royalists claimed to have lost only one man in the engagement and to have killed two hundred of the enemy, with many others wounded, including Ballard. They also claimed to have captured three guns.

The first Parliamentarian attempt to take Newark had ended in ignominious failure, but both Henderson and Sir Richard Byron, who succeeded him as Governor in the latter part of 1643, knew that a second attempt was inevitable. As a result, the defences of Newark were greatly strengthened during the course of 1643. The suburbs were burnt by Henderson not long after his arrival, and following the first siege

> they started to make new works, very high and strong, and set up a great sconce at the dovecote close called the King's Sconce. At this time they also secured the street called Mill gate.[222]

During the Royalist occupation the defences of Newark would grow steadily more elaborate. Eventually they included two massive outworks, the King's and Queen's Sconces. The former, standing near the North Gate of Newark's medieval defences, was probably not completed until after the second siege in 1644, and may have been designed by Prince Rupert's Engineer General, Bernard de Gomme. Overall, Newark's defences followed the customary pattern:

> strong bastions, earthworks, half-moons, counterscarps, redoubts, pitfalls, and an impregnable line of earth and turf, pallisaded and stockaded, and every part so furnished with great guns and cannon, that this bristling bulwark of Newark represented to the besiegers one entire sconce.[223]

Throughout 1643 Newark remained an increasing annoyance to the Parliamentarians. Royalist cavalry under the Earl of Newcastle's Lieutenant General of Horse, Charles Cavendish, in cooperation with the Lincolnshire and Midlands Royalists raided far and wide, and the Parliamentarians were forced to concentrate large numbers of troops in the threatened areas.

In June, Queen Henrietta Maria passed through Newark with her great munitions convoy, bound for Oxford. On 20 July Cavendish was killed in an action with Cromwell at Gainsborough, but the threat from Newark remained potent, a Royalist counterstroke seizing Lincoln.

However, as the autumn progressed, the Parliamentarian threat to Newark began to grow. On 11 October, at Winceby, Cromwell and Sir Thomas Fairfax routed a combined Royalist force, which included troops from Newark led by Sir John Henderson. Soon afterwards Henderson was replaced as Governor by Sir Richard Byron, who found himself under increasing threat.

With Newcastle's Northern Royalists preoccupied with the imminent Scottish invasion, Byron could expect little help from that quarter and Newark was steadily becoming more isolated. To the Parliamentarians the garrison was 'a nest of base and bloody cormorants', whose raids were a constant menace. Therefore, in January 1644, the competent Scottish professional soldier Sir John Meldrum was charged with a new attempt to take

Newark. Meldrum had gained considerable military experience on the Continent, and had seen action at the battle of Edgehill and the recent siege of Hull. He was given around 2,000 horse, 5,000 foot, 11 guns and 2 mortars, drawn from the Parliamentarian forces of Derby, Leicestershire, Nottingham and Lincolnshire – a theoretically formidable array, which led, in late January, to a desperate appeal from the Newark Royalists to the King, asking, 'how we shall be able to oppose the fury, malice, and multitudes of the rebels, if besieged, which we daily hear of and expect.'[224]

Over the next few weeks the Parliamentarians drew closer to Newark. By the middle of February Byron was reporting that the enemy were occupying the outlying villages and appearing below the defences of Newark itself. They were preventing supplies being brought into the town, and the Royalist Commissioners in Newark admitted that 'we are no better than besieged'.[225]

It was not until 29 February that Meldrum formally began his siege operations. Byron had around 1,200 foot and 6 troops of horse – inadequate to meet Meldrum in the open field – and the Parliamentarians commenced operations by storming the Spital, beating off a counter-attack by Royalist cavalry. The Spital became Meldrum's headquarters for the remainder of the siege. Sir Michael Hubbard's Lincolnshire troops, with their headquarters in the village of Balderton, completed the investment of Newark on its eastern side.

It was clearly important for the Parliamentarians to gain control of the Island and its bridges to the west of the town. Sir Edward Hartop, on his way to reinforce the besiegers with 1,000 Leicestershire and Derbyshire horse, was ordered to seize the bridge leading onto the Island, but Hartop – allegedly having 'more mind to drink than to fight' – dallied in Nottingham, allowing the Royalists to establish a fort manned by 350 men, covering the bridge.

The Parliamentarians now established a bridge of boats over the Trent to the Island from near the Spital, and on 6 March Meldrum sent a party of dragoons over the bridge to commence operations against the Royalist-held fort. A party of Byron's horse made an unsuccessful counter-attack, and Meldrum reinforced his own bridgehead with a regiment of foot and two troops of horse, who managed to get between the Royalist horse and Newark. The Royalists panicked and made off, leaving the foot in the fort at Muskham Bridge isolated. They put up a stiff fight, but the fort was stormed with 200 prisoners taken.

Meldrum was confident that Newark would fall within days, whilst an increasingly desperate Byron hoped for relief by the Midlands Royalist forces of Lord Loughborough. However, prospects of effective assistance from this quarter dwindled when a relief attempt by Royalist troops from Belvoir Castle, under Sir Gervase Lucas, was easily repulsed. The only chance seemed to be a relief attempt reportedly being planned by Prince Rupert, currently based at Shrewsbury. However, the commanders of the various contingents of Meldrum's local forces were:

> so emulous of one another, and so refractory to commands, and so piquing in all punctillos [i.e. prickly regarding their honour – ed.] of superiority, that it galled the poor old gentleman [Meldrum] to the heart; who, having commanded abroad, and been used to deal with officers that understood the discipline of war, was confounded among those who knew not how to obey any orders but disputed all his commands, and lost their time and honour in a fruitless expedition, through their own vain contentions.[226]

It proved difficult for Meldrum to conduct any coordinated operations, although the Royalists claimed that an assault made at three points on 8 March was beaten off with the loss of 500 of the attackers – likely a gross exaggeration.

Meldrum unsuccessfully asked the Committee of Both Kingdoms for reinforcements earmarked for the Army of the Eastern Association, but Parliament was unimpressed by the slow progress at Newark and was hinting that the troops could be better employed elsewhere. Sir John also made an unsuccessful appeal to the Earl of Manchester, commander of the Eastern Association, for help against Rupert's rumoured relief plans, but the Eastern Association forces were scattered over a wide area and could not be brought together before the Prince struck.

On 7 March the King had written to Rupert, requesting him to go to the aid of Newark. The Prince ordered Lord Loughborough to send 700 horses to Bridgnorth, in order to mount some of his musketeers, and on 12 March received a more urgent plea from King Charles to march to Newark's relief. Rupert was at Chester, and sent Major Will Legge to Shrewsbury with orders to muster as many musketeers as possible and send them by barge along the River Severn to Bridgnorth. Rupert himself, with his own and part of another regiment of horse, and three guns, met the 1,100 musketeers, under Major General Henry Tillier, on 15 March at Bridgnorth, and marched via Wolverhampton and Lichfield to Ashby de la Zouch, gathering reinforcements as he went. Joined at Ashby on 18 March by Lord Loughborough, Rupert now had about 3,300 horse and 3,000 foot.

The Parliamentarians at Newark believed that any relief attempt could easily be beaten off. However, a detachment of horse under Sir Edward Hartop bungled an attempt to block further reinforcements under George Porter from joining Rupert at Ashby on 19 March.

The Prince had arranged for Loughborough's troops to cut wide gaps in the hedgerows on a cross-country route from Ashby towards Newark, which would allow him a speedy approach whilst avoiding guarded roads. By 20 March Rupert was at Bingham, only 10 miles from Newark. He planned an early start next day, swinging round to the south of Newark in order to cut Meldrum's line of retreat.

That night Meldrum learnt of Rupert's arrival at Bingham and rejected suggestions that he should raise the siege. He believed that he could hold off Rupert's attack by utilising the natural defences provided by the River Trent and by garrisoning the Spital in order to protect the bridge of boats leading onto the Island. He concentrated the bulk of his foot in the Island, from where he believed they could retire northwards if necessary.

Rupert resumed his march at 2am on 21 March. As his men formed up in the moonlight, the Prince, probably with an eye to boosting their morale, told Will Legge that he had had a dream in which Meldrum was beaten. He had also slipped a message into Newark, alerting the garrison to his approach, telling them that at dawn 'let the old drum be beaten'. In the meantime, an advance party under 'Blind Harry Hastings'[227] (Lord Loughborough) was sent to engage the enemy until Rupert's main force came up.

Just before dawn on 21 March Rupert's vanguard occupied the high ground of Beacon Hill, about a mile east of Newark, driving off a small Parliamentarian detachment. Below him, the Prince could see Meldrum deploying before his bridge of boats with some foot and a party of some 1,500 horse, formed into 2 bodies, in front of them. Colonel Edward Rossiter commanded the horse on the left, Colonel Francis Thornhaugh those on the right. Rupert was eager for action:

> 'Courage' says he, let's charge them in God's name with the Horse we have, and engage them till our Rear and Foot be march'd up to us.[228]

The Royalist horse were probably drawn up in three lines. The first consisted of Rupert's Regiment and Lifeguard, about 650 men, commanded by the Prince himself. Loughborough and Porter formed the second line, with a small division under Charles Gerrard in reserve.

At about 9am Rupert charged. On the Royalist right Richard Crane, with Rupert's Lifeguard, broke through Thornhaugh's men, who behaved poorly, and drove forward as far as the Spital. On the Royalist left, however, Rossiter, doubling his files to six deep, counter-attacked, causing Rupert some difficulty. The Prince and a few companions were surrounded briefly and involved in fierce hand-to-hand fighting. Rupert was attacked by three opponents. He cut one down with his sword, while another was shot by his French aide, Mortaigne. The third grabbed Rupert by the collar but had his hand cut off by William Neale. A counter-charge by Captain Clement

Martin's troop of Rupert's Regiment, supported by Charles Gerrard, broke Rossiter's men, and Meldrum pulled his foot back to the shelter of the Spital.

The Royalist musketeers now appeared and Rupert sent Tillier to work his way along the riverbank in an attempt to seize the bridge of boats, but he found it too strongly defended. For the moment Rupert confined himself to containing the Parliamentarians on the Island, but during the afternoon he got about 500 horse across the river. Soon afterwards a sally by the Newark garrison took the fort on the far side of the Island, which commanded Muskham Bridge.

Trapped, with many of his men in a state of mutiny, Meldrum asked for terms. Those he was granted were surprisingly lenient. Next morning, after surrendering their guns and firearms, the Parliamentarians were allowed to march away. Rupert was left in possession of 11 guns, including the demi-cannon 'Sweet Lips', 2 mortars and 3,000 muskets. His disappointed men attempted to loot the departing Parliamentarians, until beaten off with drawn swords by Rupert and his officers.

Although the relief of Newark was hailed as a great victory, there was criticism in Royalist circles that Rupert had allowed Meldrum to get off too lightly. Once rearmed, his army would be able to take the field again. But the Prince's supporters argued that he had achieved his aim of relieving Newark, and *Mercurius Aulicus* pointed out:

> true though it was that the enemies were distressed, yet very wise Generals have not thought it safe to make such men desperate. Besides which, being now in the midst of their own Garrisons, they might possibly be relieved. And to confess the truth, the Prince's Horse were so over-marched, and his Foot so beaten off their legs, that he found his men less able for the present for this; in very truth too, the Rebels were more than was believed.[229]

Rupert's victory not only secured Newark, but was followed by a brief Royalist recovery of Lincoln, Gainsborough and Stamford.

Newark was left unmolested for over a year, with the Royalists in largely undisputed control of a wide swath of territory around the town. The Newark horse scoured the countryside for provisions, and to collect the assessments levied on the civilian population. The villagers attempted to court popularity with the visiting soldiers by supplying them with food and drink. The records of the village of Upton reported: 'Spent on Colonel Stanton his men when they came for the Assessment in meat and drink 1s 4d' and 'paid for tobacco and tobacco pipe for Captain Ashton when he quartered here, 2s 4d'.[230]

The great Royalist defeat at Marston Moor did not immediately threaten Newark, whose cavalry continued their raiding operations, not always successfully. In October a large Royalist force, including horse from Newark, was on its way to relieve the garrison at Crowland when it was surprised near Belvoir and suffered over 400 casualties. As the year closed Parliamentarian horse under Edward Rossiter were active once more in the area around Newark. At the end of November they surprised Sir John Girlington's Regiment of Horse, inflicting a number of casualties.

For reasons that are now obscure, Sir Richard Byron was replaced in February 1645 as Governor of Newark by a supporter of Prince Rupert, Sir Richard Willys. He faced a deteriorating situation, with the Parliamentarians drawing nearer to the town, and briefly establishing a blockade on its northern approaches. Royalist victories during the early spring at Melton Mowbray and Pontefract eased pressure once more, until the crushing Royalist defeat at Naseby on 14 June, in which some of the Newark horse were involved, served notice that the garrison might soon expect to be under threat once again.

During the summer, the pace of raid and counter-raid increased, mainly involving actions between the Newark forces and Thornhaugh and Rossiter's Parliamentarians. The latter were not yet strong enough to block up Newark, whose riders went far and wide, raising the siege of Welbeck House. Parliamentarian supporters in the East Midlands pleaded with the Committee of Both Kingdoms for assistance, and on 22 June a new Northern Association was formed to raise an army of 2,600 horse and 7,000 foot. But this force was initially absorbed in mopping up the remaining Royalist garrisons in Yorkshire, giving the garrison of Newark some additional time in which to strengthen their defences.

A double palisade and water-filled ditch were added to the fortifications, and the great gun 'Sweet Lips' was emplaced at the Goat Bridge Hornwork. Although the Island was recognised as not being defensible, it was valuable as a grazing place for the garrison's cattle and horses.

In October, following his defeat at the battle of Rowton Heath near Chester, King Charles briefly took refuge in Newark, with some of his 1,500 horse quartered in the surrounding villages. The Committee of Both Kingdoms sent an urgent request to their Scottish allies, commanded by the Earl of Leven, to move against Newark, whilst the Northern Association Army (under another professional soldier, Colonel General Sydenham Poyntz), which had been under orders to track the King, also headed for Newark. The other local commanders in the Midlands were also ordered to send all available troops, including 4,500 foot, to Newark. The Lincolnshire and Nottinghamshire horse, under Rossiter and Thornhaugh, were already in the area.

On 22 October Poyntz reached Southall, a few miles from Newark, whilst Rossiter placed piquets between Shelford and Belvoir, in the hope of intercepting the King if he tried to escape southwards. There were, as yet, not enough troops available to begin a full siege of Newark, and for the moment the Parliamentarians concentrated on reducing its outposts, some of whose garrisons had been strengthened by the horse that had accompanied the King.

The first to come under attack was Shelford Manor. On 1 November Poyntz and Rossiter occupied the adjacent village, smoking a Royalist detachment out of the church by means of burning straw. The house itself was held by a garrison of 180–200 men, including the remnants of the Queen's Regiment, a largely Roman Catholic unit, which had been among the best of the King's cavalry earlier in the war. Shelford's Governor, Colonel Phillip Stanhope, had fortified Shelford with a pallisaded rampart and a wide wet moat. He had been promised relief from Newark, so when Colonel John Hutchinson offered him terms, Stanhope returned a 'very scornful huffing reply', threatening to 'lay Nottingham Castle as flat as a pancake'. [231] Poyntz now formally summoned Stanhope:

> Sir, you may perceive I am not only master of the field, but you are also without any expectation of relief. I do therefore require the delivery up of the house and garrison of Shelford under your command for the use of King and Parliament; which if you shall refuse to do you must expect the strictest rigour of a resolved enemy, for though it fall out to be with some loss my number is so considerable that I shall compel you thereunto. You have half an hour's time to return answer. [232]

Stanhope remained obdurate:

> I keep this garrison for the King, and in defence of it I will live and die, and your number is not so great nor you so much master of the field that I am confident soon to lessen your number, and see you abroad, and for relief we need none. Therefore desire you to be satisfied with this answer. [233]

Among the prisoners earlier taken by the Parliamentarians in Shelford church was a woman corporal and a boy who had previously deserted from Hutchinson's forces. Threatened with death, the latter revealed to his captors a point in Shelford's defences where the palisade was incomplete.

At 4pm the Parliamentarians began their assault at two points. A London regiment attacked in one place and Hutchinson's Nottingham troops in another. Lucy Hutchinson related that her husband's men

> found many more difficulties than they expected, for after they had filled up the ditches with faggots and pitched the scaling ladders,

they were twenty staves too short, and the enemy, from the top of the works, threw down logs of wood, which would sweep off a whole ladderful of men at once: the lieutenant colonel himself was once or twice so beaten down. The governor [Hutchinson] had ordered other musketeers to beat off those men that stood upon the top of the works, which they failed to do by shooting without good aim; but the governor directed them better, and the Nottingham horse dismounting, and assailing with their pistols, and head-pieces, helped the foot to beat them all down from the top of the works, except one stout man, who stood alone, and did wonders in beating down the assailants, which the governor being angry at. Fetched two of his own musketeers and made them shoot, and he immediately fell, to the great discouragement of his fellows. Then the governor himself first entered, and the rest of his men came on as fast as they could. But while this regiment was entering on this side, the Londoners were beaten off on the other side, and the main force of the garrison turned upon him. The cavaliers had half-moons within, which were as good a defence to them as their first works, into these the soldiers that were of the queen's regiment were gotten, and they in the house shot from out of all the windows. The governor's men, as soon as they got in, took the stables and all their horses, but the governor himself was fighting with the captain of the papists and some others, who, by advantage of the half moon and the house, might have prevailed to cut him off and those that were with him, which were not many. The enemy being strengthened by the addition of those who had beaten off the assailants on the other side, were now trying their utmost to vanquish those that were within. The lieutenant colonel, seeing his brother in hazard, made haste to open the drawbridge, that Poyntz might come in with his horse; which he did, but not before the governor had killed that gentleman who was fighting with him. At whose fall his men gave way. Poyntz seeing them shoot from the house, and apprehending the King might come to their relief, when he came in, ordered that no quarter should be given. And here the governor was in greater danger than before, for the strangers hearing him called governor, were advancing to have killed him, but that the lieutenant colonel, who was very watchful to preserve him all that day, came in to his rescue, and scarcely could persuade them that he was the governor of Nottingham; because he, at the beginning of the storm, had put off a very good suit of armour that he had, which being musket-proof, was so heavy that it heated him, and so would not be persuaded by his friends to wear anything but his buff coat. The governor's men, eager to complete their victory, were forcing their entrance into the house: meanwhile Rossiter's men came and took away all their horses, which they had taken away when they first entered the works and won the stables, and left in the guard of two or three, while they were pursuing their work. The governor of Shelford, after all his bravadoes, came but meanly off; it is said he sat in his chamber, wrapt up in his cloak, and came not forth that day; but that availed him not, for how, or by whom, it is not known, but he was wounded and stripped, and flung upon a dunghill. The lieutenant colonel, after the house was mastered, seeing the disorder by which our men were ready to murder one another, upon the command Poyntz had issued to give no quarter, desired Poyntz to cause the slaughter to cease, which was presently obeyed, and about seven-score prisoners were saved. While he was thus busied, inquiring what was become of the governor, he was shown him naked upon the dunghill; whereupon the lieutenant colonel called for his own cloak, and cast it over him, and sent him to a bed in his own quarters, and procured him a surgeon. Upon his desire he had a little priest, who had been his father's chaplain . . . but the man was such a pitiful comforter, that the governor, who was come to visit him, was forced to undertake that office: but though he had all the supplies they could every way give him, he died the next day.[234]

About 140 of the defenders of Shelford were put to the sword, around 40 surviving. The house was set on fire, whether by troops or vengeful local inhabitants remains unclear.

However, the Parliamentarians had missed their main prize. King Charles slipped out of Newark the same night, and made his way safely to Oxford. Before leaving Newark he had been involved in an angry confrontation with Prince Rupert, who had made his way there seeking to justify his surrender of Bristol. The breach was not healed, and a number of other Royalist officers resigned their commands in support of the Prince. Among them was the Governor of Newark, Sir Richard Willys. He was replaced by Henry Lord Bellasis, whose service with the King stretched back to Edgehill. Though he had no military experience prior to the Civil War, Bellasis could be relied upon to defend his command to the last.

The example of Shelford, and the pleas of the governor's wife, caused the defenders of Wiverton, another of Newark's outposts, to surrender at once when summoned by Poyntz.

Newark was one of the most powerful of the surviving Royalist garrisons. To defend it Bellasis had retained in the town 1,000 of its best horse under Major General Rowland Eyre, together with 100 mounted gentlemen 'reformadoes' led by Colonel Conyers Darcy. He had around 3,000 foot under Colonels Gilby, Stanton, Wheatley and Jenkins. The last two men each commanded one of the big sconces. In addition there were about 1,000 armed townsmen.

Both the Scots and Poyntz were now closing in on Newark. The Scots army was led by Alexander Leslie, Earl of Leven, the illegitimate son of George Leslie of Balquhain and 'a wench in Rannoch'. He was described as an 'old little, crooked soldier', of limited education, he himself claiming, 'I got the length of the letter "g".' Though, in fact, he was rather more literate than this suggests. A canny general in his day, Leven was now probably past his best, though still well suited for the rather static operations of a siege.

Poyntz was another general of humble origins. Because of his father's poverty, he had begun his career as a London apprentice: 'a life I deemed no better than a dog's life, and base'.[235] Around 1635 he had enlisted as a volunteer in the Thirty Years War, apparently fighting on both sides without particular compunction, and surviving six years' captivity in the hands of the Turks. In 1645 he had returned to England to command, with steady reliability, the new Army of the Northern Association.

On 26 November the Scots forces came in sight on the north side of Newark, and a few days later attacked the Royalist fort at Muskham Bridge. The bridge itself now included a drawbridge section, covered by the fire of the fort. Leven placed musketeers on the opposite bank of the river, but for a few days made no progress. Then one morning the Royalist defenders made a sally from the fort in an attempt to set fire to the drawbridge. They were forced back by a Scots counter-attack before the fire took firm hold. With the bridge in enemy hands, the Royalists abandoned the fort, allowing the enemy to occupy the island.

For some time, insufficient numbers of troops prevented the allies from completely surrounding Newark. Poyntz and Rossiter arrived early in December after blocking up Belvoir, bringing with them troops from Lincolnshire, Nottingham and Derby. They took up their quarters on the eastern and south-eastern sides of the town.

A quick resolution to the siege was unlikely. As well as reorganising the garrison, Bellasis had resupplied the town, and as the blockade was not yet complete, the Royalists were able to continue raiding as far as Lincoln. On 10 December the Royalists attacked the quarters of the Nottingham and Derby forces. One of the attackers, 'in a bravado', challenged the Parliamentarians to send out a duellist. Colonel Francis Thornhaugh responded, killing his opponent's horse and taking him prisoner.

The arrival in January of more Scottish troops and units from Yorkshire and the Eastern Association enabled the allies to tighten their grip, and they were also eagerly awaiting the arrival of a mortar. However, the Royalists continued to hit back with sorties. Parliamentarian Colonel Charles Leake was killed in one such sortie, and early in January a major attack was mounted by 800 horse and 300 foot aimed at Poyntz' headquarters in East Stoke. They captured between 100 and 220 of the enemy with little loss to themselves. Poyntz himself was surprised in his quarters and, defending the doorway to his room, killed one attacker with his sword, then charging down the stairs, killed another and cut his way out.[236] That said, in another version, Poyntz ran away, leaving behind his boots and money.[237]

On another occasion, many of the Nottingham troops were absent, voting in an election in their home town:

> The Newarkers, hearing that so many of the regiment were away, fell upon their quarters, and most of the men being surprised, were rather endeavouring flight than resistance; when the lieutenant colonel and captain Poulton rallied all they could find, lined some pales with musketeers, and beat the enemy again out of their quarters, and Poyntz, mounting with as many horse as were about him, which was very few, followed them in the night up to the very works of Newark. Some loss there was in the quarters, but nothing considerable.[238]

Towards the end of January, further reinforcements arrived from the Eastern Association and Poyntz was able to occupy the village of Coddington. It was a harsh winter, and ice on the River Trent broke down Muskham Bridge. The Royalists claimed that throughout this period

> there passed scarce a day without some action, either in beating up their quarters, fighting their guards, sallying or picquering, which ever proved to their loss, especially in four or five great sallies during this siege, wherein about 1,000 of them were killed or taken.[239]

Both Poyntz and John Hutchinson had narrow escapes:

> Once, as Poyntz and he, and another captain were riding to view some quarter of the town, a cannon bullet came whizzing by them, as they were riding all abreast, the captain without any touch of it, said he was killed; Poyntz bid him get off, but he was then sliding

down from his horse, slain by the wind of the bullet, they held him up till they got off from the place, but the man immediately turned black all over. Another time the governor was in his tent, and by chance called out; when he was scarcely out of it, another cannon bullet came and tore up the whole tent, and killed the sentinel at the door.[240]

Once a thaw set in, in February, the besiegers concentrated on extending their siege lines. The English forces seem to have completed theirs by 21 March, and the Scots constructed a great fort known as 'Edinburgh'.

Also in February, the Royalists made an unsuccessful attempt to recapture Muskham Bridge fort but were repulsed. But early in March they made a renewed effort with 1,000 foot and 400 horse. The Scots were taken by surprise, their defences held by only 150 horse and 200 foot. With Muskham Bridge itself still broken, reinforcements had to be ferried over to the Scots by boat, six at a time. Eventually the Royalists were forced back into the town.

As a result of this scare, the allies began work on two bridges of boats, one at Muskham, and the other from Winthorpe to Cranley Point, both being completed by mid-March. A fort, known as Colonel Gray's Sconce, was built to protect the Winthorpe bridge. The besiegers were reinforced by the arrival of a pinnace [i.e. a light boat, propelled by sails and oars – ed.], carrying two guns and forty musketeers, which made its way up the Trent within half a mile of Newark. Poyntz, meanwhile, was trying to dam the River Devon and an arm of the Trent in an attempt to put Newark's watermills out of action. Around the same time the besiegers

> began to batter and shoot their granadoes all which (though they were very profuse of their powder) hurt us not. Our greatest want was provisions, which began to fail us, so as the soldiers fed most upon horseflesh.[241]

The greatest threat in Newark was disease, with plague raging and the houses of the infected closed up and put under guard.

The civilian population outside the town were suffering increasingly from the demands of the Scots, now commanded by David Leslie, causing mounting protests from the country folk. In February Parliament ordered that £15,000 per month be paid to the Scots to meet their needs, and Leslie ordered looters among his troops to be put to death.

Newark was now invested at cannon shot range by around 7,000 Scots and 9,000 English troops, and it was clear that the garrison's powers of resistance were weakening. On 28 March Poyntz summoned Bellasis to surrender, but after three days the Royalist commander replied asking permission to send a messenger to the King:

> I may then know His Majesty's pleasure, whether he . . . will wind up the business in general, or leave me to steer my own course. Then I shall know what to determine.[242]

Bellasis's request was refused, although the garrison were actually in touch with the outside world by means of an old woman and a 'ragged man', who sometimes concealed their messages by swallowing them encased in a lead bullet. Bellasis had received a message from the King to hold out until Charles carried out his stated intention of placing himself in the hands of the Scots. If the King had not arrived by early May, he could seek terms.

By mid–April Poyntz had diverted the course of the Trent from Newark, and his engineers were sapping towards the Queen's Sconce and completing a battery within musket shot of the Balderton Gate of the town. The Scots had taken 'Sandhills Sconce' and could direct their gun fire against the Castle. By the end of the month they were within carbine shot range of the main defences. Poyntz now had his headquarters in the village of Farndon, with Rossiter's headquarters at Balderton and the Lincolnshire troops occupying a line between Beacon Hill and the Balderton road. Colonel Theophilous Gray had his headquarters at Coddington, with his men on either side of Beacon Hill. Colonel Henry Gray held the line from Gray's Sconce almost to Beacon Hill. The Scots defended the Island.

On 27 April Bellasis agreed to discuss terms, although negotiations did not begin until 3 May. By then Bellasis had received orders from the King 'to make what conditions you can with the English not Scots that are before you'. On 5 May Charles arrived in the Scots camp and, realising his hope that the Scots might unite with the Newarkers against the Parliamentarians was pure fantasy, again ordered Bellasis to surrender. Terms were agreed at midnight on 6 May. Newark was described as 'a miserable, stinking infected town' but many of its defenders remained defiant. Bellasis was in tears on the surrender, whilst the Mayor had urged him to make a final defiant sally.

On 8 May Bellasis marched out at the head of 1,500–1,800 men, who were allowed either to go home, abroad, or to other Royalist garrisons. Colonel John Hutchinson occupied Newark and Sydenham Poyntz was rewarded by Parliament with £20 to buy a sword and two horses, and land to the value of £300.

Chapter Eleven

'No Quarter':
Basing House 1645 and Drogheda 1649

Although many feared that the outbreak of Civil War in England would entail the kind of atrocity and massacre popularly believed to be rampant in the contemporary conflicts in Germany and Ireland, this did not immediately prove to be the case. Indeed, modern research suggests that the impact of the Thirty Years War in Germany was less universally destructive than previously believed, whilst the degree of mayhem in Ireland was exaggerated for propaganda purposes.[243]

Nevertheless, methods employed by Continental armies were quickly imported into the British Isles, and whilst the partial observance by both sides of articles of war limited some of the worst excesses, disorder and harassment of civilians and prisoners – ranging through looting and rough handling to murder – was not uncommon. The Royalists have, with some justification, gained the worse reputation, but their opponents behaved in similar fashion, though sometimes from different motives.

The 'laws of war' recognised a garrison that surrendered without putting its opponents to the expense of a storm was entitled to mercy, but in the event of a defeat by assault, all such rights were forfeited. In practice, however, these distinctions would be increasingly ignored, reaching a bloody climax in Cromwell's Irish campaign of 1649–1650. It could be argued, however, that the Royalists were first to break the rules.

The opening years of the war saw a good deal of indiscriminate looting after the fall of a town or garrison, such as Rupert's sack of Birmingham in April 1643, but indiscriminate killing seems to have been limited and unauthorised. The situation changed from late 1643, and was directly linked to the arrival in England and Wales of English troops from Ireland, who had little hesitation employing the harsh methods deemed acceptable across the Irish Sea. An early, if obscure, example of their approach – on this occasion possibly the work of local Royalist troops motivated by the 'Irish' example – came in December 1643, when a number of armed Parliamentarian supporters who had attempted to defend Bartholmley Church in Cheshire were killed after surrendering.[244] But a better documented example came two months later, also on the Welsh Border. Colonel Michael Woodhouse, commander of the Prince of Wales's Regiment of Foot and Governor of Ludlow, had previously served in Ireland alongside the ruthless Sir Richard Grenville. Arriving in England in the summer of 1643, bringing several of his officers with him, Woodhouse soon adopted 'Irish' methods on the Welsh Border. In February 1644 he moved against Hopton Castle in Herefordshire, held by a small Parliamentarian garrison under Colonel Samuel Moore. The defenders put up an unexpectedly long resistance, repulsing four assaults and inflicting – according to Moore's doubtlessly exaggerated claims – several hundred casualties on the attackers, angering them considerably, with reports circulating among the Royalists that the garrison were using poisoned bullets and killing any wounded who fell into their hands.

The Parliamentarians rejected several summons before agreeing on 13 March (with their ammunition running short) to yield 'on mercy only' – a vague term, which might be taken to mean that their lives would be spared, though at the discretion of the besiegers. According to Moore, his twenty-seven men piled their arms and left the castle, 'expecting mercy', but

> command was given that they should be tied two and three then they were stripped naked as ever they were born, it being about the middle of March, very cold and many of them sore wounded in defending their own works, there they remained about an hour till the word was given that they should be left to the mercy of the common soldiers, who presently fell upon them, wounding them grievously, and drove them into a cellar unfinished, wherein was stinking water the house being on fire above them, where they were every man of them presently massacred.[245]

Apparently not suspecting what was about to happen, Moore had been separated from his men and taken into a house, where he was harangued and threatened by Woodhouse himself, and informed later by another Royalist officer of the fate of his soldiers. Moore added that his second-in-command, Major Phillips, had been stabbed to death despite offering £200 for his life, and 'all the rest, being twenty-five, were killed with clubs or such things after they were stripped naked. Two maids they stripped to their smocks and cut them, but some helped them to escape.'[246]

The massacre at Hopton Castle was apparently a premeditated action by Woodhouse – he and his officers remaining out of the way while his men were allowed to vent their anger on the prisoners. There is rather ambivalent evidence hinting that Prince Rupert may have known of the action beforehand and may even have approved it.[247] Woodhouse probably saw the massacre as a salutary warning to other enemy garrisons, notably nearby Brampton Bryan Castle. Whatever Prince Rupert's own view, the Royalist newspaper, *Mercurius Aulicus*, was noticeably reticent in its account of the affair, making no mention of the fate of the prisoners.

Perhaps the best-known 'atrocity' involving Royalist forces (Prince Rupert and troops from Ireland) was the infamous 'Bolton Massacre' of 28 May 1644. As the Prince and his forces marched into West Lancashire, local Parliamentarian troops under Alexander Rigby, who had been besieging Lathom House, took refuge in Bolton. This town, the 'Geneva of the North', was noted for its Puritanism and hostility to the King. Its defences were fairly weak, and the decision of Rigby and his officers – reinforced by about 500 armed townsmen – to make a stand was ill-considered. They nonetheless threw back the first Royalist assault and hanged a captured 'Irish' soldier in full view of the attackers. Rupert – 'highly provoked' – ordered a renewed attack, and in vicious street fighting the Parliamentarians were driven back towards the centre of the town. According to Parliamentarian accounts massacre and atrocity likened to the great sack of Magdeburg in the Thirty Years War followed:

> at their entrance, before, behind to the right, and left, nothing heard but kill dead, kill dead, was the word in the Town, killing all before them without any respect . . . pursuing the poor amazed people, killing stripping and spoiling all they could meet with, nothing regarding the doleful cries of women and children; but some they slashed as they were calling for quarter, others when they had given quarter, many hailed out of their houses to have their brains dashed out in the streets.[248]

Closer examination modifies this picture. Even the lurid version above only actually names one woman as being among those killed, and there is evidence that, for example, 700 defenders who had taken refuge in the church were given quarter. Prince Rupert's actual orders prior to the second assault appear to have been to give no quarter to 'any Person then in Arms'[249] – a definition that would have included any of the townsmen (and indeed women) not able to jettison their weapons in time. Ill treatment there certainly was, but for the most part it seems to have consisted of rough handling, insults, and widespread looting rather than systematic slaughter. The contemporary Bolton Parish Register lists seventy-eight dead townsmen and four women, who, together with several hundred of Rigby's men, seem a more probable tally of casualties than the thousands claimed in Parliamentarian propaganda.[250]

There is no doubt that religious enmity between Puritan and Catholic played a major role in events at Bolton, and these provided a foretaste of two

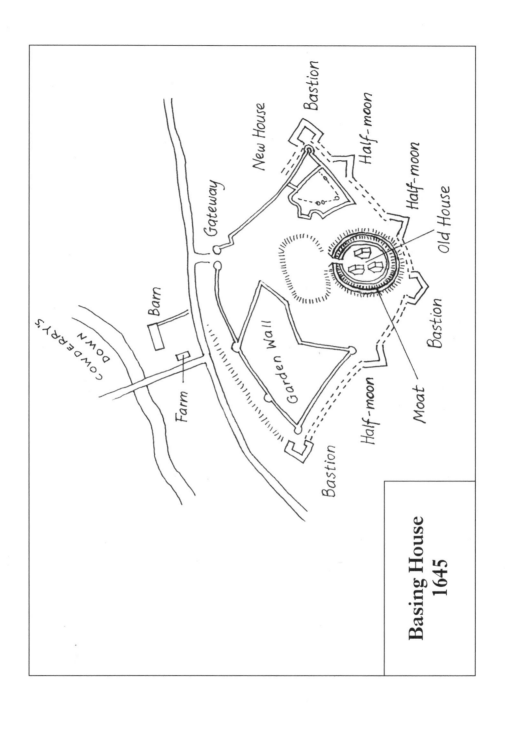

**Basing House
1645**

of the greatest examples of 'no quarter' during the war, both the work of the Parliamentarians.

Bloodbath at Basing

On an earlier fortified site, Basing House of the Civil War owed its development to the Paulet family, into whose hands it passed during the reign of King Henry VII. The complex of buildings forming Basing House was steadily expanded in line with its owners' growing prosperity. The original residence – known by the time of the Civil War as the 'Old House' – was dominated by its great four-towered Gatehouse, and surrounded by an outer rampart, strengthened with brick on its exterior side, and further protected by a dry moat. Inside were a number of small courtyards, surrounded by an array of domestic buildings, many of them with cellars beneath. A brick bridge led over the moat from the Old House to what had formerly been the castle bailey, where the huge 'New House' (built by the Paulets in their years of greatness) was situated. Said to contain 380 rooms, the New House was part mansion and part fortress, 5 stories high, with 2 great towers, built around 2 courtyards and surrounded by another dry moat, with another large gatehouse.

The complex was encircled by a defensive wall 9 feet thick, with a brick facing, and towers at intervals, roughly a mile in circumference. Inside the walls, as well as the buildings, were gardens and an orchard. The northern part of the house was partially protected by a large farmhouse known as the Grange, bordered by a high, thick, buttressed wall. The southern face of the complex would prove the weakest part of its defences, overlooking an area of parkland. In the course of the Civil War, Basing's defences were augmented by a complex of earthworks, with at least five bastions. A Royalist account describes Basing as it was in 1644:

> Basing House . . . stands on a rising ground, having its form circular, encompassed with a brick rampart, lined with earth, and a very deep trench, but dry. The lofty Gatehouse, with four turrets, looking northwards, on the right whereof, without the compass of the ditch, is a goodly building, containing two fair courts. Before them is the Grange, severed by a wall and common road, again divided from the foot of Cowdrey's Down by meads, rivulets, and a river running from Basingstoke, a mile distant upon the west. The south side of the Castle hath a park, and towards Basing town a little wood, the place scaled and built as if for Royalty, having a proper motto, 'Aimez Loyaute'.[251]

Basing was of considerable strategic importance, commanding the main road from London to the West of England, and could stifle trade between the capital and the west. This meant that an attempt by the owner of Basing in 1642 (John Paulet, 5th Marquis of Winchester) to remain neutral was doomed to failure. Eventually he sided with the King. The Paulets were staunch Roman Catholics and Basing became a refuge and rallying place for those of that faith once the war began. The capture of Basing House was of great concern to the Parliamentarians throughout the war, but siege operations in 1643 and 1644 failed, partly because the Royalist high command in Oxford had always made supporting the Basing garrison a priority. However, by the summer of 1645, the odds of capturing the garrison seemed more heavily in Parliament's favour.

For much of the war, the mainstay of Basing's defence had been the regiment of foot commanded by Sir Marmaduke Rawdon, who had served alongside the Marquis and Basing's governor, Sir Robert Peake – the latter, in civilian life, being a London print seller. However, early in 1645 a dispute broke out, apparently centred around Rawdon being a Protestant. He and his regiment were withdrawn, following a request to the King from the Marquis that Basing should be an all-Catholic garrison. It would prove a fatal decision, costing Basing the services of some 500 veteran soldiers and leaving the defence in the hands of the Marquis' own regiment, supplemented by various Catholic 'reformadoes'.

The disasters suffered by the Royalists at the battles of Naseby and Langport had left the New Model Army free to begin reducing scores of defiant garrisons. Basing became an objective in August. Colonel John Dalbier, the Dutchman who was engineer to the New Model Army, was put in command of operations. He arrived before the House on 20 August with 800 horse and foot, bringing with him 'many good engineers, and pioneers, such as are use to dig in coalpits'.[252] On 26 August orders were given by Parliament to supply Dalbier with '200 Granado shells, 9 and 10 inches in diameter . . . ' On 3 September 60 scaling ladders were also ordered. Dalbier had been promised a force of 1,700 foot and 300 horse but local authorities dragged their heels in despatching them.

By 17 September London news sheets were assuring their readers that Dalbier hoped 'to give a good account within a few days of that business'. His guns had damaged a tower of the Old House, and:

> That part of Basing House on the south side called the New House is thought most seizable [sic]; if we could gain that the other could not long hold out. There is a design to show the enemy there a

gallant stratagem of war, but I had rather let them study to find it than my pen tell tales out of school.[253]

On 22 September it was reported that:

> By letters from Basing, we were again advertised that Dalbier hath made divers shot against the Castle, and hath planted some batteries, and shot in some granadoes, some of which are believed to have done execution . . . one granado burnt two hours before they could quench it . . . [254]

But Dalbier still lacked the strength to assault Basing, and on 26 September orders were given to reinforce him with a strong detachment of the New Model Army under its Lieutenant General, Oliver Cromwell. In the meantime, Dalbier continued to hammer Basing with his artillery. On 30 September the City Scout reported that:

> the great tower in the Old House was destroyed on Monday September 22, at which time he might have taken the House had he had a considerable party to fall on. Deserters and one of our troopers, which was then a prisoner in the House, and since released by his wife, for a month's pay, say that in the top of the tower were hid a bushel of Scots twopence, which flew about their ears. The Marquis of Worcester swears that Dalbier is a greater trouble to him than ever any was that ever came against the House.[255]

On 27 September it was reported in the *Weekly Account*:

> From Basing it was certified that on Monday and Tuesday last Colonel Dalbier played with the cannon very fierce upon the New House, and after many shots against the midst of the house, which loosened the bricks and made a long crack in the wall, he made another shot or two at the top of the House which brought down the high turret, the fall whereof shook that part of the house, which before was weakened, that the outmost wall fell down all at once, insomuch that our men could see bedding and other goods fall out of the House in the court.[256]

Dalbier's persistent problem was lack of manpower to assault Basing. On 26 September he had only 1,000 foot and 4 troops of horse. This was particularly frustrating as, on 23 September, he reported that he had made 'a very great breach', and had stormed one of the outworks of the New House. Possibly referring to the 'stratagem' hinted at earlier, on 24 September the

New Informer explained: 'He hath a design to smoke them out, good store of straw being brought in from the country for that purpose.'[257]

Two days later, the *Scottish Dove* reported that 'he smokes them with sulphur of brimstone', claimed by *Mercurius Vendicus* to be a 'compounded stifling smoke'. On the 29th, the *Parliament Scout* newspaper described the 'thick and perpetual darkness which the wet and smoking straw doth make, the burning of brimstone and arsenic and other dismal ingredients doth infinitely annoy the besieged'.[258]

Morale among the defenders seems to have been falling, indicated by the increasing numbers of deserters slipping out to surrender. And to make matters worse, Cromwell was now on his way, with a force including his own regiment of horse plus those of Charles Fleetwood, Robert Hammond and Thomas Sheffield, and the foot regiments of Edward Mountagu, Sir Hardress Waller and John Pickering. Pickering's had made an enviable reputation for itself in the Army of the Eastern Association, before being transferred in its entirety to the New Model Army. It had a reputation for religious and political radicalism, exemplified by Pickering himself – 'small man but of great courage' – and a number of its officers, including its Lieutenant Colonel, a former London cobbler, John Hewson, and the fanatical Captain Daniel Axtell. Also set on whipping up religious fervour was the Chaplain to the Train of Artillery, Hugh Peters, one of the most zealous of the Independent preachers and an inveterate opponent of the King.

Cromwell moved first against Winchester, which fell on 6 October, leaving him free to turn on Basing. The Marquis of Winchester was probably aware of Cromwell's approach, and it is unclear why he remained determined to fight on against increasingly hopeless odds. The Royalists seem to have hoped that, with the approach of autumn, the weather might turn foul, forcing the Parliamentarians to lift their siege. Winchester probably realised that those within the self-proclaimed 'Catholic' garrison of Basing would receive little mercy from the enemy if they surrendered.

Parliament's Committee of Both Kingdoms was determined that matters at Basing be brought to a speedy conclusion. On 9 October orders were sent to Windsor Castle for service at Basing

> 100 whole cannon shot of 63 lb, 300 demi cannon shot of 32 lbs, 300 whole culverin shot of 18 lbs, 200 granado shells of 13 inches, 200 demi culverin shot of 9 lbs, 50 granado shells of 10 inches, and one great mortar piece.[259]

Although the defenders of Basing had nine or ten guns of various sizes, including one culverin and one demi-culverin, they were unable to match enemy firepower. All they could do was attempt to hit back in sallies against their attackers. On 14 October the *Weekly Intelligencer* reported that:

> A day or two before Lieutenant-General Cromwell's sitting down before Basing House, the enemy, being blockt only of one side, sallied out a good distance from the House, and fetcht in 45 cows out of a gentleman's grounds adjacent to the garrison.[260]

Ominously, in the light of imminent events, the same journal added:

> it is hoped they will imitate their neighbours at Winchester Castle, and accept of fair terms in due time before it is too late, for that otherwise, many of that garrison being Papists, they are like to receive little favour from the besiegers.

On 7 October Cromwell and his troops reached Alresford, and around 8 o'clock the next morning, began deploying before Basing on the side hitherto unblockaded by Dalbier. Total Parliamentarian strength was probably 6,000–7,000 men, compared with around 300 defenders of Basing. Cromwell had brought five heavy guns with him, including one whole and two demi-cannon, and as Richard Deane, his General of Ordnance, began to emplace them, Royalist troops from Oxford made a final forlorn effort to relieve Basing, but were easily driven back. Deane placed at least one mortar in position on the south-eastern side of the House, and opened fire with terrifying effect:

> one shell brake into the Countess of Winchester's lodgings, killed her waiting woman, and her chamber maid and some other, the countess herself very narrowly escaping.[261]

As his guns were brought into position, Cromwell, with Dalbier and other senior officers, rode up to view the defences of Basing more closely. In a suicidal gesture of defiance

> A cavalier of the garrison must needs peep out to see, and bid welcome our new supplies, which one of Cromwell's sees, and not enduring to be stared upon, rides up to him, pistols him in the neck, and brings off my gentleman and his horse. His body was buried, but not his clothes, for they were very good ones.[262]

The Parliamentarians expected the Catholic defenders of Basing to put up desperate resistance to an assault, and that the Roman Catholic priests in the House, 'knowing how ill it would go with them if that place were taken', were urging a fight to the death.

By Saturday 11 October all Cromwell's guns had been emplaced and Basing House was completely encircled by siegeworks stretching a mile and a half. The same evening Cromwell summoned Basing to surrender, warning that no mercy would be shown if his demand was rejected. Next day the Parliamentarian guns opened fire and by the following afternoon had battered down the drawbridge leading into the Old House.

Monday 13 October dawned misty, and early that morning about twenty Parliamentarian prisoners held at Basing were exchanged for a similar number of Royalists. About the same time, possibly hoping to use the concealment of the fog to escape, a party of horsemen rode out of Basing and captured Colonel Robert Hammond and a Major King, who seem to have mistaken the Royalists for their own men. They were taken back into Basing, whose Governor, Sir Robert Peake – possibly hoping to use the Parliamentarian officers as hostages – refused to exchange them. This brought an angry response from Cromwell, who warned that 'if any wrong or violence were offered to these men, the best in the house should not obtain quarter'. There were some reports that the prisoners were relieved of their valuables, but in fact they seem to have been fairly well treated. By nightfall

> our ordnance had done such execution, both on the part of the house where Colonel Dalbier placed his battery, and likewise where Lieutenant General Cromwell had placed his, that our men might enter.[263]

During the night, the Parliamentarians prepared their assault, Cromwell apparently passing much of the hours of waiting in prayer. About 2am, under cover of darkness, his troops began to take up their start positions. Dalbier was to attack on the north side of the House, near to the Grange, with Pickering's Regiment on his left. Hardress Waller was probably next to Pickering, with Edward Mountagu's Regiment on the far left. The onset was signalled by four guns, fired at 6am, and at around dawn the attacks began

> with great resolution and cheerfulness, and with undaunted courage got over the enemy's works, entered the breaches, and possessed part of the New House and the court betwixt that and the Old House. It is affirmed we lost but one man e'er we got within their works.[264]

The defenders of Basing may have been outnumbered as much as ten-to-one by the attacking columns, and they made little attempt to defend the mile of outworks, concentrating what they must have realised was a desperate last stand in the buildings of the House itself. The Parliamentarians forced their entry at two points: Dalbier's men on the side nearest to the town of Basing and Cromwell on the Park side of the House. According to *Mercurius Civicus*:

Tuesday morning about five of the clock, our forces began to storm
the new house adjoining to Basing House, which they took after a
hot dispute between them and the enemy, to whom on the gaining
of it no quarter was given. Who first entered is uncertain, and to
name were to disparage as worthy: all parts were entered, both by
the Lord General's party and Colonel Dalbier's. One letter saith
that some of those who had been longest before the place gave back
upon a hot charge, yet the other parties getting further ground, they
came on again.

Cromwell reported that it was Pickering's men who stormed the New House,
and one Parliamentarian writer was somewhat defensive regarding the ruth-
lessness of their assault:

Immediately the dreadful battery began the great guns
discharged . . . with great execution; many wide breaches were made
in an instant, and the besieged immediately marshalled themselves,
and stood like a new wall to defend these breaches, our men in full
bodies and with great resolution came on. The dispute was long and
sharp, the enemy, for ought I can learn, desired no quarter, and I
believe that they had but little offered them. You must remember
what they were. They were most of them Papists, therefore our
muskets and swords did show but little compassion, and the House
being at length subdued did now satisfy for her treason and rebellion by the blood of the offenders.[265]

The Parliamentarians had now taken part of the New House, together with

the court betwixt that and the Old House, where the enemy had laid
a train of powder, which they blew up; the quantity was thought to be
about three barrels, but, blessed be God, it did not much annoy us.[266]

However, Colonel Hammond, observing events as a prisoner, said:

the enemy blew up no mine, as was at first reported, only one of our
men being killed by a barrel of powder which accidentally blew up.[267]

Gaining a foothold in the courtyard of the Old House, the Parliamentarians

slid in at the windows and encompassed the New House round, for
the enemy were fled thither, then they in the house threw hand
grenadoes at our men in the court, but we made our passage into the
House among them, and by force of arms quenched their rage.[268]

Cromwell said that, once again, it was Pickering's highly motivated men who 'passed through and got the gates of the Old House'. By now the Old House was ablaze, but the doomed defenders continued their desperate resistance in what was now literally a fight to the death:

> They in the Old House hung out [four] black ensigns of defiance, and set fire to a bridge over which our men were to pass, disputing the passage at sword's point, and the rest in the house threw out grenades amongst our men, whereof many of them were killed.[269]

> This great work [the capture of the New House] being done, the batteries were forthwith made against the old house, and our men, flushed with taking of the New House, were more eager and resolute to subdue the Old. The great ordnance having torn down all before them, and made many breaches, our men did enter them. There the besieged showed incredible boldness, for although they knew that it was impossible for them to subsist, yet they fought it out to the last, and disputed every entry and pass with the edge of the sword, being all resolved to die, and as any of them fell, their seconds, with infinite boldness, adventured to avenge their fellows' death. This made our men far more resolute, who, not minding their desperate fury, cried out 'Down with the papists!' and by this means there were few of them left who were not put to the sword.[270]

One account claimed that after the gatehouse of the Old House fell, Colonel Pickering 'put those within to a parley, but the fight was hot, and the noise great, the soldiers could not hear!'[271] Cromwell, however – probably more accurately – commented of the same moment in the fighting: 'whereupon they [the defenders] summoned a parley, which our men would not hear'.[272] Their adrenalin running high amidst the fear and confusion of ferocious fighting and their already fervent religious views whipped into a ferment by Hugh Peters' fiery preaching prior to the attack, Pickering's men undoubtedly felt they were doing 'the Lord's work' by killing their opponents without mercy.

Whilst Pickering's men were engaged in this savage combat, Mountagu and Waller were attacking the main outwork or 'Court of Guard'. After fierce resistance the defenders were driven out and the Parliamentarians were left in possession of the outwork, together with a captured culverin. Taking their scaling ladders with them, the Parliamentarians crossed another part of the outworks and then assaulted the Old House at a point where the dry moat was at least 36 feet deep, with a wooden palisade on its further side:

> At last our men came on with such courage that they entered the Old House too, crying 'Fall on, Fall on, all is our own!' In this Hardress Waller, performing his duty with honour and diligence, was shot in the arm, but not dangerously.[273]

There was no formal surrender. Estimates of the length of the storm varied between three-quarters and two and a half hours. Cromwell reported grimly that he could 'give a good account of Basing', and as organised resistance ended, what was evidently indiscriminate killing began. The Parliamentarian soldiers were doubtless inflamed by their own losses, although Cromwell reported: 'We have had little loss; many of the enemy our men put to the sword, and some others of quality.' Parliamentarian accounts gave varying figures of the total dead; around 30–40 of their own men and between 100–300 of the enemy. It is clear, however, that many of the combatants in Basing died. Hugh Peters, surveying the scene with evident satisfaction, reported:

> It may be, we have found 100 slain, whose bodies, some being covered with rubbish, came not at once to our view. Among those that we saw slain, one of their officers lying on the ground, seemed so exceedingly tall, was measured; and from his great toe to his crown was nine feet in length.[274]

Once the fighting was over, the attention of many of the victorious Parliamentarians turned to loot; but 'others minded not the booty, but fell upon them and killed many'.[275] Peters claimed that 'in the several rooms about the House there were slain 74, and only one woman.' Joshua Sprigge said forty. The Marquis of Winchester and several others were saved by the intervention of Colonel Robert Hammond, under whose protection the Marquis had placed himself when the storm began. Some Roman Catholic priests, possibly Jesuits, were killed, four others were taken prisoner and 'reserved for the gallows'.[276] Major Robinson, in civilian life a Drury Lane 'comedian', was killed by Major Thomas Harrison of Cromwell's Regiment of Horse, possibly in the course of the fighting, but more likely 'after he had laid down his arms, with the words "Cursed is he who doeth the Lord's work negligently . . ."'[277]

'Divers that laboured to escape were slain, among others Major Cuffand', who was also, according to Peters, killed by Harrison, 'that godly and gallant gentleman'.

It is uncertain whether there was any organised killing of women, some of whom may have taken an active part in the defence. One account states that 'divers women were wounded, who hung upon the soldiers to keep them from killing their friends'. A notable victim was the daughter of a clergyman, Dr Griffiths:

> one of the handsome daughters, a gallant gentlewoman, fell a railing upon our soldiers at their entrance, calling them Roundheads and rebels to the King; [this] provoked our soldiers, then in heat, into a further passion, whereupon one of our soldiers cut her on the head, killing her.[278]

Some of the garrison were cut down as they attempted to flee, but others – up to 180, including the Governor, Sir Robert Peake, and the artists Inigo Jones and Wenceslaus Hollar – were taken prisoner, along with 20 'gentlewomen'. The latter probably included

> eight or nine gentlewomen of rank, running forth together [who] were entertained by the common soldiers somewhat coarsely, yet not uncivilly, considering the action in hand. They left them with some clothes upon them.[279]

The Marquis of Winchester was harangued by Hugh Peters, but remained defiant, saying

> That if the King had no more ground in England than Basing House, he would adventure as he did, and hoping That the King may have a day again.

Some of the worst horrors followed the end of the fighting. Many of the defenders had hidden in the cellars of Basing, and as the flames spread, found themselves trapped. The House burnt for twenty hours, and Hugh Peters reported:

> Riding to the House to Tuesday night we heard divers crying in vaults for quarter, but our men could neither come to them nor they to us.[280]

By the time that the flames died down 'there was nothing left but bare walls and chimneys'. Apart from the damage caused by bombardment and fire, most of the interior of the House had been torn apart by Parliamentarian soldiers in search of booty. As well as ten guns and a large quantity of arms and ammunition, the spoil of Basing included huge quantities of jewels, rich clothing and a vast range of other items. Some of this was sold by the soldiers to local country folk or in London, or kept by them and their womenfolk. Cromwell advised the House of Commons:

> I humbly offer to you to have this place utterly slighted for the following reasons: it will ask about 800 men to manage it, it is no frontier, the country is poor about it, the place exceedingly ruined by our batteries and mortar pieces and by a fire which fell on it since our taking it.[281]

On 15 October the 'Journal of the House of Commons' reported:

> Resolved that whosoever will fetch away any stone, brick or other materials of Basing House shall have the same for his or her pains.

The fate of Basing House and its defenders, as with other instances during the war, had been the result of bitter religious hatred, heightened by the fury of combat. Despite half-hearted attempts to claim otherwise, it seems most likely that the decision had been made prior to the attack to give no quarter as a warning to other Royalist garrisons. The fact that the majority of Basing's defenders were Catholic made the result more acceptable to popular opinion, and in Pickering's men, Cromwell had willing executors of his orders. But Basing proved a grim portent for what followed four years later.

'The Curse of Cromwell': Drogheda 1649

The long and troubled relationship between England and its Irish 'kingdom' had reached another bloody climax with the outbreak of the rebellion of 1641. Exaggerated claims of massacre and atrocity perpetrated on English and Scottish Protestant settlers kindled an upsurge of popular hatred in mainland Britain against the 'native' Irish population in general. However, the outbreak of the Civil War meant that it was not until 1649 that Parliament could turn its attention towards regaining control of Ireland. By then an uneasy alliance of Irish Confederates, English Royalists and Protestant settlers opposed to the execution of King Charles I, under the rather shaky leadership of James Butler, Earl of Ormonde, representing the new king, Charles II, had overrun most of the country, confining Parliament's control to the immediate vicinity of Dublin.

Fearful that this final foothold might soon be lost, Parliament prepared to send a full-scale expedition, led by Oliver Cromwell, to reconquer Ireland. Cromwell himself had mixed feelings about leaving England at a time of political ferment. Many of the troops were even less enthusiastic. Their pay was months in arrears, and some units were infected by the extreme political radicalism of the Leveller movement. It was not until the Leveller Rising of May 1649 had been ruthlessly crushed that Cromwell could begin to prepare his expeditionary force of 4,000 horse, 8,000 foot and a powerful artillery train.

In mid-August Cromwell set sail from the South Wales port of Milford Haven. Making the safety of Dublin his first objective, Cromwell landed at the Irish capital on 15 August, to find the situation considerably eased by the victory, on 2 August, of Michael Jones's Parliamentarian forces over Ormonde at Rathmines, just outside the city. This left the Irish-Royalist army too weak to face Cromwell in the open field.

Whilst reorganising Jones's men, and awaiting the arrival of the remainder of his own force, Cromwell considered his next move. He resolved to take the east coast ports, starting with Drogheda, north of Dublin, before moving inland, but knew that he would need to act quickly. Although Parliament had met the immediate expenses of the expedition, long-term supplies and reinforcements were more uncertain. With threats remaining from Scotland and unreconciled Royalists, Cromwell was unwilling to be absent from the mainland for long. Nor would the current military advantage in Ireland continue indefinitely: Ormonde was working to rebuild his field army, and in the meantime he planned to use the best of his remaining troops to tie down Cromwell in prolonged siege operations. With the aid of those inevitable seventeenth-century combatants, 'Colonel Hunger' and 'Major Sickness', Cromwell's advance might be slowed until winter ended active campaigning.

Objective Drogheda

A key factor in Ormonde's strategy was the town of Drogheda. Situated at the mouth of the River Boyne, about 30 miles north of Dublin, Drogheda controlled the main route between the capital and the north, and could threaten the flank of any Parliamentarian advance west or south from Dublin. On 23 August the Irish-Royalist commanders, meeting in Drogheda, decided to hold the town, 'judging that if Cromwell could there be foiled, or kept before it but for a time, it would much advantage us that had so lately received so great a blow, as required time to recover'.[282]

One of the minority who voted against this plan was Drogheda's governor, Sir Arthur Aston, an English Roman Catholic Royalist. A professional soldier with a long and distinguished record on the Continent and in the English Civil War, Aston was noted for his arrogance – and for his wooden leg, fitted after a riding accident: 'There was not in the King's army,' claimed an optimistic Royalist, 'a man of greater reputation or one of whom the enemy had a greater dread.'[283]

Drogheda's garrison consisted of about 3,600 troops, 500 of them horse and the remainder foot. The foot included four of Ormonde's best infantry

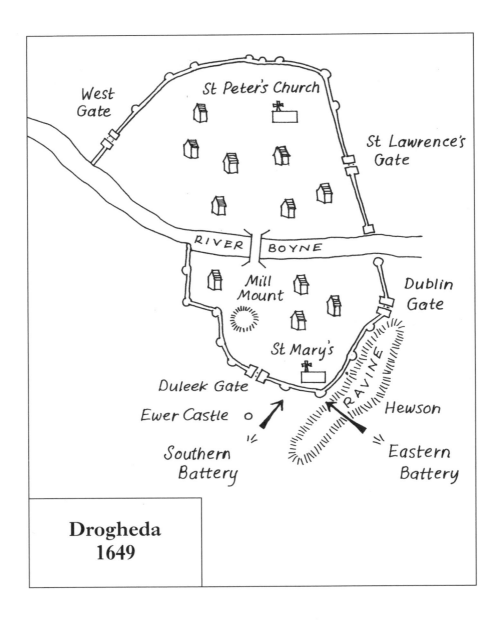

West Gate

St Peter's Church

St Lawrence's Gate

RIVER BOYNE

Mill Mount

Dublin Gate

St Mary's

RAVINE

Duleek Gate

Ewer Castle

Hewson

Southern Battery

Eastern Battery

**Drogheda
1649**

regiments, two of them, including his own, mainly consisting of Protestants, and two Irish Confederate Catholic units. He had little artillery and insufficient gunpowder to make use of it anyway. The majority of the 3,000 townspeople were of English Protestant origin, probably with a slight leaning towards Parliament, though their overriding concern was to keep clear of the fighting. Some favoured surrender to Cromwell, and there is no evidence of any of them taking part in the defence of the town.

Aston's slim hope was that Drogheda's formidable medieval defences could withstand Cromwell. The larger part of the town lay on the northern bank of the Boyne, connected by a drawbridge to the smaller area, known as the 'Irish' town, on the southern bank. Drogheda was protected by medieval walls, 20 feet high and 4 to 6 feet thick. The gateways were flanked by towers, and there were also several detached towers, or 'tenalia', covering their approaches. On the southern side of the town the defences were strengthened in places by a deep ravine. Aston appears to have lacked time to strengthen his defences with any outworks.

Cromwell formed a 'marching' army of 6 cavalry and 8 foot regiments, about 12,000 men in all. His powerful siege train was to be transported by sea. Early on 1 September Cromwell left Dublin, bound for Drogheda, promising severe penalties for any of his men who might 'abuse, rob and pillage . . . and . . . execute cruelties upon the country people'. Not wishing to have his army divided by the Boyne, Cromwell decided to concentrate his attack on the southern portion of Drogheda. He sought a quick conclusion in order to spare his troops the effects of foul weather and disease.

Arriving before the town on 3 September, Cromwell's men spent several days digging trenches and emplacing their artillery. Despite several ineffective sorties to disrupt the besiegers, morale among the defenders remained high. On 9 September the English Royalist Sir Edmund Verney, Lieutenant Colonel of Ormonde's Regiment of Foot, wrote to the Earl that he had

> great hopes and expectations that the service I am engaged in will receive a happy issue . . . [our] men are all in heart and courage . . . and we do little fear what the enemy can presently do against us.[284]

This hope of prolonged and successful resistance ignored the power of Cromwell's artillery. His guns included several heavy pieces, among them at least four 'whole' cannon, two 48-pounders, and two 42-pounders. Cromwell's plan was to bring the siege to a swift conclusion by blasting breaches in Drogheda's walls with his heavy guns, and then, taking partial advantage of the cover provided by the ravine, launch his veteran infantry in a full-scale assault.

The attackers concentrated their artillery in two batteries at the south-eastern corner of the town. Their converging fire was intended to create two breaches into the walled church yard of St Mary's Church. In response, Aston feverishly began constructing a double line of trenches behind the wall running from St Mary's Church to the Duleek Gate and from east of the church to the point where the wall overlooked the ravine. On 10 September, his guns in position, Cromwell summoned Aston to surrender, warning: 'If this be refused you have no cause to blame me.' [285] Though this was a common threat in siege warfare, memories of the fate of Basing after a similar warning might have given Aston pause for thought.

His summons rejected, Cromwell's guns opened fire, and kept up their bombardment throughout the day. By nightfall the tower of St Mary's Church had been demolished, and a nearby outlying 'tanalia' damaged. Breaches had begun to appear, and that night Aston sent his final desperate appeal to Ormonde:

> The soldiers say well, I pray God [they] do well. I will assure your Excellency speedy help is much desired. My ammunition decays apace, and I cannot help it. I refer all things to your Excellency's provident care. Living I am, and dying will end, your Excellency's most obliged servant.[286]

But, apart from a handful of reinforcements, Ormonde could do little to help Aston, and at dawn on 11 September the remorseless bombardment resumed. Throughout the day the two breaches were steadily widened, whilst behind them Aston's men worked frantically on their entrenchments.

The Assault

By 5pm, after 200–300 shots had been fired, Cromwell judged the breaches to be assailable. His attack was spearheaded by three veteran foot regiments, The southern breach would be attacked by Castle and Ewer's Regiments; Colonel John Hewson's men would attack the eastern one. As at Basing, Hewson's Regiment would play a sinister role. Hewson had taken over Pickering's old unit in November 1645, and its reputation for deep ideological motivation grew. It was prominent in the Army's defiance of Parliament in 1647, with Hewson, a close ally of Cromwell, vociferously advocating the use of martial law against civilians. He was one of the judges who tried and sentenced to death Charles I.

If Hewson was first and foremost an advocate of military rule, a religious militant and unquestioning supporter of Cromwell, his Lieutenant Colonel, Daniel Axtell, was more complex. By late 1649 he had a reputation for cruelty and brutality. Responsible for security during the King's trial, he had narrowly been prevented from ordering his men to fire on a woman protester (probably the wife of the General of the New Model Army, Sir Thomas Fairfax). He incited his troops to call out loudly for Charles's execution, and Axtell's views on the Irish were particularly vehement. Years later, when on trial for his own life, Axtell proclaimed defiantly:

God did use me as an instrument for the suppression of the bloody
enemy, and when I considered their bloody conduct in the murder
of so many thousands of Protestants, and innocent souls, that word
was much in my heart: 'Give her blood to drink, for she is worthy',
and sometimes we neither gave nor took quarter.[287]

Most of the rank and file mirrored the views of their officers. Cromwell could
rely upon Hewson to carry out his orders without question, whilst Axtell
would eagerly perform – or indeed exceed – any instructions for reprisals
against the hated Catholic and Irish foe.

In places the Parliamentarian assault was hindered by the steep slopes of
the ravine, which limited any cavalry support, whilst the defenders, with few
illusions as to their probable fate, resisted desperately. The attackers first took
an outlying tower, putting its fifty defenders to the sword, but the main
fighting centred on the two breaches. At the southern breach, held by Colonel
Garret Wall's Irish Confederate Regiment, supported by fire from the fortified mound within the walls, known as Millmount, resistance was ferocious.
Parliamentarian Colonel James Castle was shot dead at the head of his men,
who began to fall back:

the breaches, not being made low enough, the horse could not go in
with the foot, but the foot alone stormed and entered the town, but
by reason of the numerousness and stoutness of the enemy, who
maintained the breach as gallantly as ever men did, and by the death
of Colonel Castle . . . our men were disheartened and retreated.[288]

The story was similar at the eastern breach. Hewson admitted:

We entered the breach, but not so orderly as was appointed; [we]
were stoutly resisted, and after a short dispute, did retreat dis-
orderly, tumbling over the breach and down a steep hill [the ravine]
which ascends up to the wall.[289]

Both assaults had been repulsed and, with the outcome in the balance,
Cromwell – who had not been personally involved in close combat for years –
was forced to intervene at the western breach. According to Edmund Ludlow,
a Parliamentarian officer:

the enemy defended the breach against ours from behind an earthwork which they had cast up within, and where they had drawn up
two or three troops of horse which they had within the town, for the
encouragement and support of their foot . . . The Lord Lieutenant
[Cromwell], well knowing the importance of this action, resolved to
put all upon it; and having commanded some guns to be loaded with

bullets of half a pound and fired upon the enemy's horse . . . himself
with a reserve of foot [Ewer's Regiment] marched up to the breach,
which giving fresh courage to our men, they made a second attack,
with more vigour than before. Whereupon the enemy's foot being
abandoned by their horse, whom our shot had forced to retire,
began to break and shift for themselves.[290]

The gallant Colonel Garret Wall had been mortally wounded, perhaps by a
cannon shot, which carried off both of his feet, though he attempted to fight
on, balanced on their stumps. As the Parliamentarian foot secured the breach,
their cavalry passed through and began scouring the streets of Drogheda.

The Killings

Resistance was collapsing rapidly. Hewson's men also now entered, possibly
finding their opponents had abandoned their entrenchments. As
Parliamentarian cavalry drove on across the drawbridge into the northern part
of the town, Aston attempted to organise a last stand on Millmount.
Cromwell describes what happened:

> The enemy retreated, divers of them to Millmount, a place very
> strong and of difficult access, being exceedingly high, having a good
> graf and strongly pallisadoed. The Governor, Sir Arthur Aston, and
> divers considerable Officers being there, our men getting up to
> them were ordered by me to put them all to the sword. And indeed
> being in the heat of the action, I forbade them to spare any that were
> in arms in the town, and I think that night they put to the sword
> about two thousand men . . . [291]

Cromwell had a furious and occasionally violent temper, probably exacer-
bated on this occasion by his rare involvement in front-line action. In fact,
events were rather more complicated than Cromwell suggests. Some of his
men had actually begun to offer quarter to their opponents, but Aston – with
about 250 officers and men on Millmount – initially continued to bid
defiance. However, according to a Royalist officer who probably spoke to
eyewitnesses of the general collapse:

> they thought it vain to make any further resistance, which if they
> had, they could have killed some hundreds . . . before they had taken
> it. Lieutenant Colonel Axtell . . . with some twelve of his men went
> up to the top of the mount and demanded of the Governor the
> surrender of it, who was very stubborn, speaking very big words,
> but at length was persuaded to go to the windmill on top of the

mount, and as many more of the chiefest of them as it would contain, where they were all disarmed and afterwards all slain.[292]

It was said that the soldiers had thought Aston had gold concealed in his wooden leg and, finding none there, used it to beat him to death.

The quarter that had initially been granted on an unofficial basis by individual officers and soldiers was now revoked on Cromwell's orders and the prisoners killed. Supposedly, Cromwell was influenced by Michael Jones, who pointed out that he had 'the flower of the Irish Army' in his hands. Cromwell was evidently unwilling to see them go free to fight again and seems to have entrusted Hewson's men with their executions. Similar actions had occurred during the English Civil War but the killings at Drogheda were notable in being more systematic, prolonged, and on a much larger scale. The massacre was repeated in other parts of Drogheda, with Hewson's Regiment closely involved. Its commander stated:

> The rest fled over the bridge [into the northern part of the town] where they were closely pursued and most of them slain. Some got into two towers on the wall, and some into the steeple [of St Peter's Church] but they, refusing to come down, the steeple was fired and then fifty of them got out at the top of the church, but the enraged soldiers put them all to the sword, and thirty of them were burnt in the fire, some of them cursing and crying out 'God damn them', and cursed their souls as they were burning.[293]

The killing, as Cromwell himself confirmed, was done on his orders, the steeple being set alight by a bonfire of burning pews after an attempt to blow it up had failed. Perhaps a thousand of the defenders were killed in or around the church.

The bulk of the killings took place in the first few hours after Drogheda was stormed, though instances occurred for at least two days. Some isolated pockets of resistance remained to be mopped up, and a number of prisoners – including officers and several Catholic priests – were killed, although the majority of surviving common soldiers were shipped off as slaves to Barbados. Some senior officers, including Sir Edmund Verney, were killed at least a day after fighting ended, presumably because they were no longer needed to persuade their men to surrender.

The most severe charge against Cromwell, which has blackened his name in Ireland ever since, was that he ordered his men to massacre the civilian population of Drogheda. In fact, there is no evidence that the bulk of the townspeople took any part in the fighting. Most of them probably remained barricaded inside their homes, and there are no reliable reports from either side that many were killed, although a number of houses were looted. Body counts carried out by the Parliamentarians estimated a total of 150 of their own men and 3,500 others dead. The latter figure corresponds almost exactly with the number of troops in Drogheda's garrison. Cromwell's report of the killings to Parliament was an uneasy mixture of self justification and defiance:

> This is a righteous judgement of God, upon these barbarous wretches who have imbrued their hands in so much innocent blood . . . it will tend to prevent the effusion of blood for the future, which are satisfactory grounds to such actions, which otherwise cannot but work remorse and regret.

The killings at Drogheda were undoubtedly intended to intimidate other Irish towns into surrender, but in October similar killings on a slightly smaller scale took place when the port of Wexford was stormed whilst negotiations were still in progress. Again, it is unclear what orders had been given by Cromwell, though he made no attempt to halt the killings. Though a number of Irish garrisons did surrender thereafter, others resisted ferociously, and in April 1650 the New Model Army suffered the most bloody defeat in its history when it was repulsed in its attack on Clonmel.

It was not until 1653 that organised resistance in Ireland came to an end. Far from hastening the end of hostilities, Cromwell's actions at Drogheda probably prolonged the war, and cast a stain on his name that successive centuries have failed to wipe clean.

Chapter Twelve

Aftermath

Towards the close of the First Civil War, the Royalist poet Andrew Marvell wrote sadly:

> Shall we never more
> That sweet militia restore
> When gardens only had their towers,
> And all the garrisons were flowers;
> When roses only arms might bear,
> And men did rosy garlands wear?

Harlech Castle, the last Royalist garrison in mainland Britain, surrendered in March 1647 but peace had scarcely been restored when, in 1648, the series of Royalist uprisings and Scottish invasion – known as the Second Civil War – broke out. This resulted in several major sieges, notably those of the castles at Pembroke, Scarborough and Pontefract, before Parliament eventually regained control. Even then, prolonged fighting lay ahead in Ireland and Scotland before an uneasy peace was restored. A large number of towns – and even more villages, country houses and castles – had suffered major damage in the course of the fighting. It is difficult to produce reliable figures, for the natural tendency when claiming compensation – either from Parliament or out of the estates of the defeated Royalists – was to exaggerate the amount of damage suffered. It has, however, been estimated that within England and Wales in the region of 150 cities and towns, 100 villages, and over 200 country houses and castles suffered significant damage.[294]

As might be expected, the towns suffering the most damage tended to be those of strategic importance, generally possessing at least some pre-war defences. Parliamentarian-held towns on the whole suffered least damage, and received a more sympathetic hearing when petitioning for compensation than was the case with pro-Royalist settlements. The latter – and indeed others that had been Royalist garrisons for most of the war – suffered more damage, partly because of the generally increased rate of destruction in the latter stages of the war, resulting from the larger number of heavy guns then available, and greater professionalism and knowledge of siegecraft.

167

The extent of the destruction varied according to length and intensity of fighting. Chester, which had come under prolonged attack, suffered severely. The suburbs were virtually all destroyed, mainly by the defenders, together with the cloth fulling mills, which stood beneath the medieval walls, along the bank of the River Dee. Within the cramped confines of the old medieval city:

> The destruction of divers other houses in the city, with grenades, not a house from Eastgate to the middle of Watergate St on both sides but received some hurt from them, many slain by the fall of houses which were blown up, St Peter's Church much defaced and pews torn, and all windows broken by two granadoes that fell therein.[295]

A number of large country houses in the vicinity of the city were destroyed and the total cost of the war to Chester was estimated as around £200,000, 'so far hath the God of Heaven humbled this famous city'.[296]

A further blow came with the onset of plague, probably caused by the crowded conditions within the town during the siege, which between 22 June 1647 and 20 April 1648 cost the lives of over 2,000 people – roughly 20 per cent of the population. Chester was said to have been so depopulated that grass was growing in the streets. Recovery was fairly rapid, however, with large-scale rebuilding during the 1650s, as the city regained its pre-war prosperity. Even so, it took some considerable time for particularly hard-hit civilians to find their economic feet again. One Chester citizen to suffer was John Johnson, a Royalist alderman and shoemaker, who

> in time of the late siege, he had received great loss by fire, having had two houses and a kiln burnt to the ground, besides many household goods, and that he had all his boots, shoes, materials for his trade, and other things, burnt in his shop, and he had a wife and six small children to maintain . . . [297]

In many places, however, rebuilding took much longer. Severe though the damage suffered at Chester had been, in other places it was as bad or worse. Banbury, Taunton and Pontefract were all devastated by prolonged siege, either of the towns themselves or of the castles within them. At Exeter the town's water supply was not restored for a decade. Faringdon, where the Royalist garrison had put up prolonged resistance in the closing stages of the war, was described in 1649 as 'a good handsome market town turned into ashes and rubbage',[298] with, at Banbury, 'scarce the one half standing to gaze on the ruins of the other'.[299] Hereford and Worcester lost most of the suburbs as a result of the destruction carried out by their Royalist garrisons, as did Gloucester, in this case mainly at the hands of its Parliamentarian defenders.

Smaller towns also suffered. The destruction at Lyme, in Dorset, under siege by Prince Maurice in 1644, was considerable – partly as a result of prolonged bombardment by incendiaries of various kinds. Bridgewater, in Somerset, had been stormed in 1645 by the New Model Army, and a large number of houses burnt during the fighting. On the Welsh Border, Bridgnorth lost an estimated 300 houses worth £60,000 in total. Even the little town of Holt, whose Royalist-held castle underwent prolonged siege, suffered the destruction – at the hands of its garrison – of 103 houses, effectively most of the town.

At Newcastle, besieged by the Scots in 1644, several hundred houses in the suburbs had been destroyed, whilst Liverpool, savagely stormed by Prince Rupert in June 1644, and undergoing a second siege later in the year, was described as 'in a great part destroyed or burnt'.[300]

In 1648 Parliament authorised a number of national subscriptions to raise money for the relief of specific towns, those which had been Parliamentarian in sympathy naturally getting more generous support than the pro-Royalist. Some of the latter, such as Bridgnorth, got little assistance until after the Restoration. Even for Parliamentarian towns, Westminster was not able to produce adequate funds, and to some extent these were supplemented by Royalist resources. In some cases, for example Liverpool, timber for rebuilding was obtained from the estates of local Royalists.

Some wartime Royalist garrison commanders and fortress governors were later sued for compensation for alleged damage as a result of their actions. Sir John Boys, Governor of Donnington Castle, was detained after his surrender until 'he gave satisfaction for the Damage to the Neighbour Inhabitants'.[301]

The immediate problem facing the victors was what to do with the scores of Royalist garrisons that had fallen into their hands. Indeed, this question had arisen for both sides during the course of the war. In most cases a successful besieger had to decide whether to garrison or destroy his prize. Adequate garrisons would quickly drain the manpower of a victorious army, whilst, as the Royalists discovered at Evesham in 1645, an insufficient force of defenders would fall easy prey. In May 1645 Prince Rupert destroyed the magnificent house at Chipping Camden in order to add its garrison to his field army.

Whilst, during the war, there were often compelling military reasons to continue manning a captured garrison, these became much less pressing after fighting ceased, when the continued existence in a defensible condition of a castle or country house, which might fall into the hands of opponents of the regime, was to be avoided. In general, most of the damage to castles that can be seen today was the result of 'slighting' of defences after the war rather than the result of destruction suffered during it. After the First Civil War

Parliament made efforts to limit the amount of destruction of country houses in particular. In April 1646, the Committee of Both Kingdoms counter-manded instructions from the Shropshire County Committee for the demolition of High Ercall House, a notorious Royalist garrison for much of the war, in favour of merely slighting its defensive works and draining the moat, for Parliament

> did not think it fit that all houses whose situation and strength render them capable of being made garrisons should be pulled down. There would then be too many sad marks left of the calamity of this war.[302]

But there had been cases where such moderation came too late. Basing House, for example, had been destroyed partly by the victorious Parliamentarian soldiery and partly by vengeful local inhabitants who had suffered from the depredations and demands of its garrison, and Lathom House was so thoroughly dismantled by the local population that its site was eventually forgotten.

Officially, the work of 'slighting' was carried out by County Committees or Deputy Lieutenants under instructions from the Committee of Both Kingdoms or the Council of State. Surviving records are incomplete, and many slightings were undertaken without higher authority. In August 1646, with hostilities in their area ended, the Committee for Oxfordshire, Buckinghamshire and Berkshire met to consider 'what garrisons are fit to be continued, and what are fit to be slighted'.[303] Their deliberations were replicated across the country, and early in 1647 a long list of fortifications was placed before the House of Commons for its decision. The House of Lords was opposed to wholesale demolition so the result was a compromise, under which only new fortifications at a site should be slighted. The result, in 1648, when the Second Civil War broke out, was that castles such as Scarborough and Pontefract were reoccupied by the Royalists, for often only the earthen outworks had been demolished.

Learning from the experience, after hostilities again ceased, Parliament took a much more severe line. Pontefract, Belvoir, Nottingham, Bolingbroke, Montgomery and Aberystwyth Castles were among those whose thorough slighting was ordered. In November 1648 a Committee was set up to consider again the fates of individual castles, garrisons and 'places of strength'. In March 1651, at a time when the new English Commonwealth was still involved in war in Scotland, the Council of State was asked to consider 'what castles and garrisons are fit to be demolished and disgarrisoned, and how and when; what walled towns are fit to be dismantled; and report their opinion therein to the House'. Inevitably, following the battle there that September,

Worcester was one of the places whose defences were to be dismantled, and further consideration took place after the 1659 Rising.

In practice, many problems were encountered. Some castle owners objected, despite being offered compensation, and the massive masonry of many castles proved resistant to attempts at demolition. For this reason, in some cases orders for demolition were ignored or only partially carried through. The work also proved considerably lengthier and more expensive than had been anticipated. On average a castle slighting might occupy 50–100 men over a period of 6 months. At Montgomery, for example, as many as 180 men were at work. However, some of the costs could often be recouped by the sale of materials obtained in the slightings.

Greenhalgh Castle, Lathom House and the castles at Banbury, Wallingford, Winchester, Nottingham, Belvoir, Bolingbroke, Pontefract, Montgomery and Aberystwyth suffered the most comprehensive demolition. Usually the work included demolition or undermining of parts of the keep or towers, and the reduction of the linking walls to a uniformly low level. With local people eager for free building materials, the authorities sometimes had to discourage over-enthusiastic destruction. At Bolsover, for example, orders had to be given that 'so much only be done to it as to make it untenable as a garrison, and that it may not be unnecessarily spoiled and defaced . . . '

In the interests of security and national defence it was necessary for some garrisons still to be maintained. As invasion was thought more likely than serious internal rebellion, priority was given to coastal garrisons. The Scottish Border also continued to be fortified, and on the Welsh coast garrisons were maintained at Caernarvon, Conwy, Beaumaris, Chepstow, Cardiff and Carmarthen, with remaining castles being slighted.

The work of slighting was never really reversed after the Restoration in 1660, and the majority of unoccupied castles continued a steady deterioration due the continuing demand for building material. Among the key former Royalist garrisons to have suffered slighting were: Ashby de la Zouch, Banbury, Belvoir, Bolton (Yorks), Denbigh (in this case mainly after 1660), Donnington (mostly during the war), Dudley, Flint, Hawarden, Knaresborough, Lathom, Montgomery, Nottingham, Pontefract, Raglan, Rhuddlan, Sherbourne, Sudeley, Tamworth, Wallingford and Worcester.

The massive earthen outworks constructed around many towns disappeared more gradually. In some cases they had to be removed before the job of rebuilding razed suburbs could begin. And at times military requirements, at for example Liverpool, meant that earthen defences were retained for a decade after the end of the war, despite the protests of the townspeople. The task of demolition was often immense and daunting, particularly as, in peacetime, local authorities were unable to use forced labour. In some cases financial incentives were given to tenants of land on which defences stood to encourage them to undertake the work. Even so, at places like Gloucester and York remains of the earthen defences were still clearly visible in the eighteenth century, and a few for considerably longer, with sometimes significant vestiges remaining still today at Newark, Chester and Fort Royal, Worcester.

Places to Visit

Very few of the earthen fortifications or siegeworks of the Civil War still remain. Most were demolished after fighting ended, and many more have succumbed to the demands of agriculture, town expansion and the effects of weather. Other possible remains are little more than irregular lumps or mounds, difficult to identify with any degree of certainty.

However, in several places some important examples of Civil War military construction may still be seen. Most important are the remains of the defences and siegeworks at Newark-on-Trent. Most impressive, and still clearly visible, is the Queen's Sconce, the most important surviving Civil War earthen fortification. Also important is the fort known as Gallant's Bower, built by the Royalists above the town of Dartmouth as part of its defences. Significant remains of its Civil War outworks may still be seem at Basing House, and at Worcester the important outwork known as Fort Royal. Although most of Donnington Castle, near Newbury, was demolished at the end of the war, the outworks built by its Royalist garrison can still be traced.

Siegeworks are equally scarce, although some traces may be seen at Raglan Castle in Monmouthshire, and also in the Queen's Meadow at Chester, where there are the remains of a sconce constructed by the Parliamentarians to guard the approaches to the bridge of boats, which they built spanning the River Dee.

Many castles garrisoned during the Civil War may still be visited, although the main visible legacy is usually the 'slighting' of their defences carried out after the war. Among those of particular interest for their Civil War associations are Beeston Castle, Cheshire, Goodrich and Raglan Castles, Monmouthshire, Pontefract and Scarborough Castles, Yorkshire, and Pendennis Castle in Cornwall. Equally rewarding are the largely intact medieval walls of York (as well as St Mary's Tower, where damage suffered in an attempt to mine it may be seen. Just outside Micklegate Bar is 'the Mount', site of a gun battery during the siege) and Chester. The latter retain significant evidence of the Civil War leaguer, including the clearly defined breach made near the new Gate, the impact of cannon shot on Thimbley's Tower and gun ports pierced in the defences near the Water Tower.

Chronology of Selected Sieges

'P' = *'Parliamentarian-held;* *'R'* = *Royalist-held.*

1642

30 July	First Siege of Hull (P) fails.
6 August	Siege of Portsmouth (R) begins.
22 August	King Charles I raises standard at Nottingham signalling official start of hostilities.
2 September	Earl of Bedford lays siege to Sherborne Castle (R).
6 September	Siege of Sherborne (R) raised.
7 September	Portsmouth (R) surrenders.
23 October	Battle of Edgehill marginal Royalist victory.
18 November	First Siege of Exeter (P).
21 November	First Siege of Exeter raised.
1 December	Waller storms Farnham Castle (R).
30 December	Second Royalist attempt on Exeter fails.

1643

6 February– March	Parliamentarians besiege and capture Lichfield Close.
9 February	Parliamentarians storm Preston (R).
27 February	Parliamentarian assault on Newark (R) fails.
3 April	Prince Rupert storms Birmingham (P).
7–21 April	Prince Rupert takes Lichfield Close (P).
15 April	Parliamentarians lay siege to Reading (R).
27 April	Reading surrendered to Parliamentarians.
1–8 May	Siege of Wardour Castle (R) taken by Parliamentarians.
21 May	Parliamentarians storm Wakefield (R).
24–27 July	Bristol (P) besieged and stormed by Prince Rupert.

10 August–6 September . . .	Royalists unsuccessfully besiege Gloucester.
2 September–11 October . .	Second Siege of Hull (P) Royalists failure to capture.
4 September	Prince Maurice takes Exeter (P).
20 September	First Battle of Newbury marginal Parliamentarian victory.
1 October–22 December . . .	Royalists unsuccessfully besiege Plymouth (P).
6 October	Prince Maurice takes Dartmouth (P).
6–14 November	Parliamentarians fail to take Basing House (R).
9 December	Hopton takes Arundel Castle (P).
13 December	Royalists take Beeston Castle (P).
20 December–6 January . . .	Parliamentarians besiege and capture Arundel Castle (R).

1644

10–25 January	Siege of Nantwich (P) Royalists defeated and siege raised.
28 February–27 May	First Siege of Lathom House (R) Parliamentarians fail to capture.
29 February	Parliamentarians besiege Newark (R).
21 March	Rupert relieves Newark.
20 April–15 June	Prince Maurice unsuccessfully besieges Lyme (P).
21 April–1 July	First Siege of York (R).
28 May	Prince Rupert storms Bolton (P).
7–11 June	Rupert takes Liverpool (P).
2 July	Battle of Marston Moor Royalist defeat.
11 July	Second Siege of Basing House (R) begins.
16 July	York (R) surrenders.
28 July–22 October	Scots besiege and take Newcastle upon Tyne (R).
22 October	Donnington Castle (R) relieved.
25 October	Banbury Castle (R) relieved.
27 October	Second Battle of Newbury marginal Royalist victory.
1 November	Liverpool (R) surrenders.
19 November	Basing House (R) again relieved.

December–19 July . . . .   Parliamentarians besiege and capture Pontefract Castle (R).

1645

January–12 July . . . .   Parliamentarians besiege and capture Scarborough Castle (R).

22 February . . . .   Parliamentarians surprise and capture Shrewsbury (R).

1 March . . . .   Royalists briefly relieve Pontefract.

24 April . . . .   Bletchingdon House (R) surrenders to Cromwell.

20 April . . . .   Cromwell repulsed at Faringdon (R).

31 May . . . .   Rupert storms Leicester (P).

14 June . . . .   Battle of Naseby Royalist defeat.

25 June . . . .   Carlisle (R) surrenders.

July–15 November . . . .   Second Siege of Beeston Castle (R) taken by Parliamentarians.

30 July–27 August . . . .   Scots besiege but fail to take Hereford (R).

1–16 August . . . .   Parliamentarians besiege and take Sherborne Castle (R).

August–14 October . . . .   Final Siege of Basing House (R) taken by Parliamentarians.

10 September . . . .   Parliamentarians storm Bristol (R).

19 September–3 February .   Final Siege of Chester (R) taken by Parliamentarians.

28 October–9 April . . . .   Final Siege of Exeter (R) taken by Parliamentarians.

15 November–6 May . . . . . .   Final Siege of Newark (R) taken by Parliamentarians.

18 December . . . .   Parliamentarians surprise Hereford (R).

1646

27 February . . . .   Parliamentarians take Corfe Castle (R).

17 March–17 August . . . . . .   Parliamentarians besiege and capture Pendennis Castle (R).

3 May–27 June . . . .   Parliamentarians besiege and take Oxford (R).

31 May–19 July . . . . Parliamentarians besiege and take Worcester (R).

June–31 July . . . . Siege and surrender of Goodrich Castle (R).

4 June . . . . Caernarvon Castle (R) surrenders.

1647

January . . . . Holt Castle (R) surrenders.

March . . . . Surrender of Harlech Castle last Royalist garrison in mainland Britain.

1648: Second Civil War

May–11 July . . . . Parliamentarians besiege and take Pembroke Castle (R).

June–28 August . . . . Siege of Colchester (R) taken by Parliamentarians.

July–17 March . . . . 1649 Siege and capture of Pontefract Castle (R).

Glossary

Abbatis	Defences of felled trees with sharpened ends facing outwards.
Approaches	Trenches built by attackers leading towards the place under attack.
Bastion	Forward projection from the curtain on the side or at the angle of a defensive work, providing flanking cover of adjoining defences.
Battery	Fortified position mounting cannon.
Breastwork	Parapet, usually of earth.
Bulwark	Similar to a bastion.
Circumvallation	Linear works constructed by a besieger around a besieged garrison.
Counterscarp	Outer face of a ditch.
Curtain	Run of wall or rampart between towers or bastions.
Enceinte	Main line of bastions and curtain of a fortified town, as distinct from the outworks.
Faggots	Bundles of wood used by attackers to fill ditches or moats.
Fascines	Bundles of wood used for cover from enemy fire.
Fort	Detached stronghold.
Gabions	Large baskets filled with earth providing protection for gunners and cannon.
Glacis Slope	On which attackers are exposed to the fire of the defenders, usually in front of a rampart.
Graf	Ditch.
Half-Moon	Outwork, usually with two faces forming a salient angle, placed outside the main work in front of the curtain or bastion.
Hornwork	Advanced work consisting of a short curtain between two demi-bastions, often joined to the main work by long sides.
Leaguer	Either a fortified camp or a prolonged siege operation.
Mount	Fort or battery.
Outworks	Fortifications outside the main defences of a garrison, often protecting the suburbs of a town.

178

Palisade	Defence of timber stakes, usually set upright.
Parapet	Low mound or wall, usually along the front edge of a rampart, giving protection to those behind it.
Pitfall	Trap, usually a concealed pit.
Ravelin	Work similar to a half-moon.
Redoubt	Small detached stronghold without provision for flank defence.
Sconce	Detached fort with bastions.
Storm Poles	Horizontal timber stakes projecting from the face of a defence work to prevent scaling.

Notes

1. Charles Carleton, *Going to the Wars*, London, 1992, pp.206–7.
2. Ibid., p.263.
3. George Monck, *Observations on Military and Political Affairs*, London, 1671, p.119.
4. Mike Osbourne, *Sieges and Fortifications of the Civil War*, Southend-on-Sea, 2004, p.81.
5. Carleton, pp.172–3.
6. John Barratt, *Happy Victory: The Siege and Battle of Nantwich, 1644*, Birkenhead, 1995, p.6.
7. Osbourne, p.99.
8. Ibid., pp.105–6.
9. Ibid., p.113.
10. Joshua Sprigge, *Anglia Rediviva*, London, 1647, p.27.
11. Osbourne, p.21.
12. Carleton, p.161.
13. Ibid., p.151.
14. Ibid.
15. Stephen Porter, *Destruction in the English Civil War*, Stroud, 1994, p.29.
16. Bulstrode Whitlocke, *Memorials of English Affairs*, London, 1682, I, p.540.
17. Quoted Porter, p.29.
18. John Barratt, 'A Most Unfortunate Man: the Case of Frank Windebanke', in *English Civil War Times*, 59, pp.14–18.
19. See John Barratt, *Great Siege of Chester*, Stroud, 2004, pp.153–4.
20. Ibid., p.142.
21. Ibid., pp.54–5.
22. Ibid., p.51.
23. Carleton, p.244.
24. Richard Gough, *History of Myddle* (ed. David Hey), Harmondsworth, 1981, pp.73–4.
25. W. Prynne and N. Walker, *Trial of Nathaniel Fiennes*, London, 1643, p.25.
26. Bernard de Gomme, 'Siege and Capture of Bristol', in Eliot Warburton, *Memoirs of Prince Rupert and the Cavaliers*, London, 1849, II, p.243.
27. Ibid., p.240.
28. Ibid.
29. John Lynch, *For King and Parliament*, Stroud, 1999, pp.39–41.
30. Ibid.
31. Ian Roy (ed.), *Royalist Ordnance Papers Pt II*, Oxford, 1975, pp.226–8.

32. Warburton, II, p.243.
33. Ibid., p.242.
34. Ibid., pp.243–4.
35. Ibid., pp.244–5.
36. Ibid., p.248.
37. Ibid., pp.248–9.
38. Edward Earl of Clarendon, *History of the Great Rebellion*, Oxford, 1888, VII, p.295.
39. Warburton, II, p.249.
40. Ibid., pp.250–2.
41. Ibid.
42. Ibid., p.254.
43. Ibid.
44. Ibid., p.255.
45. Prynne and Walker, p.35.
46. Lynch, pp.83–4.
47. Prynne and Walker, p.31.
48. Clarendon, p. 295.
49. Anon., *Tragedy of the King's Army's Fidelity*, London, 1643, p.6.
50. Ibid.
51. Warburton, III, p.151.
52. *Mercurius Aulicus*, 4 September 1645, p.1621.
53. Ibid.
54. Anon., *Heads of Some Notes . . .* , London, 1645, p.7.
55. Warburton, III, p.175.
56. Thomas Rainsborough, *True Relation of the Storming of Bristol*, London, 1645, p.19.
57. Oliver Cromwell, *Letter to the House . . .*, London, 1645, p.5.
58. Warburton, III, p.170.
59. Cromwell, p.6.
60. Sprigge, p.116.
61. Cromwell, pp.5–6.
62. Warburton, III, p.176.
63. S. Iremaine, *An Exact Relation of Prince Rupert His Marching Out of Bristol*, London, 1645, p.1.
64. R. Stewart Brown (ed.), 'Records of the Chamberlain's Accounts of the County of Cheshire, 1301–1360', in *L.C.A.S.*, 59, 1911.
65. George Ormerod, *History of the County Palatine of Cheshire*, Chester, 1882, ii, p.275.
66. Nathaniel Lancaster, *Chester's Enlargement . . .*, London, 1647, p.10.
67. Ibid.
68. Ibid.
69. Ibid.
70. British Library, *Harleian MS 2135*.

71. Thomas Malbon, 'Memorials of the Civil War in Cheshire', in *L.C.A.S.*, 19, 1884, p.15.
72. *Mercurius Aulicus*, 16 December 1643, p.716.
73. Lancaster, p.16.
74. Warburton, II, p.238.
75. Malbon, p.28.
76. R. Morris and P.H. Lawson, *Siege of Chester*, Chester, 1923, p.92.
77. R.N. Dore, 'Beeston Castle in the Great Civil War', *L.C.A.S.*, 65, 1975, p.14.
78. R.N. Dore (ed.), 'Letter Books of Sir William Brereton', in *L.C.A.S.*, 123, 1983, item 142.
79. Ibid., item 202.
80. Ibid., item 212.
81. Ibid.
82. Malbon, pp.32–3.
83. Dore (ed.), 'Letter Books', I, item 175.
84. Ibid., item 439.
85. Ibid., item 459.
86. Ibid., item 460.
87. Lancaster, p.16 .
88. Ibid.
89. Dore (ed.), 'Letter Books', II, item 762.
90. Ibid., item 775.
91. Ibid., item 872.
92. Ibid., item 885.
93. Ibid., item 868.
94. Ibid., item 875.
95. Malbon, p.37.
96. Dore, 'Beeston Castle', p.24.
97. Philip Photiou, *Plymouth's Forgotten War*, Plymouth, 2005, p.15.
98. John Barratt, *Civil War in the South West*, Barnsley, 2005, pp.22-5.
99. Photiou, p.81.
100. Barratt, *Civil War*, pp.31-7.
101. Bodleian Library, *Nalson MS*, f.194.
102. John Barratt, *Cavalier Generals*, Barnsley, 2004, pp.61–76.
103. Photiou, pp.145–6.
104. Ibid., p.209.
105. Barratt, *Cavalier Generals*, p.152.
106. *C.S.P.D.* 1644–45, p.296.
107. Barratt, *Cavalier Generals*, p.153.
108. Joseph Jane, 'Relation of the State of the Parties in Cornwall', n.d. (Bodleian Library, *Clarendon MS 2074*).
109. John Barratt, 'A Drubbing for Skellum: Sir Richard Grenville's Attack on Plymouth, 1645', in *English Civil War Times*, 55.
110. Ibid.

111. Sir Richard Grenville, *Narrative of the Affairs of the West, Clarendon MS 37*, f.76.

112. John Barratt (ed.), 'John Byron's Account of the Siege of Chester', in *Cheshire Sheaf*, 4th Series, Chester, 1971, p.12.

113. Ibid., p.21.

114. Dore (ed.), 'Letter Books', II, items 417 and 458.

115. M.B. Williams and M.J. Lawson, *The Better Soldier: The First Siege of Lathom House*, Liverpool, 1999, pp.30–40.

116. J. Seacombe, *History of the House of Stanley*, Preston 1793, pp.104–5.

117. Edward Halsall, *Journal of the Siege of Lathom House, Harleian MS 2043*, pp.12–13.

118. Ibid.

119. Ibid., p.13

120. Ibid.

121. Seacombe, p.107.

122. Edward Robinson, *Discourse of the War in Lancashire*, Chetham Society, Manchester, 1864, p.21.

123. Seacombe, p.108.

124. Halsall, *Journal*, p.14.

125. Warburton, II, p.231.

126. Ibid., p.233.

127. Halsall, *Journal*, p.15.

128. Ibid., p.16.

129. Ibid., p.17.

130. *Mercurius Aulicus*, 21 April 1644, p.1051.

131. Halsall, *Journal*, p.17.

132. Ibid. Presumably the gunners suspected that the Royalists had damaged the inside of the barrel.

133. Ibid., pp.17–18.

134. Ibid., p.18.

135. Ibid., pp.19–20.

136. Robinson, p.23.

137. Halsall, *Journal*, p.20.

138. Ibid., p.21.

139. Ibid.

140. Ibid. Presumably spiked them.

141. Ibid.

142. Colin Pilkington, *To Play the Man*, Preston, 1991, p.96.

143. Ibid.

144. Seacombe, p.284.

145. *C.S.P.D.* 1644–45, p.5.

146. Robinson, pp.60–1.

147. Seacombe, pp.274–5.

148. *Perfect Occurances*, 28th week, 4–11 July 1645.

149. Seacombe, pp.262–4.
150. Ibid., p.276.
151. Robinson, p.63.
152. Seacombe, p.264.
153. Robinson, p.63.
154. Barratt, *Cavalier Generals*, p.132.
155. Ibid, pp.194-5.
156. Malcolm Atkins, *Civil War in Worcestershire*, Stroud, 1995, p.101.
157. Ibid., p.105.
158. J.W. Willis-Bund, *The Civil War in Worcestershire*, Worcester, 1905, p.180.
159. J.W. Willis-Bund (ed.), *Diary of Henry Townsend*, Worcester, 1915, ii, p.102.
160. Atkins, p.107.
161. Ibid., p.108.
162. Ibid., p.109.
163. Willis-Bund (ed.), *Diary*, ii, p.129.
164. Ibid., p.140.
165. Ibid., p.142.
166. Ibid., p.160.
167. Ibid.
168. Willis-Bund, *Civil War*, p.189.
169. Willis-Bund (ed.), *Diary*, p.174.
170. Ibid., p.171.
171. Ibid., p.177.
172. Ibid., p.179.
173. Atkins, p.115.
174. Willis-Bund (ed.), *Diary*, p.192.
175. Samuel Pasfield Oliver, *Pendennis and St Mawes*, Truro, 1875 p.41.
176. Ibid.
177. Ibid., pp.40–1.
178. Ibid.
179. Ibid.
180. Ibid., pp.42–3.
181. *Weekly Account*, 25–31 March.
182. *Moderate Intelligencer*, 56.
183. *Clarendon MS 2184.*
184. *Perfect Diurnal*, 147.
185. *Weekly Account*, 25.
186. *Clarendon MS 2251.*
187. Sprigge, pp.302–3.
188. Ibid.
189. Ibid., p.303 .
190. Ibid.
191. Ibid.
192. Oliver, *Pendennis*, p.51.

193. q. Ibid., p.54.
194. J.W. Webb, *Memorials of the Civil War in Herefordshire*, London, 1879, II, p.118.
195. Ibid.
196. Ibid.
197. Ibid., II, p.277. The purpose of the boards is not stated, although they may have been intended as hoardings to give additional cover to men on the ramparts.
198. Ibid., p.414.
199. Ibid., p.415.
200. Ibid.
201. *Copy of another Letter from Colonell Birche's Leaguer*, London, 1646.
202. L.A.S. Butler, *Denbigh Castle and Town Walls*, Cardiff, 1990, p.3.
203. J. Williams, *Ancient and Modern Denbigh*, Denbigh, 1849, p.215.
204. Norman Tucker, 'Denbigh's Loyal Governor', in *Denbighshire Historical Society Transactions*, 1955, p.17.
205. Williams, p.219.
206. Ibid., p.223.
207. Ibid., p.224.
208. Ibid., p.225.
209. Ibid.
210. Ibid., p.226.
211. Ibid.
212. Ibid., p.227.
213. Ibid.
214. Ibid.
215. Ibid.
216. Ibid., p.228
217. Ibid.
218. Ibid., p.229.
219. C. Brown, *History of Newark*, Newark, 1904, II, p.49.
220. Lucy Hutchinson, *Memoirs of Colonel Hutchinson* (ed. C.H. Firth), London, 1896, pp.114–5.
221. Ibid.
222. Brown, II, p.49.
223. Ibid., p.59.
224. Bodleian Library, *Firth MSS*, I, ff.60–1.
225. Ibid., ff.120–1.
226. Hutchinson, p.173.
227. So called because he had lost the sight of one eye in action.
228. *Mercurius Aulicus*, 23 March 1644, p.899.
229. Ibid.
230. *Staunton Account Books*, quoted in Peter Young, *Newark on Trent: the Civil War Siegeworks*, London, 1964, p.20.

231. Hutchinson, p.226.
232. Ibid.
233. Ibid.
234. Ibid., pp.227–9.
235. *D.N.B.*
236. *Perfect Diurnal*, 5–12 January 1646.
237. *Moderate Intelligencer*, 8–15 January 1646.
238. Hutchinson, p.230.
239. H.M.C. *Ormonde MS*, N.S. ii, p.392.
240. Hutchinson, p.231.
241. *Ormonde*.
242. John Rushworth, *Historical Collections*, London, 1704, vi, pp.250–2.
243. Carleton, pp.18–19.
244. John Barratt, *Cavaliers*, Stroud, 2000, pp.193–4.
245. H.M.C., *Bath MS*, I, p.29.
246. Ibid., p.40.
247. Barratt, *Cavaliers*, p.145.
248. George Ormerod (ed.), *Civil War in Lancashire*, Chetham Society, II, 1844.
249. John Barratt, *Siege of Liverpool and the 1644 Campaign in Lancashire*, Bristol, 1994, p.10.
250. Statistics support a sharp drop in marriages recorded in Bolton in the years after 1644, suggesting noticeably fewer younger people in the town. The dead listed in the Parish Register may have accounted for many of these, and there were undoubtedly other casualties from among Bolton's male population during the course of the Civil War in Lancashire.
251. *Description of the Siege of Basing Castle*, Oxford, 1644, p.1.
252. R.N. Godwin, *Great Civil War in Hampshire*, Southampton, 1904, p.320.
253. Ibid., p.321.
254. Ibid., p.323.
255. Ibid., p.324.
256. Ibid.
257. Ibid., p.325.
258. Ibid., p.326.
259. Ibid., p.345.
260. Ibid.
261. Ibid., p.347.
262. *Moderate Intelligencer*, 13 October 1645.
263. Godwin, p.350.
264. Ibid., p.351.
265. *Kingdom's Weekly Post*, 15 October 1645.
266. Godwin, p.352.
267. Ibid.
268. Ibid. This account has been confirmed by the remains of grenadoes found in the ruins in recent excavations.

269. *Mercurius Civicus.*
270. Godwin, pp.352–3.
271. Ibid., p.353.
272. Ibid.
273. Ibid.
274. Whilst this is undoubtedly an exaggeration, some years ago farm workers digging out rabbits uncovered the skeleton of a man well over 6 feet in height, which was later reburied in the garrison cemetery at Basing.
275. *Moderate Intelligencer.*
276. Godwin, p.355.
277. It is not impossible that Robinson can be identified with the 'giant' mentioned by Peters.
278. Godwin, p.358.
279. Ibid.
280. Ibid., p.359.
281. Ibid., p.365.
282. Bodleian Library, *Carte MS* 25, f.53.
283. Ibid., f.56.
284. Ibid., f.59.
285. J.G. Sims, 'Cromwell at Drogheda', in *Irish Sword*, 11, 1974, p.218.
286. *Carte MS* 25, f.501.
287. J. Gilbert, *Continued History of Affairs in Ireland*, Dublin, 1875, ii, p.259.
288. Occasional Passages (q. C.H. Firth and G. Davies, *Regimental History of Cromwell's Army*, Oxford, 1940, ii, p.629).
289. Sims, p.220.
290. Ibid., p.223.
291. T.T.E. 533 (15) *Perfect Occurrences*, 28 September–4 October 1649, pp.1275–6.
292. *Letter from Sir Lewis Dyve*, The Hague, 1650, p.25.
293. *Perfect Occurrences.*
294. Porter, p.65.
295. Barratt, *Great Siege*, p.213.
296. Ibid.
297. Ibid.
298. Porter, p.64.
299. Sprigge, p.251.
300. *Commons Journals*, IV, 1644–46, p.277.
301. Porter, p.62.
302. *C.S.P.D.* 1645–47, pp.402–3.
303. *Commons Journals*, p.191.

Bibliography

Manuscript Sources
British Library: *Harleian MS 2043, 2135*
Bodleian Library: *Carte MS 25; Clarendon MS 37*

Printed Sources

Atkins, Malcolm, *Civil War in Worcestershire*, Stroud, 1995

Barratt John, 'A Drubbing for Skellum: Sir Richard Grenville's Attack on Plymouth, 1645', in *English Civil War Times*, 55

Barratt, John, 'A Most Unfortunate Man: the Case of Frank Windebanke', in *English Civil War Times*, 59

Barratt, John, *Cavalier Generals*, Barnsley, 2004

Barratt John, *Cavaliers*, Stroud, 2000

Barratt, John, *Civil War in the South West*, Barnsley, 2005

Barratt, John, *Great Siege of Chester*, Stroud, 2004

Barratt, John, *Happy Victory: the Siege and Battle of Nantwich, 1644*, Birkenhead, 1995

Barratt, John (ed.), 'John Byron's Account of the Siege of Chester', in *Cheshire Sheaf*, 4th Series, Chester, 1971

Barratt, John, *Siege of Liverpool and the 1644 Campaign in Lancashire*, Bristol, 1994

Brown, C., *History of Newark*, Newark, 1904

Butler, L.A.S., *Denbigh Castle and Town Walls*, Cardiff, 1990

Calendar of State Papers Domestic 1643–46, London

Carleton, Charles, *Going to the Wars*, London, 1992

Clarendon, Edward, Earl of, *History of the Great Rebellion*, Oxford, 1888

Copy of Another Letter from Colonell Birche's Leaguer, London, 1646

Cromwell, Oliver, *Letter to the House . . .* , London, 1645

Description of the Siege of Basing House, Oxford, 1644

Dore, R.N., 'Beeston Castle in the Great Civil War', in *L.C.A.S.*, 65, 1975

Dore, R.N. (ed.), 'Letter Books of Sir William Brereton', in *L.C.A.S.*, 123–4, 1983, 1991

Duffy, Christopher, *Siege Warfare*, London, 1979

Firth, C.H. and Davies, G., *Regimental History of Cromwell's Army*, Oxford, 1940

Gilbert, J., *Continued History of Affairs in Ireland*, Dublin, 1873

Godwin, R.N., *Great Civil War in Hampshire*, Southampton, 1904

Gough, Richard, *History of Myddle* (ed. David Hey), Harmondsworth, 1981

Harrington, Peter, *English Civil War Archaeology*, London, 2004

Harrington, Peter, *English Civil War Fortifications*, Oxford, 2003

Historical Manuscripts Commission, Bath MS

Historical Manuscripts Commission, Ormonde MS, N.S.

Hutchinson, Lucy, *Memoirs of Colonel Hutchinson* (ed. C.H. Firth), London, 1896

Lancaster, Nathaniel, *Chester's Enlargement . . .* , London, 1647

Lynch, John, *For King and Parliament*, Stroud, 1999

Malbon, Thomas, 'Memorials of the Civil War in Cheshire', in *L.C.A.S*, 19, 1884

Mercurius Aulicus, Oxford, 1643–45

Monck, George, *Observations on Military and Political Affairs*, London, 1671

Morris, R., and Lawson, P.H., *Siege of Chester*, Chester, 1923

Oliver, Samuel Pasfield, *Pendennis and St Mawes*, Truro, 1875

Ormerod, George, *History of the County Palatine of Cheshire*, Chester, 1882

Ormerod, George (ed.), *Civil War in Lancashire*, Chetham Society, II, 1844

Osbourne, Mike, *Sieges and Fortifications of the Civil War*, Southend-on-Sea, 2004

Photiou, Philip, *Plymouth's Forgotten War*, Plymouth, 2005

Pilkington, Colin, *To Play the Man*, Preston, 1991

Porter, Stephen, *Destruction in the English Civil War*, Stroud, 1994

Prynne, W. and Walker, N., *Trial of Nathaniel Fiennes*, London, 1643

Rainsborough, Thomas, *True Relation of the Storming of Bristol*, London, 1645

Robinson, Edward, *Discourse of the War in Lancashire*, Chetham Society, XLV, Manchester, 1864

Roy, Ian (ed.), *Royalist Ordnance Papers Pt II*, Oxford, 1975

Rushworth, John, *Historical Collections*, London, 1704

Seacombe, J., *History of the House of Stanley*, Preston, 1793

Sims, J.G., 'Cromwell at Drogheda', in *Irish Sword*, 11, 1974

Sprigge, Joshua, *Anglia Rediviva*, London, 1647

Stewart Brown, R. (ed.), 'Records of the Chamberlain's Accounts of the County of Cheshire, 1301–1360', in *L.C.A.S.*, 59, 1911

Tucker, Norman, 'Denbigh's Loyal Governor' in *Denbighshire Historical Society Transactions*, 1955

Warburton, Eliot, *Memoirs of Prince Rupert and the Cavaliers*, London, 1849

Webb, J.W., *Memorials of the Civil War in Herefordshire*, London, 1879

Whitlocke, Bulstrode, *Memorials of English Affairs*, London, 1682
Williams, J., *Ancient and Modern Denbigh*, Denbigh, 1849
Williams, M.B. and Lawson, M.J., *The Better Soldier: The First Siege of Lathom House*, Liverpool, 1999
Willis-Bund, J.W., *Civil War in Worcestershire*, Worcester, 1905
Willis-Bund, J.W. (ed.), *Diary of Henry Townsend*, Worcester, 1915
Young, Peter, *Newark on Trent: the Civil War Siegeworks*, London, 1964

Index